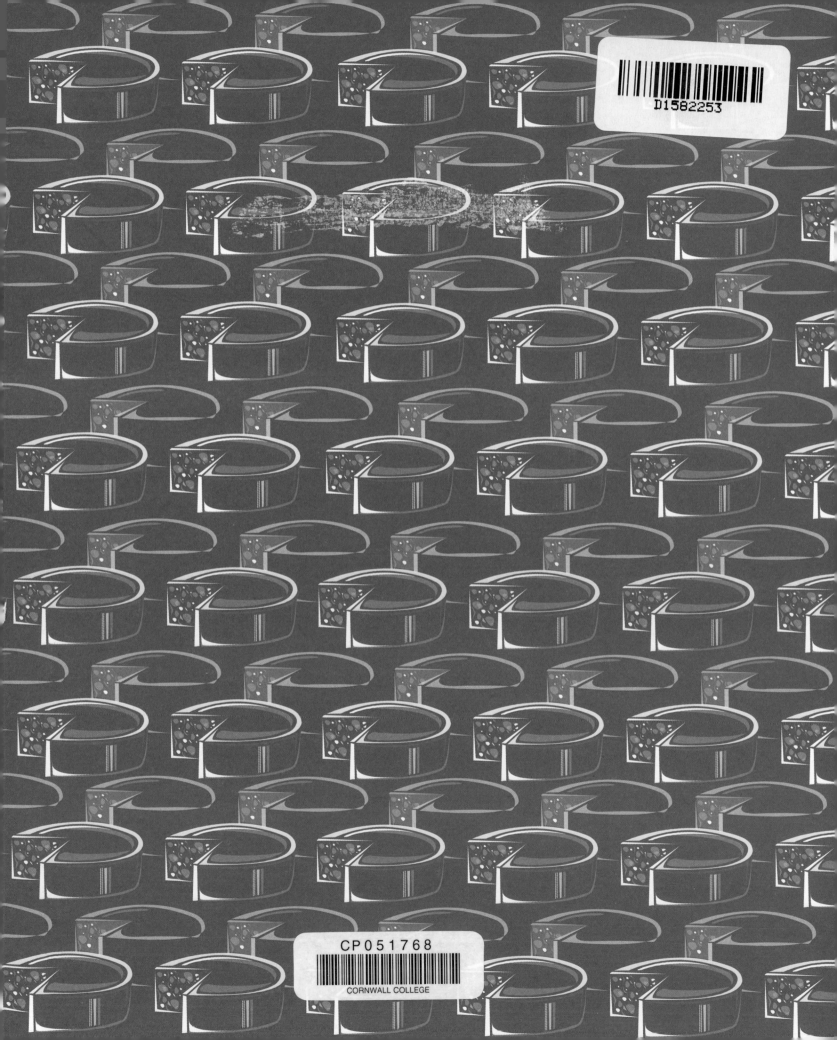

THE CULINARY INSTITUTE OF AMERICA®

IDENTIFICATION · CLASSIFICATION · UTILIZATION

CHEESE

John W. Fischer

KITCHEN PRO SERIES

Join us on the web at
culinary.delmar.com

THE CULINARY INSTITUTE OF AMERICA®

IDENTIFICATION · CLASSIFICATION · UTILIZATION

CHEESE

John W. Fischer

DELMAR
CENGAGE Learning™

Australia · Brazil · Japan · Korea · Mexico · Singapore · Spain · United Kingdom · United States

KITCHEN PRO SERIES

DELMAR
CENGAGE Learning

KitchenPro Series: Guide to Cheese Identification, Classification and Utilization
John W. Fischer

The Culinary Institute of America

President: Dr. Tim Ryan '77

Vice-President, Dean of Culinary Education: Mark Erickson '77

Senior Director, Continuing Education: Susan Cussen

Director of Intellectual Property: Nathalie Fischer

Editorial Project Manager: Margaret Wheeler '00

Editorial Assistant: Shelly Malgee '08

Editorial Assistant: Erin Jeanne McDowell '08

Photography:

Keith Ferris, Photographer

Ben Fink, Photographer

Vice President, Career and Professional Editorial: Dave Garza

Director of Learning Solutions: Sandy Clark

Acquisitions Editor: Jim Gish

Managing Editor: Larry Main

Product Manager: Nicole Calisi

Editorial Assistant: Sarah Timm

Vice President, Marketing, Career and Professional: Jennifer McAvey

Executive Marketing Manager: Wendy Mapstone

Marketing Manager: Kristin McNary

Marketing Coordinator: Scott Chrysler

Production Director: Wendy Troeger

Content Project Manager: Glenn Castle

Senior Art Director: Bethany Casey

Technology Project Manager: Chris Catalina

Production Technology Analyst: Tom Stover

For product information and technology assistance, contact us at
Cengage Learning Customer & Sales Support, 1-800-354-9706
For permission to use material from this text or product,
submit all requests online at **www.cengage.com/permissions.**
Further permissions questions can be emailed to
permissionrequest@cengage.com

Library of Congress Control Number: 2009942321

ISBN-13: 978-1-4354-0117-4

ISBN-10: 1-4354-0117-4

Delmar
5 Maxwell Drive
Clifton Park, NY 12065-2919
USA

Cengage Learning is a leading provider of customized learning solutions with office locations around the globe, including Singapore, the United Kingdom, Australia, Mexico, Brazil, and Japan. Locate your local office at: **international.cengage.com/region**

Cengage Learning products are represented in Canada by Nelson Education, Ltd.

To learn more about Delmar, visit **www.cengage.com/delmar**

Purchase any of our products at your local college store or at our preferred online store **www.CengageBrain.com**

Notice to the Reader

Publisher does not warrant or guarantee any of the products described herein or perform any independent analysis in connection with any of the product information contained herein. Publisher does not assume, and expressly disclaims, any obligation to obtain and include information other than that provided to it by the manufacturer. The reader is expressly warned to consider and adopt all safety precautions that might be indicated by the activities described herein and to avoid all potential hazards. By following the instructions contained herein, the reader willingly assumes all risks in connection with such instructions. The publisher makes no representations or warranties of any kind, including but not limited to, the warranties of fitness for particular purpose or merchantability, nor are any such representations implied with respect to the material set forth herein, and the publisher takes no responsibility with respect to such material. The publisher shall not be liable for any special, consequential, or exemplary damages resulting, in whole or part, from the readers' use of, or reliance upon, this material.

Printed in the United States of America
1 2 3 4 5 6 7 XXX 13 12 11 10

Contents

ABOUT THE CIA

THE WORLD'S PREMIER CULINARY COLLEGE

The Culinary Institute of America (CIA) is the recognized leader in culinary education for undergraduate students, foodservice and hospitality professionals, and food enthusiasts. The college awards bachelor's and associate degrees, as well as certificates and continuing education units, and is accredited by the prestigious Middle States Commission on Higher Education.

Founded in 1946 in downtown New Haven, CT to provide culinary training for World War II veterans, the college moved to its present location in Hyde Park, NY in 1972. In 1995, the CIA added a branch campus in the heart of California's Napa Valley—The Culinary Institute of America at Greystone. The CIA continued to grow, and in 2008, established a second branch campus, this time in San Antonio, TX.

From its humble beginnings more than 60 years ago with just 50 students, the CIA today enrolls more than 2,700 students in its degree programs, approximately 3,000 in its programs for foodservice and hospitality industry professionals, and more than 4,500 in its courses for food enthusiasts.

LEADING THE WAY

Throughout its history, The Culinary Institute of America has played a pivotal role in shaping the future of foodservice and hospitality. This is due in large part to the caliber of people who make up the CIA community—its faculty, staff, students, and alumni—as well as their passion for the culinary arts and dedication to the advancement of the profession.

Headed by the visionary leadership of President Tim Ryan '77, the CIA education team has at its core the largest concentration of American Culinary Federation-Certified Master Chefs (including Dr. Ryan) of any college. The Culinary Institute of America faculty, more than 140 members strong, brings a vast breadth and depth of foodservice industry experience and insight to the CIA kitchens, classrooms, and research facilities. They've worked in some of the world's finest establishments, earned industry awards and professional certifications, and emerged victorious from countless international culinary competitions. And they continue to make their mark on the industry, through the students they teach, books they author, and leadership initiatives they champion.

The influence of the CIA in the food world can also be attributed to the efforts and achievements of our more than 40,000 successful alumni. Our graduates are leaders in virtually every segment of the industry and bring the professionalism and commitment to excellence they learned at the CIA to bear in everything they do.

UNPARALLELED EDUCATION

DEGREE PROGRAMS

The CIA's bachelor's and associate degree programs in culinary arts and baking and pastry arts feature more than 1,300 hours of hands-on learning in the college's kitchens, bakeshops, and student-staffed restaurants, along with an 18-week externship at one of more than 1,200 top restaurant, hotel, and resort locations around the world. The bachelor's degree programs also include a broad range of liberal arts and business management courses to prepare students for future leadership positions, as well as a Wine and Food Seminar travel experience in one of the world's top culinary regions.

CERTIFICATE PROGRAMS

The college's certificate program in culinary arts is designed for students interested in an entry-level position in the food world and those already working in the foodservice industry who want to advance their careers. The CIA also offers an accelerated culinary arts certificate program (ACAP), which provides graduates of baccalaureate programs in hospitality management, food science, nutrition, and closely related fields with a solid foundation in the culinary arts and the career advancement opportunities that go along with that skill base.

PROFESSIONAL DEVELOPMENT PROGRAMS AND CONSULTING

The CIA offers food and wine professionals a variety of programs to help them keep their skills sharp and stay abreast of industry trends. Courses in cooking, baking, pastry, wine, and management are complemented by stimulating conferences and seminars, online culinary R&D courses, and multimedia training materials. Industry professionals can also deepen their knowledge and earn valuable ProChef® Certification and Certified Wine Professional™ credentials at several levels of proficiency.

In addition, the college offers expert culinary consulting to the industry through its CIA Consulting group. Headed by a seasoned team of Certified Master Chefs and supported by the college's acclaimed international faculty, CIA Consulting offers foodservice businesses a rich menu of custom consulting services in areas such as product innovation, menu R&D, restaurant strategy and design, and culinary training.

FOOD ENTHUSIAST PROGRAMS

Food enthusiasts can get a taste of the CIA educational experience during the college's popular Boot Camp intensives and Weekends at the CIA courses offered at all three campuses. In addition, the college's CIA Sophisticated Palate programs at Greystone offer the very best of Napa Valley's food and wine scene, including exclusive visits to area growers, vintners, and purveyors.

CIA LOCATIONS

MAIN CAMPUS—HYDE PARK, NY

Bachelor's and associate degree programs, professional development programs, food enthusiast programs

The CIA's main campus in New York's scenic Hudson River Valley offers everything an aspiring or professional culinarian could want. Students benefit from truly exceptional facilities that include 41 professionally equipped kitchens and bakeshops; five award-winning, student-staffed restaurants; culinary demonstration theaters; a dedicated wine lecture hall; a center for the study of Italian food and wine; a 82,000-volume library; and a storeroom filled to brimming with the finest ingredients, including many sourced from the bounty of the Hudson Valley.

THE CIA AT GREYSTONE—ST. HELENA, CA

Associate degree programs, professional development programs, certificate programs, food enthusiast programs

Rich with legendary vineyards and renowned restaurants, California's Napa Valley offers students a truly inspiring culinary learning environment. At the center of it all is the CIA at Greystone—a campus like no other, with dedicated centers for flavor development, professional wine studies, and menu research and development; a 15,000-square-foot teaching kitchen space; demonstration theaters; and the Ivy Award-winning Wine Spectator Greystone Restaurant.

THE CIA, SAN ANTONIO—SAN ANTONIO, TX

Certificate program, professional development programs, food enthusiast programs

Created to promote Latino diversity in the U.S. foodservice industry, the CIA campus in San Antonio, TX provides a variety of educational opportunities. In addition to a 30-week certificate program in culinary arts, the CIA's southwest campus also hosts Latin American cuisine courses for foodservice professionals as well as programs for food enthusiasts. The campus is currently undergoing an expansion that will grow its facilities from 5,500 to 25,000 square feet. Opening in fall 2010, it will include three new kitchens, one bakeshop, a 125-seat demonstration theater, and an outdoor cooking facility.

AUTHOR BIOGRAPHY

John W. Fischer, C.H.E., M.S.

Associate Professor in Hospitality and Service Management

The Culinary Institute of America

John Fischer is an associate professor in hospitality and service management at The Culinary Institute of America (CIA) in Hyde Park, NY. Mr. Fischer serves as maître d' instructor in the college's Escoffier Restaurant. The Ivy Award–winning restaurant, which is also a classroom for students in the CIA's culinary arts degree program, features the culinary traditions of France with a light, contemporary touch.

His front-of-the-house class, titled "Advanced Table Service," emphasizes high-quality customer service, wine and spirits, restaurant trends, and sales. Mr. Fischer's students also study reservation and point-of-sale systems, managing costs, and managing service. Mr. Fischer is the author of the CIA's book about service and customer relations, *At Your Service: A Hands-On Guide to the Professional Dining Room* (John Wiley & Sons, 2005) and co-author of *Bistros and Brasseries* (Lebhar-Friedman, 2008).

A 1988 CIA graduate, Mr. Fischer completed his externship field experience at Le Bernardin in New York City. Prior to returning to his alma mater in 2000 as a faculty member, Mr. Fischer held managerial positions at renowned New York City restaurants. He was general manager of Morrell Wine Bar & Café, Cellar Master at The Rainbow Room, manager and wine director of Fresco by Scotto, wine and floor manager at Manhattan Ocean Club, wine director and beverage manager at Campagna and Hudson River Club, and maître d' and wine director at Mondrian.

A Certified Hospitality Educator (C.H.E.), Mr. Fischer also holds a Bachelor of Arts degree from Swarthmore College in Swarthmore, PA and a Master of Science degree in Education from Walden University.

ACKNOWLEDGEMENTS

It's not easy being cheesy. I have received help and support from many directions during this project, and everyone who joined in deserves credit. First and foremost, Maggie Wheeler, my editor, combines a sharp mind, eagle eye, and soft voice. Thanks to her for keeping me on track and reminding me that not every sentence makes sense. Also on the inside, Shelly Malgee and Erin McDowell for helping to make my cooking look good, and Joe Saenz for helping to prepare many of the dishes as well. Thanks to David Barillaro for actually finding all of these marvelous cheeses for the photographs. Without him, the book would be much less interesting. On that note, Keith Ferris did wonders with the many, many cheese photographs, along with those of a few cows. Thanks to my students who, over the years, have helped me to refine my methods of teaching the subject of cheese. And thanks to Tim Ryan, president of the CIA, his administration, and my fellow faculty members for supplying support and even recipes to make this book better.

As for support from outside the Institute, Ben Fink could make a puddle look appetizing, and did so with the food here as well. Colin McGrath and the folks at Sprout Creek Farm were generous with their time (and cheese) and helped me to more organically understand where cheese really starts and what it can become. Two great cheese retailers also helped; Artisanal Premium Cheese supplied many of the hard-to-find cheeses for the identification photographs (and tastings), and my tour of the caves at Murray's Cheese, arranged for by my friend Jamie "Pickles" McAndrew, which helped me to understand why different cheeses are happier under different storage conditions.

From inside my world, I would not be where, and who I am without my family and friends, especially my brother Tom, sister Mary, and sainted mother Mary Ellen Fischer. Speaking of sainted, my wife Nathalie has eaten a lot of cheese over the past year but seems okay with it. Thank goodness she was there to provide quality control. Finally, my late father Robert E. Fischer is the reason I write. He was the editor of *Architectural Record* magazine and was especially good at explaining complex engineering concepts to architects in simple terms. In my teaching and writing, I try to use concept rather than data, and this is certainly my father's legacy.

INTRODUCTION

While cheese has been an important part of food culture in Europe for hundreds of years, Americans are just now learning that there's more to cheese than just Cheddar and Mozzarella. With the huge increase in Americans' awareness and curiosity regarding fine cheese has come a need for clear, easy-to-understand information on good cheese and its uses.

To understand the product fully, though, there are some areas where we can enlighten the reader. In that cheese was first a method to preserve excess milk during the early days of animal domestication, there is a lot of history — thousands of years worth, but herein will only be enough to provide a solid foundation. Other subjects covered will be the basics of cheesemaking, differences between the most popular source milks, and the major factors like rinds and aging that have the greatest effect on flavor profiles.

That said, rather than presenting the cheeses in alphabetical order, their descriptions are organized by flavor profile. Thus the Medium Cheese chapter includes aged Gruyère, Comté, and other cheeses that have some power. The Stinky & Strong Cheese chapter obviously includes Taleggio, Cabrales, Époisses, and Pont l'Évêque while the Mild Cheese chapter includes fresh goat cheese and Brie. By doing this, readers do not have to plow through a list of names to find the flavor they're looking for . . . people in search of cheese don't typically think alphabetically when zeroing in on what they might want to eat that night.

Other benefits of this approach include a simplification of beverage pairing, as well as an easier way to plan a cheese board or plate ... by flavor, not from an intellectual construct. Altogether, this book will provide both the information and structure to not only understand cheese a bit better, but also to manage its use in your business as well as your personal life. You will have the opportunity to learn a lot more about more than one hundred and twenty-five cheeses and why they all taste so different. But even before you have the subject all figured out, there are two things that will help you immediately; the chapter structure can help you to build an assortment before you truly know the differences, and the preparation chapters will give you immediate access to cooking with cheese as well as a conceptual method to pair beverages and other food items with your cheese choices. That said, relax and start to enjoy the ease and complexity of a truly great renewable food.

WHY CHEESE?

Simple answers abound here. Most simply, people love cheese. On average, Americans eat 32 pounds a year per person. The Italians each eat 51 pounds, the French 53 . . . and the Greeks 60 pounds of cheese (most of it Feta) per year! Why, though? Why do we love preserved milk? Because humans have acquired a taste for a food that is practical. For the thousands of years that we have been making cheese, it has been a way to keep the calories around. Our domesticated mammals, first sheep and goats, then cows, produced milk for immediate consumption. But the stuff went sour, and then bad without some form of preservation. Modern refrigeration has only been around for two centuries, and ice harvesting was not always practical or affordable. The removal of some water from the milk, however, made it less perishable. In temperate regions, cheeses could be stored in a cool place (such as a cellar) alongside cured meats, wine, beer, and sturdy root vegetables. It's no surprise that these foodstuffs are still around — they've been part of our diet for thousands of years.

This is not a history book but some knowledge of whence cheese came will help you to have a more conceptual understanding of the product. That is, it was easier to keep cheese in the colder regions, and more difficult in the warmer ones. This means a couple of things — that, in the colder regions, cheese could have a higher water content and still last for a while. In hotter areas, fresh and creamy cheeses didn't last as long, so more moisture was removed from the milk to yield a harder cheese; that or you had to eat the fresh cheeses right away. For example, you could have a creamy, soft Brie in Île-de-France, which is near Paris and a pretty cool region; but on Corsica, in the Mediterranean, some of the cheeses are so hard (Tomme de Chèvre) that you almost need to take a hammer and chisel to them.

Hard cheeses were eventually made in cooler places, of course, but that was just a matter of time and desire — they didn't *have* to be produced out of necessity. And in hotter places like Naples, you can have a fresh cheese like Mozzarella di Bufala, but you buy it and should probably eat it that same day.

Some turophiles (cheese lovers) will argue that the best and most complex flavors in cheese don't arrive until after some aging, but I would argue that there is also pleasure to be found in the simplest of young cheeses, which can be thought of as only one step beyond fresh milk.

THE ANATOMY OF A CHEESE

There will be two terms in this book that refer to the cheese's morphology. One is the rind. Just like that of an orange, it is the outermost surface, and can be edible or inedible, hard or fuzzy, artificial or naturally occurring — or totally absent. The other term is paste. This is the interior of the cheese, which can be consistently of one texture, vary a little bit, have holes or streaks of mold, and is an important part of each cheese's description.

MILK

This mammalian baby food has been around for a long time. Mammals began to develop their physical traits about 300 million years ago, but the animals responsible for most of the milk we use evolved around 270 million years later. Ruminants developed their chambered stomachs so they could extract nutritional value from plant material that was indigestible to most other animals, including humans. Straw and hay can be stored pretty easily, and these fine animals turn it into large amounts of a highly nutritious liquid. Thus, milk cows have been selectively bred in Europe for about 5,000 years, whereas goats and sheep have provided us with milk for thousands of years longer, mostly because they require less effort to maintain.

Milk is a product of whatever the animal has been eating and will bear some vestige of its origin. It's intriguing that a type of cheese can have seasonal differences because of what the animal is fed. In Italy, Parmigiano-Reggiano has distinct seasons; the cows are eating fresh grass in spring and dried hay in the winter, and a gradually changing blend of the two in summer and fall. The milk is different, and so are the cheeses.

COW'S MILK

As farm machinery became available during the Industrial Age, cattle were no longer needed as draft animals, and were now able to spend time and energy making more milk. Newly available fast and affordable long-distance transportation (trains and trucks) made it possible for city dwellers to drink farm-fresh milk. These and other advancements in agricultural practices that developed around the same time coincidentally led to a huge increase in milk production and consumption. It should come as no surprise that most cheese in temperate regions is made from cow's milk because there is so much more produced than sheep's and goat's milk.

Cow's milk is usually around 3.7 percent fat and 87 percent water with the balance being made up of lactose, protein, and some minerals. It has much less lactose than human milk, but more protein. When unpasteurized, milk is initially quite alive; some living cells come from the cow, but also millions of bacteria are present. Some of these bacteria can lead to spoilage, but many of them are actually beneficial to the cheese-making process. So raw milk is more perishable, but many cheesemakers are willing to deal with the inherent challenges to produce a more complex set of flavors in the final product.

In India, the large and long-horned cow, called a zebu, is still used as a beast of burden. It produces much less milk than its European counterparts, like the ubiquitous Holstein, but its milk is 25 percent higher in butterfat. So, milk products in India are quite a bit richer. Keep that in mind next time you're cooking Indian food — you might have to find a local zebu farm.

FIGURE **1.1** Black Angus bull

FIGURE **1.2** Black Angus cow

FIGURE **1.3** Charolais bull

FIGURE **1.4** Charolais cow

FIGURE **1.5** Brahman bull

FIGURE **1.6** Brahman cow

FIGURE **1.7** Hereford bull

FIGURE **1.8** Hereford cow

FIGURE **1.9** Holstein cow

FIGURE **1.10** Limousin buil

FIGURE **1.11** Chianina bull

FIGURE **1.12** Simmental cow

FIGURE **1.13** Texas Longhorn

BUFFALO MILK

The water buffalo is very popular in tropical Asia, but also has a very significant presence in the Campania province of Italy. Though there is not a definitive explanation for its presence in both places, it is most likely that Arabs brought the buffalo to Sicily in the tenth century, and they made it to southern Italy from there.

The buffalo's popularity is driven by two things; their large feet spread out to allow them to walk in marshy areas, and their milk is very high quality. Campania is where the lovely and prized *mozzarella di Bufala* comes from. The milk is considerably richer than that of cows because of the higher butterfat content, and the cheese therefore has a creamier taste and texture than mozzarella made from cow's milk.

GOAT'S MILK

Goats originally thrived in mountainous and arid areas near present-day Iran and Iraq. Their natural ability to survive, even prosper, in marginal conditions was a plus. Goats can subsist on a wide range of foods that other animals won't touch. The fact that they produce a large quantity of milk proportional to their body size made them that much more attractive as an animal to domesticate. Because of these factors, they became popular in areas with a meager food supply more than 10,000 years ago.

The milk is chalky-white and has slightly lower lactose levels than cow's milk. Because of this, it is often recommended for children, or even adults who are lactose intolerant. Goat's milk has a higher level of acidity (lower pH) than the other popular milks, and thus yields a tangier cheese, especially when it's young or fresh. Although many think

of goat's cheese as the log of white stuff that you get in the supermarket, there is a broad range of many interesting goats' milk cheeses from around the world, from the freshest ricotta to the funkiest Bleu de Chèvre.

SHEEP'S MILK

These animals are somewhat less about mountains than goats are and tend to be happier in foothills and rolling glades. A good example is the foothills of the Pyrénées, where the justly famous Brebis family of cheeses is made. Essentially, *brebis* means "mountain sheep cheese." While not as scrappy and low-maintenance as goats, sheep have the extra benefit of providing a lot of wool for clothing. In cold regions, sheep are multi taskers.

Their milk has more fat and protein than cow's or goat's milk, and more minerals as well. While not produced in as great a volume as its two closest competitors, there are many famous cheeses made from it — some that might surprise you. Roquefort is one of those; the other being any cheese from Italy that has the word *pecorino* in it. As you might imagine, the Old Chatham Sheepherding Company produces quite a few examples, all of which are lovely. As with goat cheese, the range in style is very broad, and there are sheep's milk cheeses made wherever sheep are raised.

France is arguably the most important cheese-producing country in the world. Those arguments will come from all corners with the Italians and Belgians saying that their cheeses are of higher quality and Americans disputing such a statement because they make more cheese than any other country. However, the French export more cheese than any other country, which points to both volume production and high quality. In France, there is everything from the smallest farmer hand-milking animals and then making cheese from that milk, to factories that accumulate milk from many farms and make cheese using modern technology.

These examples, and many in between, can be seen all over France. Cheese must have its milk, so some regions produce more because they are better suited for raising domesticated dairy animals. Also, different animals survive and thrive under different conditions; this plus the overall regional climate has a direct influence on the final product. Because of this influence, and many years of history (often centuries), most regions in France are known for either a specific class of cheeses (bloomy rinds from Île-de-France, for instance), or a grouping of cheese styles. Here's a quick "tour de France" in a roughly clockwise direction starting in the North.

Alsace and Lorraine

Lorraine is the larger of these two regions, but Alsace is more famous for its comestibles. Perhaps it is the proximity to Germany that has given Alsace a bit more of a multicultural flavor, and so a more varied collection of food products. It could also be that the Vosges Mountains that lie on the border between Lorraine and Alsace act as a rain shadow for the land below, creating ideal sunny and relatively dry growing conditions for grapes on the hillside, and grain, geese (for foie gras), and cattle on the plains. This confluence of conditions makes Alsace a particularly wonderful region for both food and drink. The wines of Alsace are some of the best in the world for pairing with food (Riesling, especially), there are great beers like Kronenbourg, and the bounty of fruits is often fermented and then distilled into *eaux de vie* — clear, strong, and very pure spirits. Most notable of these is Kirsch, made from cherries but there are many others; Alsatians will ferment and distill just about anything they can, including pine tree buds.

The most famous cheese of the region is Munster. This is not your deli Munster, though. It is a washed-rind cow's milk cheese that has some serious funk in its aroma. It is popular in its home region, both in a fresh state (while still a bit chalky inside) or aged to its stinky and unctuous state, considered by many to be when this cheese is best.

Lorraine is not without its own version of this cheese, called Géromé or Munster-Géromé. It is slightly larger than its Alsace sister, but is covered under the same A.O.C.

Although some other cheeses are produced there, they don't come close to the popularity of Munster, which is part of the *Alsacien* diet along with the other products of the region. It would be criminal not to mention the most famous dish from this part of France, *Choucroute Garnie*. It means "garnished sauerkraut" and consists of its named ingredient with a variety of sausages and other pork bits like bacon, hocks, and shoulder meat.

Together, Alsace and Lorraine are known for the quality of their foodstuffs. Climate, geography, and cultural influence conspire to create a French-German hybrid cuisine based on excellent local ingredients and beverages. Oh, and it's also a beautiful place to visit as well (if the food isn't enough to draw you there).

Franche-Comté

Just south of Alsace is the rural region of Franche-Comté. It borders Switzerland and is dominated by the Jura Mountain range. In fact, the slopes increase from west to east, offering a range of altitudes and types of grazing (and growing) regions. There is some wine production in the Jura, *vin jaune* ("yellow wine") being perhaps the most famous. It is an intentionally oxidized wine somewhat similar to a dry sherry. There are some un-oxidized dry wines as well, which lie stylistically between the wines of Burgundy to the west and Switzerland to the east. Conveniently, they happen to go quite well with the cheeses of the area, the characteristic oxidized flavors of the *vin jaune* pairing nicely with the nutty sweetness of the aged cheeses from there.

Given that the pastureland ranges from fairly broad, low altitude sites to alpine mountain meadows, the milk from the famous Montébeliard cows that graze in them also range in complexity of flavor . . . as well as in the volume produced. As you might have guessed already, the alpine milk usually has more complex flavor than the milk from the plains, and leads to more flavorful cheeses. The alpine milk's complexity is due to the cows' more varied diet. The most famous cheese of the region is Comté (sometimes called Gruyère de Comté), one of the most popular cheeses in France. Two other notables are Morbier and Bleu de Gex, also called Bleu de Haut-Jura. For a rather small region, quite a bit of cheese is produced, Comté being the largest production A.O.C. cheese in France. Their cuisine leans toward that of nearby Switzerland, with a reliance on pork and locally available ingredients such as wild mushrooms. Two famous smoked sausages, the *Saucisse de Morteau* and Montbéliard sausage are very tasty and are smoked in the chimneys (called *Tuyé*) of traditional houses in the area.

Savoie

This is a beautiful part of France that lies just to the south of Burgundy and the Jura, and to the west of Switzerland and Italy. A quick glance at a topographic map shows that it is a region defined by the Rhône Alpes mountains. This means that farming for crops is not as popular (or possible) as cattle grazing. In addition to the previously mentioned Montébeliard cows, the famed Abondance and Tarentaise cattle all produce milk for the cheeses the area is famous for.

Perhaps the best known is Reblochon, but Abondance, Beaufort, and Tomme de Savoie are not far behind in popularity. The dish called *Tartiflette* is from here and was created by a trade council not too long ago to act as a vehicle for Reblochon. The cheese and the dish are quite famous here, but the region is almost more known as a place to visit — tourism is one of its largest industries year-round. Beautiful alpine views are available at all times, and winter sports draw many when there is snow. That same snow drives the cattle to lower elevations in the cold months, where they are fed silage. The cheeses made with winter milk do not hold a candle to those from summer alpine milk. Look for the younger cheeses in the spring, and the aged cheeses in winter (a year later). The cheeses from a region famous for having held the Winter Olympics once in Albertville are usually at there best around the same time. The wines of Savoie are similar to those from Jura. Most of it is white, and fairly light without a whole lot of complexity. This is not a criticism, of course; they are great wines for casual consumption, and go quite well with the cheeses of the region. The main grape is Chasselas, a white grape that might be better known for its use in Switzerland. A small amount of red is produced in Savoie, usually from Gamay or Pinot Noir. None of the wines are intended for long-term aging, and they should be appreciated for their alpine charm.

Burgundy

Burgundy is one of the most important food regions in France. Made up of rolling hills and older (thus, smaller) mountain ranges, it ranges from just south of Paris to just north of the Rhône Valley. The Morvan Massif runs roughly down the center of Burgundy, with the Saône River to the east and the Loire to the west. The most important (and costly) wines are from the Côte d'Or, famous for having an escarpment

that is rich in limestone, which is beneficial for wine growing. The red and white wines of Burgundy are generally some of the most significant and famous wines made in France, which is saying something. Based mostly on Chardonnay and Pinot Noir, burgundies are some of the most food-friendly wines in the world. Home to the famous and name-protected Bresse chicken (*Poulet de Bresse*) as well as some pretty good mustard from the region's capital, Dijon, Burgundy means food. Both Beef Bourguignon and Coq au Vin are dishes that originated there, along with the wonderful *Oeufs en Meurette*, eggs poached in red wine then served in a rich wine-based sauce with mushrooms and bacon.

Ironically, there aren't very many famous cheeses from Burgundy. There is a ringer, though. Often referred to as a favorite, even by Napoleon, Époisses de Bourgogne is considered one of the great connoisseur's cheeses in the world. Stinky and with a spoonable consistency when ripe, it is as important to food lovers as Gevrey-Chambertin is to oenophiles. Other notable cheeses are Chaource and Langres (a calmer Époisses-type). But in this region known for its wines and other foods, Époisses retains the title "King of Cheeses," given it by eighteenth century gastronome Brillat-Savarin.

Provence and Rhône

The Rhône river begins in the Alps of Switzerland, and winds its way down through the mountains, eventually splitting in two at its mouth. There are many hills, and the valley itself acts as a funnel for the famous Mistral wind that comes down from the northwest. The hills and Alps continue down through Provence as does the Mistral, a dry cool wind that can reach over fifty miles per hour. This creates a rather inhospitable environment for plants, animals, and people, but all are somewhat toughened by the experience.

As the climate warms, dairy farming become less likely because cows produce less milk at hotter temperatures. A few other factors lead farmers to the animals more likely to survive the heat, sheep and goats. These two animals produce much less milk than cows, though, so cheese production decreases.

Provence and Rhône, famous for their wines, olives, tomatoes, and the like, are not quite as well known for their cheeses. One exception is Banon, a goat cheese (sometimes with cow's milk added) that is washed with eau de vie and then wrapped in chestnut leaves. It does, admittedly, come from the northern reaches of Provence but it still counts as a Provençal cheese. Another A.O.C. cheese from the region is Picodon, a relatively small goat cheese available in several guises, as well as varying levels of quality.

Provence has a more famous cuisine than the Rhône, with dishes such as Ratatouille and Bouillabaisse which rely on the produce of the area as well as the Mediterranean Sea's bounty. Also, any dish described as *provençal* should have some combination of tomatoes, peppers, olives, garlic, herbs, and olive oil.

Corsica

The birthplace of Napoleon Bonaparte (1769) is the fourth-largest island in the Mediterranean Sea, and sits southeast of Provence. It has been occupied by Greeks, Etruscans, Romans, and Genoese over the years, but became part of France in 1768. *La Corse* is one of the most mountainous Mediterranean isles, and relies on both tourism and agriculture to supply its economy. The topography precludes what many would consider mainstream agriculture, so fruit, olive, chestnut, and cork trees are grown, with honey production and wheat bringing up the rear. Most important to us, though, is the sheep population on the island that provides milk for cheese. Some fresh and high-quality, if nondescript, cheeses are sold locally and exported, but the impressive Brin d'Amour is worthy of attention and notice. It is a sheep's milk cheese (with some goat versions available) coated in dried herbs that include rosemary, thyme, juniper, and savory — with the occasional whole dried hot pepper or two. The exterior of the cheese reveals the interior of the island and also flavors the paste underneath. Some say that the aromatic "brush" on Brin d'Amour can bring back memories of what the island smelled like when you were there.

There are quite a few food products that Corsica is famous for, especially its honey, nuts, charcuterie, and olive oil. Pork is the predominant meat used for the charcuterie, and other sources of protein include

their famous whey cheese called Brocciu, and fish caught along the coastline. Most of the indigenous dishes are similar to the rustic cooking of nearby regions, but one interesting specialty is *pulenda*, a chestnut-flour polenta that is used as a side dish.

French Pyrénées

The western end of the Pyrénées mountain range is Basque country, mostly south of the mountains in Spain, but with a sizable population on the French side. The climate is rather lush because moisture comes in from the Atlantic (over the Bay of Biscay), and the mountains themselves are more rounded than their Alpine counterparts. Still, they are rather formidable, and not easy for people (or cows) to navigate. This is sheep country, and cheeses have been made from their milk for thousands of years.

The Basque people have been considered their own ethnic group for centuries, and speak a unique language that bears little resemblance to any other, although it has slowly acquired some words and idioms from Spanish and French. Food is very important in Basque culture, and they are justifiably proud of their sheep cheeses.

The best known of these is Ossau-Iraty, an A.O.C. *Brebis* (the French term for female sheep *and* the cheese made from their milk) that comes in several different shapes and sizes, but is always delicious. It tends to be eaten on its own rather than in recipes, and is sometimes served alongside the delicious Jambon de Bayonne, a ham from nearby that is very similar to the Spanish Jamón Serrano.

Gascony and Périgord

Here in the foothills of the Pyrénées there is an interesting mixture of hills, cliffs, and caves. It was here in the caves of Lascaux that some of the best-preserved cave paintings from the Paleolithic era were found. The varied soils do provide a range of farming conditions, and the rolling hills that make up most of the landscape lead right into the Pyrénées to the southwest.

Although somewhat sparsely populated, this southwestern portion of France is quite famous for a number of reasons beyond the Three Musketeers. In fact, a trio of luxury culinary products from here would leave the food world a very sad place should they disappear. Black truffles, foie gras, and Armagnac brandy have enriched the lives of many gourmands for hundreds of years. Throw in some roast goose, or lamb with potatoes browned in goose fat, and you begin to understand how impressive (and rich) the food is there. This isn't just in Gascony, though, as you probably know that *Sauce Périgueux* or *Périgourdine* is a Madeira sauce with black truffle.

There aren't many famous cheeses from this region, but there is one, *Cabécou* (which means "little goat"). In particular, the Cabécou de Rocamadour is a good example of this type. It's a little surprising that the region known for such over-the-top rich foods is also known for a diminutive (about one ounce each) and somewhat light goat cheese. There is also a famous cow cheese from Aveyron (to the east) called Laguiole.

Auvergne

Coiling in from the left, we come to Auvergne, a region largely defined by the Massif Central, a collection of mountains and defunct volcanoes that dominates south-central France. This range is truly massive, covering about one sixth of France, and is the source of several important rivers. However, its highest peak, the Puy de Sancy, tops out at just shy of 6,200 feet. Interestingly, industry is an important part of the economy here, with Michelin based in Clermont, a high concentration of thermoplastics firms in Thiers, and Volvic water in the town of the same name. Still, agriculture is about as important, with meat, grain, and dairy products being the most prominent.

The old, defunct volcanoes (450 of them in the region) have provided both soil and space to raise cattle in this somewhat arid place. These conditions combine for the production of great milk, and there are several famous cheeses from Auvergne. Some of the greatest blues come from here, including Fourme d'Ambert and Bleu d'Auvergne. They are somewhat milder and easier on the constitution than Roquefort, which actually comes from the southern reaches of this region. Also, there are Cantal and Salers that are somewhat like a more refined version of farmhouse cheddars.

The Loire

Referring to "the Loire" as a region is about as defining as it would be to say "the Mississippi" or "Amazon" and expect that we were both thinking about the exact same spot. The Loire River is about 700 miles long and meanders through a few very different geographical regions on its trip from south-central France to its estuary to the northeast. The regions have a few things in common, though — physical beauty and great growing conditions. In fact, the Loire valley is known as the "garden of France," and the country wines from there are known by the name *Vin de Pays de la Jardin de France*. Such beauty and bounty have not gone unnoticed, as there are more than 300 chateaus lining the river, mostly along the part closest to Paris. These were originally built as country homes for royalty, nobility, and the wealthy.

Having mentioned wine, it should come as no surprise that this is an important growing region, mostly for white wines based on Chenin Blanc and Sauvignon Blanc. Most versions (e.g., Sancerre and Vouvray) go marvelously with the local cheeses. And those cheeses are almost exclusively made from goat's milk. In fact, the goat cheeses of the Loire Valley are some of the finest in the world, and a listing of the smaller regions and towns within reads like a buying guide. Poitou, Charentes, Valençay, Chavignol, Sainte-Maure, Sell-es-sur-Cher, and especially Berry are names to seek out when looking for a great goat cheese. Just as the towns are individual and separated by distance, the cheeses come in dozens of shapes and sizes, though they all tend toward the diminutive. You can find logs, balls, small barrel shapes, pyramids, and even truncated pyramids. They are perfectly good when young and fresh, but will not have developed much character. Most fanciers of *Chèvre* have their own idea of when the cheese (often a specific favorite) is at its best, and many French will buy the cheese fresh and age it themselves at home.

Whether you do this or not, the region and its products are worth exploring, either on your next visit to France, or your next visit to the cheese and wine stores.

Normandy

The region of Bordeaux is busy making wine, and to the north, Brittany is gone fishing. Brittany also produces a huge amount of milk and butter for French consumption, but there isn't much important cheese made in the region. Maybe it's because they don't even try to compete with the bounty of great cheeses made by their neighbors in Normandy.

While Normandy's place on the coast of France does ensure a certain amount of seafood in the Norman diet (especially scallops and mussels), the region is much more famous for its apples and cattle. In fact, if you see a dish described as *à la Normande*, you can be quite certain that there will be either apples, cream, or butter, but most likely all three of them in the preparation. The quality and availability of these ingredients has led to a cuisine that is rather rich and there are a few specialty items that depend on them. Pastry (often with apples) is a specialty, as well as a few apple-based drinks that Normandy is known for, especially cider (alcoholic or not), and Calvados, which is perhaps the finest apple-based brandy in the world. Inevitably, the high-quality milk makes its way into a number of excellent cheeses, which conveniently pair nicely with the apple-based local beverages.

One of the best examples of bloomy rind cheese in the world is Camembert de Normandie, of which the finest examples are not available in the United States because the milk used to make the cheese isn't pasteurized. There are some others, though, that are available. Livarot is a soft, stinky cheese that is recognizable by the raffia strips wrapped around its circumference. Perhaps more famous is another washed-rind cow's milk cheese, Pont l'Évêque. One of the most popular cheeses in France, and now in the United States, it was even part of the "Cheese Shop" sketch from *Monty Python's Flying Circus*. Pont l'Évêque is forceful but restrained — stinky but not horribly so. Its popularity is convenient in that large quantities are imported, and so its freshness can almost be guaranteed. Also, a good cheesemonger will have individual cheeses available at their peak condition, ready to purchase and serve at their best.

Two less intense, and perhaps less impressive cheeses from Normandy are Brillat-Savarin and Petit-Suisse. Brillat-Savarin, named for the famous gastronome, is a very rich, triple cream, bloomy rind cheese best known for its luxurious nature. Petit-Suisse isn't known for much other than the simple pleasure it provides, and it is often served with sugar or fruit preserves, much as one might do with yogurt. Remember, though, it doesn't have to be "serious" to be tasty.

There is a cheese from Normandy at the opposite end of the durability spectrum, which is helpful if you are worried about shipping to a remote location. Mimolette is a nearly spherical cheese that can be eaten at almost any age from six months to four years. During that time, it gets harder and the flavor develops, eventually tasting like a union of aged cheddar and Parmigiano Reggiano. This makes it particularly attractive to Americans, and puts it alongside Pont l'Evecque in popularity. Not to be missed from this area is one more dairy product, fine butter. Often seasoned with local sea salt, it is a real treat on good bread.

Île-de-France

Paris. That's what this region in north-central France is about. The city and its immediate suburbs take up most of the region's area. The landscape is dominated by a large limestone basin that is freckled with rolling hills. As you might imagine, this is pretty crowded territory — it is one of the most densely populated regions in Europe with urban architecture and quite a bit of industry dominating the landscape. But, as it was with New York City many years ago, there was farmland not too far away from the city center. In both cities, urban sprawl has well overtaken most forms of agriculture that were there. Still, there are some towns on the outskirts that still produce milk and cheese. Most famous is the town of Meaux, where one of the two name-protected Brie cheeses (Brie de Meaux) is made. If you find this cheese in the United States, it is undoubtedly made with pasteurized milk, and is most likely from the caves of Pierre Rouzaire, an *affineur* (negociant and cheese-aging specialist) who is based in Tournan-en-Brie in the Seine-et-Marne department southeast of Paris.

Having mentioned Rouzaire, his company makes and sells a number of other cheeses, including Fougerus, with its real fern leaf decoration on top, and Pierre-Robert, a triple-crème bloomy rind cheese that is earthy and incredibly rich with 75% butterfat, measured as percentage of solids. This is not the only bloomy rind triple-crème, and most of the other famous ones come from Île-de-France as well. Explorateur and Brillat-Savarin (originally made in Normandy, but now here) along with Pierre-Robert make up a triple threat of triple-crèmes that are all made in Seine-et-Marne, only a short distance from the center of Paris. In a way, it makes sense that some of the most luxurious cheeses in the world (including Brie, of course) are made in the region of Paris, one of the richest cities in the world.

Champagne

The Champagne region is just to the northeast of Paris and is (of course) known for its sparkling wine. There are a few cheeses from here, although you might imagine that the Champenoise can make a lot more money growing grapes and selling wine. Still, both Chaource and Langres are from this region that is actually farther north in latitude than Fargo, North Dakota, which makes it very cold. Bloomy and washed, respectively, they are both complex and luxurious. Considering the neighborhood, they'd probably be run out of town if they weren't.

Nord-Pas-de-Calais

"Le Nord", as many French refer to it, is the northernmost tip of the country, bordering Belgium and jutting into the English Channel. It has fertile plains and rolling hills and is not as cold there in the winter as you might think because the temperature is modulated by the nearby ocean. It is quite densely populated and has been for years, and was known for its industries, mainly coal and steel. Industry has become less important though — in fact unemployment was very high for a while, but the building of the Chunnel (English Channel Tunnel) brought jobs and tourism to the area.

Fittingly, with industry having been the most important part of their economy, an aggressive, strong cheese is the most popular in the region. Maroilles is one of the stinkiest cow's milk cheeses made in France, and many versions of it, some going by other names (e.g., Gris de Lille), are produced up there. It is powerful, salty, and highly odiferous — not for the faint of heart, and just what a French factory worker or coal miner needs for lunch. Traditional dishes show Flemish influence and include *Carbonnade*, a beef and beer stew, as well as game from nearby forests — the fare tends to be hearty, and not as dependent on fish from the nearby coast.

OTHER INGREDIENTS

SALT

Almost all cheeses are salted or brined at some point during their production. This is a practical addition — it's a preservative. Just as in corned beef and salt cod, salt draws out liquid, which in turn makes it less perishable. Salt also drastically (and positively) affects the flavor of the cheese, just as it does many other foodstuffs. So, most cheeses are basically preseasoned.

RENNET

It contains enzymes, most notably *chymosin*, that are elemental to cheese production. It is found in the fourth stomach of young ruminant animals, and helps them to digest their mother's milk. The animal's production of rennet ceases after awhile, so there isn't a huge window of opportunity to obtain it from calves' stomachs. Other types of rennet are available, some from plants (like nettles and thistles), and some from microbes, such as certain molds. Also, genetic engineering has provided us with rennet from genetically modified microorganisms (for better or worse).

Although cheese can be made using acid (ricotta, for example), the use of rennet after the initial souring yields a stronger and more elastic curd. This is because the chymosin affects only one type of casein protein (the kappa type) and breaks that protein in only one spot, creating a curd that is more durable. Acid alone produces a brittle curd and allows a lot of protein and calcium to bleed out into the whey.

MICROBES

In the squeaky-clean world of the American food marketplace, it upsets some who find out that one of their favorite foods is the product of controlled microbial activity.

The two main categories include bacteria and molds. These two families are largely responsible for the decomposition of our organic world; they also contribute extensively to the flavor and texture of most cheeses.

BACTERIA

This may not sound like an ingredient, and it isn't. It's millions of ingredients that have a fundamental role in the production of cheese. Broad subcategories of bacteria have different effects on cheese. The aptly named starter bacteria are in the milk to begin with and create lactic acid that sours the milk, resulting in yogurt, crème fraîche,

and many other fermented milk products. In cheesemaking, the bacteria usually die off during the process, but their enzymes endure, breaking proteins down into aromatic (flavor) molecules. One of the most famous starter bacteria is *Propionibacterium shermanii*, which is used in the Swiss-type cheeses. One of the enzymes it produces creates both diacetyl (butter smell) and acetic acids in the cheese, resulting in the characteristic flavor. During the process, it also creates carbon dioxide, which creates the holes.

Fermentation isn't just for alcohol. It's when a microorganism changes the chemistry of a substance, often giving off CO_2 and creating other chemicals such as alcohol or diacetyl. Interestingly, it is *not* correctly used when describing the "fermentation" of tea leaves. The browning of tea leaves is actually a form of enzymatic oxidation, and has nothing to do with bacteria or fungi. Cheese, however, can be considered a fermented product when living bacteria and fungi are used.

Smear bacteria, such as *Brevibacterium linens*, are used to varying degrees. They are, indeed, the bacteria responsible for the odor of stinky cheeses such as Taleggio, Epoisses, and (real) Munster. Smear bacteria are tolerant of salt and need oxygen, and so are found only on the surface of cheeses that are likely to have been salted. They also like moisture, so "washing" the cheeses with brine and keeping them in humid environments encourages the formation of a rind. Their somewhat more subtle use is found in Camembert and Gruyère, which are both known for a certain earthiness, but not a profoundly odiferous funk. Note that smear bacteria, which are surface-grown, create flavor compounds that can diffuse deep into the cheese. Luckily, these flavors are usually more pleasant than the aroma would indicate. In addition to flavor compounds, the bacteria can break down the protein structures within the cheese, and this can result in a creamier or even runny texture. In fact, a truly runny cheese is usually one in which the bacteria have been allowed to go too far, and have virtually destroyed the protein matrix in the paste of that cheese.

MOLD

"It's moldy, throw it out!" Well, there wouldn't be any blue cheese dressing at the salad bar or brie baked with almonds if you did. Molds, a type of fungus, appear in and on many cheeses. The blue molds, of course, give us "bleu" cheese. *Penicillium roqueforti* gives Roquefort its distinctive piquancy by breaking some fats down into fatty acids. Other blue molds create similar qualities to cheeses such as Gorgonzola and Stilton, where the effects can be subtly different. White molds need more oxygen, so they tend to grow on the surface of Brie, Camembert, and other "bloomed" cheeses. In

fact, these molds often belong to the *Penicillium camemberti* family. They form a white fuzzy felt-like coating, but also contribute to flavor and texture by breaking down proteins to create the characteristically soft, waxy texture as well as aromas of earth, mushrooms, and eventually ammonia, which is usually considered a fault in cheese.

TIME

If it weren't for this final ingredient, all cheese would be the color of this page and taste like fresh milk. As tasty as milk can be, it is the combined work of bacteria, mold, their enzymes, and Father Time that create the alchemy that brings us such wonderful, exciting, delicious, and nutritious foods. It takes two years of work and patience to yield the complex simplicity in a bite of salty, sweet, nutty, spicy Parmigiano-Reggiano, one of the best eating cheeses on the planet.

THE MAKING OF CHEESE

Although the flavors in the base milk have a lot to do with flavors in the final product, the myriad types of cheese vary almost as much because of the process they go through. Cheesemaking has thousands of variables, in fact, too many to cover in this book. However, a simple description follows.

CURDLING

The cheesemaker usually adds a combination of starter bacteria and rennet to the milk at the outset. If using only acid, it slowly produces a rather fragile curd that retains its moisture — think ricotta. Rennet, however, acts quickly and creates a broader, firm curd that can be cut into smaller pieces. The type of curd achieved is basic to the final product; softer cheeses start out as larger curds, or pieces of curd, so that more whey is retained. To create a hard cheese, the curds are cut into smaller pieces to increase surface area and allow for more whey to leak out.

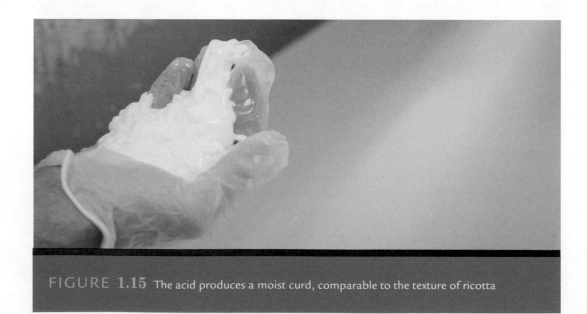

FIGURE **1.15** The acid produces a moist curd, comparable to the texture of ricotta

DRAINING, SALTING, AND SHAPING

If the cheese is meant to be soft, more moisture needs to remain, so the curds are handled gently — sometimes not cut up at all, but gently ladled into their forms so they can drain by gravity and be salted later.

Harder cheeses begin life as smaller pieces of curd, sometimes drained but also pressed to expel more whey. Cooking the curd helps squeeze out even more liquid by denaturing the proteins that squeeze out the whey. Cheeses are almost always salted, by mixing salt with the curd, allowing formed cheeses to float in a brine solution, or even rubbing the cheese with a brine or dry salt.

Obviously salt enhances flavor, but it also removes more water from the cheese, and inhibits unwanted microbial activity. Once the curds have been put in their forms, they are sometimes pressed to expel even more liquid. Mechanical presses can be used, also the weight of other cheeses, stacked one on top of the other.

FIGURE **1.16** The curds are poured into forms to drain

FIGURE **1.17** Cheeses draining in forms before salting

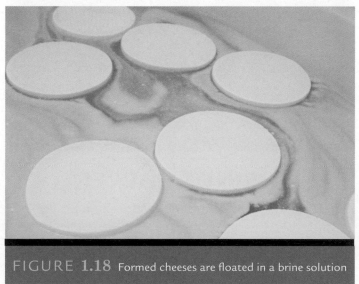

FIGURE **1.18** Formed cheeses are floated in a brine solution

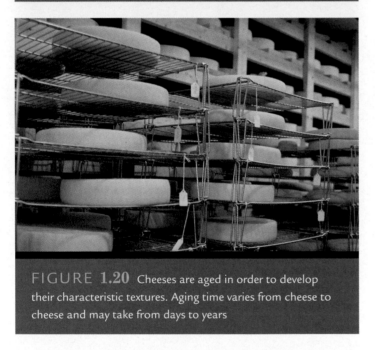

RIPENING/AFFINAGE

This is the period during which the cheese will reach its familiar stage. For instance, if you cut open a brand-new Camembert, the inside would look like fresh cheese — white, chalky, and not un-like farmer's cheese or a log of Chèvre. As it ages, though, the texture slowly changes from the surface inward. After four weeks, the entire paste of the cheese has the characteristic creamy/waxy tex-ture that one expects. At this point the cheese is ready to eat. In fact, if you don't eat it soon, its quality will decline quickly because of the relatively high moisture content. This demonstrates the point that the moisture content of a cheese deter-mines, largely, how long it will take to ripen, and also how long it will remain in good condition. So, Mimolette will ripen and live for a couple of years; Camembert is overripe and virtually inedible after a couple of months.

Now, while the ingredients and basics of cheesemaking are good to know in order to better understand the product, you can do pretty well by just concentrating on a few basic aspects of a cheese. What milk is it made from? Is it soft, semi-soft, or hard? What kind of rind does it have? The first two have been covered previ-ously. The last follows.

FIGURE **1.19** Formed and salted cheeses at the outset of the ripening process

FIGURE **1.20** Cheeses are aged in order to develop their characteristic textures. Aging time varies from cheese to cheese and may take from days to years

RINDS HAPPEN

Jean-Francois was feeling a bit peckish, and went to the cellar to fetch some cheese for a quick snack. But, *q'eul horreur*, the last wheel of cheese was covered with a hairy, white mold! Although wary, J-F grabbed the wheel, ran upstairs, and hesitantly ate the cheese along with some simple *vin de table*, a fresh baguette, and a few green grapes. It was delicious. While I have no idea if this is how rinds were discovered (and it probably isn't), something like this scenario took place in thousands of places over the same number of years, and some people realized it was a good thing.

Rinds are good for many cheeses, but not all cheeses have rinds. Fresh ones such as mozzarella and Queso Blanco don't have the time to form, nor do they need one. High-volume cheddars are wrapped in aluminized cellophane, and are fine that way.

But many venerable cheeses have a rind that is good for them (and us) in several ways, for a number of reasons.

1. Protection — Cheese starts out with fairly high water content. As it ages, one of the simplest changes is that of evaporation. A coating helps to retain moisture, either to keep the cheese at a preferred texture, or to allow the cheese to slowly age and lose some of its water content more gradually.

2. Flavor — Depending on what type of rind is present, there can be a desirable addition of flavor to the cheese, such as that of some herbs or spices — or even the flavor of a bloomy (moldy) rind. In some cases, the mold or bacteria that form the rind also create enzymes that can break down fats and/or proteins into smaller, flavorful molecules.

3. Texture — A very appealing characteristic of the bloomy mold is that it adds textural interest to the mouthfeel of a soft, creamy cheese such as Brie or Pierre Robert. Sure, the creamy rich pastes of these cheeses are lovely, but that goo can use a little contrast to show it off.

4. Identification — Along with the actual shape of the cheese, the type of rind it has can identify it as a specific variety. Taken to the extreme, some cheeses even have their name imprinted in the rind, such as with Parmigiano-Reggiano or Grana Padano, both natural rind cheeses.

TYPES OF RIND

FRESH CHEESE

This actually denotes the absence of any sort of rind. When the cheese is first produced, the outside is essentially the same as the inside. The interior of the cheese is called the paste or *pâté*, and unless the cheese has been brined or coated in some way, it's the same as the outside.

NATURAL RIND

Technically the simplest of rinds, it's not necessarily that easy to create. Consider that a cheese such as Grana Padano has to sit on a shelf long enough for its leathery coating to form, but can't be allowed to get moldy or slimy in any way and still has to

be at a warm enough temperature that it can age. Some cheeses with natural rinds are brined, which can help to preserve them, and many are regularly brushed or rubbed with an oiled cloth to abate the growth of mold.

BLOOMY RIND

Most Americans are now aware of and comfortable with these cheeses, especially Brie and Camembert. Not all know, however, that the rind is actually edible. Many bloomy-rind cheeses are served rather young, while their bloom is still pristinely white. Camembert is ready to be shipped after three to four weeks of aging, and *à point* (ready to eat) after the paste has been transformed by fungal enzymes from a chalky-looking fresh state to the familiar creamy consistency. The rind, or coating on these cheeses is actually a type of mold. Although it used to happen naturally because of airborne (ambient) mold spores, today's cheesemakers will usually inoculate their product with purified strains of *Penicillium candida* or *Penicillium camemberti* molds. This coating won't last forever in its prime state, so these cheeses tend to be eaten rather young. In fact, once the interior of the cheese is runny, the cheese has gone too far. Smooth and creamy — good. Running out onto the cheese board — gone.

WASHED RIND

Welcome to Funkytown. Whereas bloomy cheeses are covered by a relatively benign mold, washed rind cheeses have a coating created by bacteria belonging to the "smear" family. This group of *Brevibacteria* is actually native to both seashores and human skin — both briny, hence the fact that many of these cheeses are washed with salty solutions. These same bacteria do not like acid, need oxygen to grow, and thus stay outside the cheese. Brevibacteria break down some of the proteins and fats, and also produce a pigment similar to carotene, creating the orange to red-orange or tan color on some of these cheeses. Ever wonder why grocery-store Muenster has that orange-colored coating? Because the real thing, from Alsace in France, is a washed-rind cheese! The Danish, German, and American versions do not have that coating, nor do they have the character of the true Alsatian Muenster, a truly stinky cheese. Just why do these cheeses smell so bad? First of all, bacteria, along with fungi, are the most populous and efficient degraders of organic material on the planet — and you know what that can smell like. Also, the smear bacteria that create these rinds are similar to those found on human skin, and thus can smell like sweat, fish, or even garlic. These compounds can sometimes find their way into the cheese and affect both flavor and texture. Yum!

ARTIFICIAL RIND

Notice that the term manmade is not used here. Sure, a person put the red wax coating on a wheel of Gouda, but the same with the dried herbs on the Brin d'amour and the ash on the log of goat's cheese. Artificial means that the coating did not *originate on that cheese*. It can be of a perfectly natural (and edible) character, but it was put there by some*body* — it didn't grow there. The rinds in this case are all intended to carry out the protection part of the deal, and some of them actually add to the flavor or textural sensation while eating the cheese.

ARTISANAL VS. INDUSTRIAL

There are a few terms that will appear with some regularity in this text that refer to the size and style of production facility that the cheese comes from. The first, and perhaps most overused term, is artisanal. This *should* mean that the cheese was made by hand and presumably by someone who is an artisan. When I say that it can be overused, this is not by the people to make or sell these products. It is usually consumers and innocently ignorant sellers who will refer to any small-production cheese as "artisanal." As you will soon see, not all small-production cheeses are made by hand.

Another concept is described by two terms; both *fermier* and *farmhouse* mean that the cheese was made at the farm where the milk is produced. It is usually made by artisanal production but not necessarily. This, of course, depends on the size of the farm and the amount of mechanization they use. There are, of course huge farms in the United States and abroad where almost the entire milk and cheese production are automated, so that would technically be a farmhouse cheese without being artisanal.

Finally, the term *industriel* or "industrial" describes those cheeses just mentioned, but doesn't always carry negative connotations. Having visited such a facility in Normandy, France, I can tell you that the product was of superior quality and consistency, but perhaps lacked a little bit of complexity or individual personality that an artisanally produced cheese from a farmhouse would have.

There is not much value judgment to be made here. If you increase individuality and character, consistency may suffer; but if you want to get the same cheese every single time, the cheese might not be reaching the dizzying heights of its potential character. Luckily, as the buyer, you usually have a choice and can purchase the product that best fulfills your needs. If you are serving a knowledgeable and experienced clientele from your cheese board, character and individuality are prized qualities; but if you need to produce a large quantity of prepared foods for a constant, high-volume outlet, the cheese's consistency can be even more important than its absolute quality.

FRESH AND YOUNG CHEESES

CHEESES BY FLAVOR

In this book, the cheeses are in order of increasing flavor intensity. Some cheeses are available at more than one stage of maturity, so they will appear in more than one chapter. For instance, some cheeses such as Mimolette are edible during different stages of their maturation process. When young, around six months, they have the slightly rubbery texture and somewhat tangy flavor of a young Edam, after which they are modeled. But after a year or two of aging, the texture approaches that of a Parmigiano-Reggiano, and the flavor is like a cross between Parmigiano and sharp cheddar.

The main listing for each of these variable cheeses will lie in the chapter that defines the cheese at what is considered by most to be its best state. Its other states of edibility will be included in the appropriate chapters, with a reference to its main listing elsewhere in the book.

FRESH AND YOUNG CHEESES

Some turophiles might argue that fresh cheese is too young to be interesting — that it hasn't had the time to develop any character. However, it is worth countering that the blush of youth does indeed hold some virtue. The appeal of fresh cheese is it was fresh milk seemingly moments ago. The freshness and the flavor of the meadow are right there, largely unadulterated. Mascarpone, for instance, is such a simple and luxurious pleasure that you don't need the complexity, you just revel in the voluptuous texture and light sweetness. Other fresh and young cheeses have their attractions as well, but there is one caveat. Because their water content is so high, fresh cheeses are highly perishable. Many of them really should be eaten (or served) the same day that they are purchased. Be very conscious of any expiration dates printed on the packaging and avoid products nearing that date unless they're going to be used immediately.

The flavor profile of these cheeses is dominated by the milk, and varies from species to species, breed to breed — even members of the same breed that are raised under different conditions will produce different milk. It depends largely on the animals' diets because what they eat ends up in the milk. Also the fat content of the milk (whole or skim) has an effect on the final product. Some might say the cheeses are bland, but they have a refreshing simplicity; in fact, there is a lot of subtlety here. Depending on the animal and how the cheese is made, there will be slightly different levels of acidity and salinity. Textures vary widely as well, from the velvety Mascarpone, to the crumbly Paneer of India. Some can actually be made at home or in a professional kitchen, and you'll find instructions for some of them in Chapter 6.

FIGURE 2.1 · Mascarpone

MASCARPONE

Mascarpone is barely cheese. In fact, it's even more like milk than its cousins, yogurt and sour cream. Essentially, it is a cultured product usually made from a milk product high in butterfat. One example would be the cream skimmed off the milk that is then used to produce Parmigiano-Reggiano. Mascarpone is a rich, thick, lush, and creamy product that is vital to the making of Tiramisu, and is sometimes used to enrich savory dishes such as risotto or polenta. Thoroughly hedonistic, the word *cheese* doesn't quite do it justice.

COTTAGE CHEESE/FARMER'S CHEESE

Some of the simplest, though some might say the most bland, flavors in the cheese world are found in a tub of cottage cheese. It is thought to have originated as a by-product of butter-making in cottages, so even then it was relatively low in fat but high in protein content. During production, some whey is left in the curds by letting it drain, but not pressing it, which leaves the final product with a high moisture content. Pressing turns it into farmer or farmer's cheese, which is still rather mild, but has a much firmer texture. Cottage cheese can be used in a number of simple preparations, and even to replace ricotta in some recipes, but I can't help but think, where do all those tubs of cottage cheese in the grocery store go?

FIGURE **2.2** Cottage Cheese

FROMAGE BLANC/FRAIS

Either name gives away the nature of this cheese. Whether called "white" or "fresh," there is something else about the name that is significant — there is no place name in it. Fromage blanc can be and *is* made in many regions of France, but these cheeses are more similar than not. Because there isn't (and shouldn't be) any aging, the type and quality of milk (and sometimes, cream) are most important to the flavor of the final product. A goat's milk fromage blanc will be quite different from a cow's milk version, but it really doesn't matter where it's from. The factors that affect the flavor of the milk, though, do matter. Animal feed, season, breed, and even time of day figure in, as well as whether any fat is removed by skimming. Raw milk versions have more complexity but are also illegal in the United States.

The French have quite a few fresh cheeses, under different names and from various parts of the country. They all share the same background flavor — that of fresh milk — but some are flavored with herb mixtures, some have fresh bay leaves or other herbs on the outside, and some are even enriched with additional cream. Following is a list of some of them, along with their places of origin.

- Brousse du Rove (Provence)
- Cervelle de Canut (Lyon; often mixed with shallots, garlic, and *fines herbes*)
- Chèvre Frais (Loire, especially Berry; goat's milk)
- Fontainebleau (Iles de France)
- Fromage Frais de Nîmes (Languedoc; the one with a bay leaf on top)
- Gastanberra (Aquitaine; sheep's milk)
- Petit Suisse (All over France; popular with bread, jam, and coffee)
- Ségalou (Quercy, in the Midi-Pyrénées)

The flavor is mild, often with a light tanginess. The added herbs lend their characteristic flavors, and the texture is delicate and moist. These cheeses can become somewhat crumbly with a few days' age.

FIGURE **2.3** Queso Fresco

QUESO BLANCO/FRESCO

This means the same exact thing as the previous *fromage blanc/frais* heading. It also refers to a very similar family of cheeses that originated in Spain and that are used in Mexican and Southwestern American cuisine. It is a staple in Mexican cooking, is made from cow's milk or a combination of cow's and goat's milk, and usually has a crumbly texture and fresh, slightly salty flavor. It does not melt when heated (see sidebar below), and so will hold its shape when crumbled over a casserole. It is also sometimes eaten as is, with (or between) warmed corn or flour tortillas — which was, perhaps, the original quesadilla. As Mexican food has become more popular in the United States, its availability has increased dramatically and it remains a mild cheese. If the queso fresco was made with some goat's milk, it will be tangier. Let's face it, though, complexity is not supposed to be its strong suit, just its creaminess and use as a foil for the spicy and stronger-flavored foods that lie beneath.

GOAT CHEESE/CHÈVRE

This is the first category in which some members will reappear in later chapters. As mentioned earlier, if they are best known for their fresh versions, the full listing will appear here.

NOPE, THEY WON'T MELT

There are some cheeses that will not melt, no matter how much heat is applied. They include ricotta, paneer, halloumi, queso fresco, and most goat cheeses. What they all have in common is that they are curdled with acid and little or no rennet. Rennet creates a protein structure that can be weakened with heat and thus, a cheese that will melt. But when heat is applied to an acid-curdled cheese, the curds tighten up and force out the water, maintaining structure and actually allowing them to be sautéed and browned like a piece of meat. It is also why ricotta-based ravioli filling doesn't ooze out when you cut one open or why that disk of goat cheese will get softer, but not melt all over the salad greens. This is neither detriment nor outright benefit — it's just one of the properties of these cheeses that should be noted, and that can be taken advantage of or avoided.

There are a few regions around the world known for the production of fine goat's milk cheeses. Perhaps the most celebrated is the Loire Valley in France, which is responsible for some of the most famous cheeses of this ilk, er, milk. Indeed, some of the best goat cheeses around the world have been modeled on those from the Loire. Speaking of modeled, the French offer these cheeses in a myriad of shapes — pyramid, log, spheres, little spheres on sticks, logs molded *around* a stick as with the pictured St. Maure. Each one has its own local name, but all have fairly similar flavor profiles. There are slight differences depending on the breed of goat, the milk, and their diet. Also, differences in fat content can lead to different mouthfeels and richer (or leaner) flavors.

FIGURE **2.4** St. Maure

CAPRI

Milk – Goat (pasteurized)

Origin – Westfield Farm, Hubbardston, Massachusetts, United States

Rind – None

Paste – Bright white, moist, and slightly fudgy texture

Aging – 1 week

Westfield Farm has been making cheese since 1971 and offers a range of styles from this cheese, their simplest and freshest, to a fascinating aged version with a bluemold surface. The fresh and uncomplicated "Plain Capri" has a light lactic sourness, but is better represented by describing the freshness and lovely citrus notes it has. It is one of the most popular fresh goat cheeses at Murray's Cheese in New York, which could be due to proximity — the dairy is only a few hours from Manhattan. In this case, freshness matters.

FIGURE **2.5** Capri

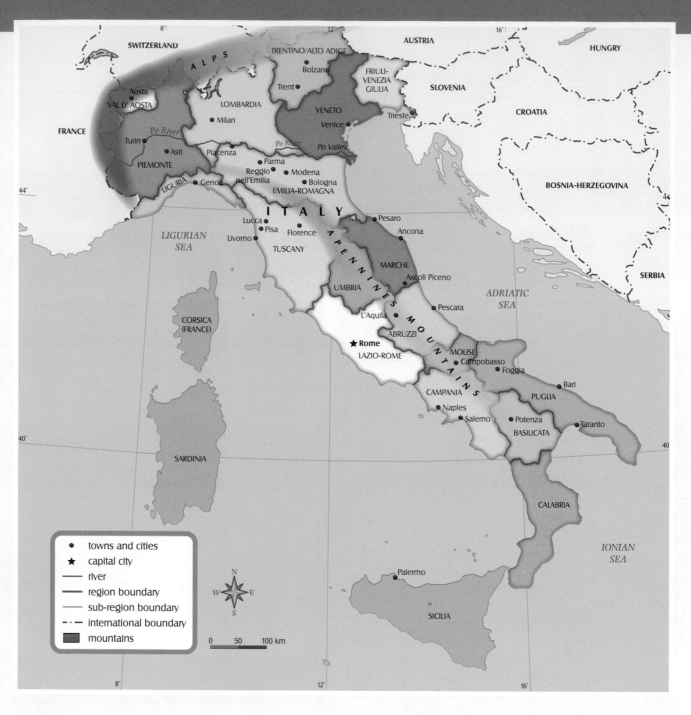

This is one of the greatest nations on earth for eating and drinking . . . and relaxing. The Italians are as passionate about food and drink as the French — maybe even more so. But there is a big difference. A French cheese shop is likely to carry all or most of the "important" cheeses of France, no matter where they're from. There might be a somewhat larger selection of the regional specialty, but you will still find Roquefort in Paris, although the blue cheese was made four hundred miles to the south. This is not going to happen in Italy.

Italians are proud people. They fiercely promote their regional products (cheese, wine, produce, and clothing) and virtually ignore those from elsewhere, even right across regional borders. This is one reason that Italian wine is one of the most difficult subjects in the world of beverages — the grape and wine names change whenever you cross over into another region. It does, however, preserve the integrity of local products and perhaps even makes it easier to compartmentalize food and wine information in your brain. For example, if you hear

"Sangiovese," it is most likely that the subject of conversation is Tuscany.

Moving on to cheese (and concerning wine, to a degree), Italy has quite the collection of climates because of its positioning, length, and geology. There are the Dolomites and Italian Alps in the north, the spine of Apennines running down the center, and the seas that surround it. Virtually every type of environment is available from Alpine cold to blisteri heat and from very dry to quite rainy. This allows for a very wide range of agricultural conditions, and for a broad variety of cheeses and wine to be produced.

Let's start, as we did in France, with the northeast of Italy and move around in a clockwise direction.

Alto Adige, Friuli, Venezia-Giulia, and Veneto

These regions combine to form the upper-right corner of the boot. It is seriously mountainous and hilly country, with the Alps up north giving way to first hills, and then fertile plains as you move south. The regions take turns bordering Austria, and Friuli also borders Slovenia. These are very important wine regions, producing quite a bit of white wine, but also some very important reds such as Valpolicella and Amarone della Valpolicella in the Veneto. Also, the current thirst for Prosecco sparkling wine is slaked by the voluminous production of bubbly from the same region. Speaking of thirst, Pinot Grigio is the cash crop of the Alto Adige and Friuli regions where they also make wine with the more German-sounding grape varieties such as Gewürztraminer. Although a lot of inexpensive and nondescript wine is made in northern Italy, some of the finest white wines made anywhere are from Friuli and the Alto Adige.

The regions are, of course, also known for their indigenous foods, including white polenta (Veneto) and one of the finest hams of the world, Prosciutto di San Daniele (Friuli). Though a large amount of cheese is produced in these regions, they are best known for Asiago, Montasio, and Piave. They are all made from cow's milk, and are heartily satisfying.

Emilia-Romagna

It's true that Italians cling closely to their home regions and will rarely, if ever, admit to the existence of another. However, most will admit that there is something special about the food of Emilia-Romagna, and especially its capital, Bologna. The list of foods produced there includes some of the most famous, important, and high-quality unique foods in the world. Their wheat makes fine pasta, the true balsamic vinegar (Aceto Balsamico di Modena) comes from Modena, and the most famous ham in the world hails from nearby Parma (Prosciutto di Parma). About half of the region is made up of hills and mountains, but the other half is mostly fertile plains. So, beautiful produce is available everywhere, the butter is remarkable, and is only overshadowed by one of the greatest cheeses made, Parmigiano-Reggiano. Many expert cheese-lovers consider true Parmesan to be the finest cheese on the planet. With the surfeit of amazing food products in this region, it's hard to describe how overwhelming Emilia-Romagna can be for a food lover. The local cuisine is obviously based on the unfair bounty of perfect ingredients from the surrounding area. Of course, *ragù alla bolognese* is the most famous meat sauce in the world, but when combined with or served alongside the other wonderful food from there, the overall experience is enveloping. If the food itself wasn't enough, perfection is carried out in other arenas as well, such as the automobile industry. Ferrari, Maserati, and Lamborghini all call this region home, as does the Ducati motorcycle manufacturer. So, yes, Emilia-Romagna is rich in many ways, financially and with an overabundance of near-perfect — even perfect products.

Southern Italy (not Sicily, yet)

Heading south, before hitting the islands and moving back up the shin of the boot, some important territory must be covered. The thing is, there is not a lot of variety among the cheeses produced in Apulia, Basilicata, Calabria, and Campania. These regions have unique cuisines and traditions, but the geography and climate limit both the species of animals that will thrive, and also what kind of foods can be produced. The relatively hot and infertile environment is, however, good for sheep. The *pecorino* cheeses of each region are eaten either fresh or are highly salted and aged, then used for grating. One other important animal, though, lives in the swampy areas of the south . . . the water buffalo. Some consider *mozzarella di Bufala* to be the finest mozzarella made. It is wonderfully rich and flavorful, but must be eaten very fresh — its high-moisture content causes it to sour very soon after production. The high-volume cow's milk cheeses from the south do not suffer the same fate, especially when they are salted and aged to become Provolone or Caciocavallo. These will last, but lack the delicate nature, richness, and sweetness of the water buffalo cheese.

There happen to be some great wines from these regions. They are mostly red and rustic, and are typically big and a little rough around the edges. Puglia (the heel of the boot) is home to Salice Salentino, the town and the wine, which tends to be a great value. Another value red from Basilicata (the arch of the boot) is called Aglianico del Vulture. It is a mouthful in more ways than one. To the west is a region that is perhaps better known for its wines, Campania. It is home to the noble red, Taurasi, which is also based on the Aglianico grape. Because it's a fairly hot climate there, it is surprising to find a few great whites as well, including Greco di Tufo, Fiano di Avellino, and Falanghina. These wines are more full-bodied than you might expect from Italian white wine, and can have lots of interesting, ripe flavors. They might change what you think of Italian white wine.

The Islands — Sicilia (Sicily) and Sardegna (Sardinia)

These islands (the two largest in the Mediterranean) have climates that are quite similar to the mainland regions nearby. Both islands are quite mountainous, and Sicily is home to Mount Etna, Europe's largest active volcano. The soil in these regions is excellent for growing crops, but the Mediterranean climate leads to very dry summers and rather frequent droughts. So rather than lush vegetation, the preferred crops are wheat, olives, almonds, citrus, cotton, and wine grapes. Similarly, while there are some cattle, sheep are the predominant dairy animals. So, the cheeses

are not that different from the pecorinos of the nearby mainland, although a few name-protected versions have their own characters. Sardinia's version is Fiore Sardo, a cheese that has many imitators — almost counterfeiters. There are producers who will name their cheese with a similar name hoping to dupe the casual buyer. *Caveat emptor.* As for Sicily, their famous cheese of this type is Pecorino Siciliano. Both the *incanestrato* (made in a basket) and *pepato* (peppered) versions are worth seeking out. One other Sicilian specialty of note is Ricotta Salata. Also a sheep's milk cheese, it is salted but not salty, mild but not boring. It is a highly versatile cheese for use on pasta, in salads, or as part of an antipasti platter. It also happens to be delicious when served with ripe pears, which is a simple, light, and delicious dessert just by itself.

The fierce heat of Sicily creates a very high level of ripeness in the grapes grown there, so the wines tend to be big and red. The advent of affordable refrigeration in wineries has allowed winemakers to produce some balanced white wines, but red wine still dominates this island. The popularity of the Nero d'Avola grape is undeniable and has become the source of juice for quite a few value-oriented wines. The most important wine from Sicily, though, is Cerasuolo di Vittoria, which acquired its DOCG status (the highest certification available in Italy) in 2005. As famous as it may be in Italy, it is still relatively unknown in the United States, and is still a very good value.

Lazio (Rome)

Returning to the mainland, the region around Rome is known for one very famous and confusing cheese, Pecorino Romano. As you might imagine, the area around Rome is highly populated, and not exactly cow or sheep country. As the cost of doing business (especially agriculture) has gone up in Lazio, much of the *Romano* production has moved over to Sardinia. The true Pecorino Romano, from Lazio, is still available, but the name-protected version is allowed to come from Sardinia. To get the real thing, look for the word "genuino," or one of these brand names — Brunelli, Fulvi, Locatelli, or Lopez.

The coast of Lazio is low-lying, and moving toward the interior of the region, there are some smaller mountain ranges as well as the foothills of the Appenines. There is agriculture, and the wines tend to be more for local consumption and lack individual character. The most famous wine of the region is Frascati, a slightly fizzy and uncomplicated wine that can be found in pitchers and carafes at bars and restaurants throughout the region. It is a simple and satisfying wine that is great for washing down a casual meal.

Toscana (Tuscany) and Umbria

The landscape of rolling hills with lines of cypress trees, stone outcroppings, and fields of sunflowers in Tuscany fill your eyes and head with romantic thoughts. It doesn't hurt that you had a pitcher of Chianti with your lunch, either. The entire region, with some of the finest and most friendly food, wine, art, and people contrives to keep you there. While the term "Tuscan cuisine" has been hijacked by hundreds of restaurateurs, the genuine article uses a broad range of regional produce including white beans, rosemary, lemons, and olives (and their oil), as well as the magnificent Chianina beef cattle that are responsible for one of the finest steaks in the world, *la Bistecca Fiorentina*.

With all the other great foods available in this region, the cheesemakers have their work cut out for them. Luckily, there is a fine and distinctive cheese made from sheep's milk in Tuscany, predictably called Pecorino Toscano. There is also a sub-category called Pecorino di Pienza (from the town of Pienza) that is considered the best version of this lovely cheese. On a visit to the area, I had been informed as to the quality of this cheese, but was also warned to stay away from counterfeit cheeses being peddled by nefarious types on the street. There were only a few shops in Pienza that were considered (at least by my nervous friend) trustworthy, and we only went to those. Luckily, all you need to do is buy from a reputable cheesemonger . . . but look 'em straight in the eyes when asking if it's an authentic cheese.

Piemonte/Piedmont

This region of Italy is contentedly contained. Surrounded on all sides by mountains (its name means "feet of the mountains"), there is a long history of industrial and agricultural success. With the Alps to the north and Appenines to the south, the flatter regions are quite fertile and provide excellent growing conditions for cereal grains and rice, especially in the province of Alessandria. This is where the best types of rice for risotto such as Carnaroli and Arborio are grown. There is also cultivation of produce, and in the slightly less arable lands apple, peach, and pear orchards thrive.

One of the most important crops is not cultivated, but is probably fertilized more by prayer and hope than with compost. The prized, powerful, and extravagantly pricey white truffles of Alba and the surrounding Langhe are one of the most coveted forms of fungus on the planet. Having been lucky enough to work with (and occasionally eat) them, I can honestly say that there is no other single ingredient as seductive and engaging. Although they tend to be found in the same locations every year, especially around the roots of certain species of trees (hazel, alder, and others), their appearance is rarely a sure thing. Although pigs have famously been used to find these nuggets of fungi, dogs are increasingly popular because they can be trained not to eat these underground mushrooms that can cost from \$1,200 to \$2,300 a pound during their season in the fall.

In many ways, there is a more reliable important crop grown in Piedmont, and that is wine grapes. Two of the most important and expensive wines in the world come from this region, especially from the area in and around the towns of Alba and Asti. They are Barolo and Barbaresco, both made from the Nebbiolo grape. Often the most expensive wines on an Italian list, these are serious red wines that can easily live on for decades, continuing to develop complexity while having their tannins tamed. Less expensive, but still important wines include Barbera, Dolcetto, Gavi, Asti Spumante, and Moscato d'Asti. Altogether, they make Piedmont one of the most important quality wine regions in Italy.

This has all been a set-up to explain why cheese is an important part of the food picture in this region. Frankly, with all these other world-famous and world-class ingredients around, there is a lot of pressure on the cheesemakers to produce great stuff as well. They don't disappoint. The most luxurious is Robiola, a fresh cheese that is allowed to age for a week or so to acquire a lightly sour flavor. Even more luxurious and maybe even sinful is La Tur. More than one cheese expert has described this almost fresh cheese as "sexy." Onto somewhat less racy territory, the Aosta area of Piedmont is known for producing the finest Fontina in the world. Fontina Val d'Aosta is the real thing, and unlike any supermarket "fontina." It is unpasteurized and aged at least three, but usually seven months to a year. The sweet earthiness and fine melting characteristics make it the perfect cheese for Fonduta, the Italian *fondue*, with one regional twist here — shaving white truffles into the melted cheese right before serving will blow your mind, and budget.

Lombardia (Lombardy)

This region borders Switzerland on the north and Emilia-Romagna on the south. It is home to Milan, one of the most important business (and style) centers in Italy. A land of mountains, plains, hills, lakes, and rivers, Lombardy has been important to the Italian economy for hundreds of years, initially because of its central location for trade, and its agricultural potential. The fashion world is based in Milan, and Lake Como is a center of silk production. The region is densely populated (second in density after Campania), but there is still room and plentiful water for agriculture, with grains grown on the lowest plains. The higher plains produce grain and vegetables, and the hills are home to fruit trees and grape growing for wine. A very good red wine called Valtellina is made from Nebbiolo grapes, and tends to be much more affordable than its rich cousins from Piedmont — Barolo and Barbaresco. Good value wines come from the Oltrepò Pavese and are made from a range of grapes. Perhaps most important, though, are the sparkling wines from Franciacorta, called Franciacorta

Brut. These are the highest-quality bubbles made in Italy, and some can actually rival wines from Champagne. Just a hint, they also are a great choice for pairing with the local foods.

The most impressive cheese made in Lombardy is Taleggio, a washed-rind cow's milk cheese that can be impressively stinky. It is rich, elastic, creamy, and a little salty, and can have meaty, nutty aromas accompanying the funk. Another variety is essentially a mini-taleggio, and that is Robiola Lombardia. It is *not* interchangeable with the Robiola of Piedmont, because as close as the two regions may be, the cheeses could not be more different.

Although Taleggio is arguably the finest, most complex cheese from Lombardia, one of the most famous blues in the world comes from there as well, and that is Gorgonzola. It is available in its young state as *dolce* (sweet) or the spicier, drier, aged version often referred to as *piccante* (spicy). Both are delicious and Gorgonzola is one of the Four Big Blues.

Finally, we have a cheese that is not really a cheese. Mascarpone is a triple-cream dairy product that is just this side of being butter. Its simple richness is so hedonistic that you might find yourself looking guiltily over your shoulder as you eat it with a spoon. Used for both savory and sweet recipes, it can be stirred into risotto or polenta and is also the base for tiramisu, the famous ladyfinger and espresso dessert. There is also a wonderful combination of Mascarpone with Gorgonzola called a "torte," which is layers of the two cheeses that can be served as is. They are perfect together, and might even convert self-proclaimed blue cheese haters. Oh, and that Franciacorta Brut a few lines up? Crack open a bottle to go with the torte, some fresh pears, and walnuts.

PASTA FILATA

This is a family of cheeses that will be familiar to every American. Even if you haven't heard of Provolone, chances are pretty good that you have had some of the number one cheese (by weight) sold in the United States, mozzarella. *Pasta filata* translates to "spun paste," and that's how the cheeses are made. Fresh curd is heated, often in water or whey, and then stirred until a ropy consistency is achieved. At this point most pasta filata cheeses are formed into any number of shapes — balls, logs, animal shapes (Scamorza from Lombardy), or the part-melted snowman shape of Cacciocavallo. Although most of these cheeses are served as fresh as possible, as with mozzarella, they can be aged if handled properly. In fact, Provolone is essentially an aged mozzarella. There are certainly some differences in exact procedures and recipes, but you get the idea. Another well-known spun cheese is Armenian String Cheese. It is usually sold in a braided, continuous loop that is dotted with black seeds, *Nigella sativa*, a commonly used spice in Asia sometimes referred to in English as "black cumin seed," although there's no relation to cumin — in fact, they taste a bit more like oregano. In any case, string cheese is fun to eat and quite tasty, and has a bit longer shelf life than mozzarella because of its lower moisture content.

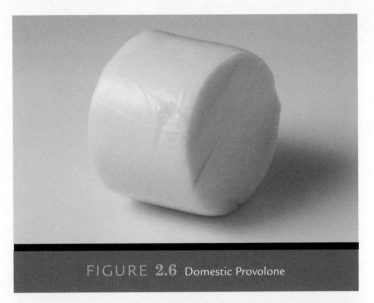

FIGURE **2.6** Domestic Provolone

FIGURE **2.7** Imported Provolone

FIGURE **2.8** Armenian String Cheese

BURRATA

FIGURE **2.9** Burrata

Milk – Cow (usually pasteurized)
Origin – Puglia, Italy
Paste – Spun-curd (mozzarella) surrounding a creamy center
Aging – None, best within 24 to 36 hours of production

Eating Burrata is a hedonistic experience. Cut one open and a creamy mass of soft mozzarella scraps pours out of its mozzarella "bag." It is thought that the cheese originated as a way to use up the little scraps left over after making mozzarella. They are mixed with cream and poured into a "pouch" made of fresh mozzarella that is then pulled together and tied at the top. Traditionally, the cheese was then wrapped in leaves of *asphodel*, a rustic herb. This practice has diminished somewhat with the production of Burrata becoming a little more industrial, but occasionally an image of leaves is printed on the plastic wrapping in a nod to tradition. The cheese is highly perishable, and can't be put back together, so it must be consumed entirely once served.

MOZZARELLA

Mozzarella might have surpassed Cheddar as the number one cheese in America in 2003 (according to the USDA), but most of those 10.3 pounds/4.67 kilograms eaten each year per person are made up of the flavorless, rubbery stuff used on industrial-grade pizzas. The first true mozzarella was produced in southern Italy from the milk of water buffalo. Salerno and Napoli (Naples) are often mentioned as historical centers of production. Water buffalo, an Asian species, were by most accounts introduced to Europe during the Middle Ages some time after 700 C.E. Buffalo milk is much higher in fat and protein than cow's milk, with just a little bit less water. This makes the whole milk *Mozzarella di Bufala* a much richer cheese than its Italian cow's milk counterpart, *Mozzarella Fior di Latte*. It also has a more complex set of aromatics, sometimes described as mushroomy or grassy. Whatever the case, true buffalo mozzarella is a delicacy in the truest sense of the word. Its freshness fades rather quickly, and it should be consumed as soon as possible after its production.

When mozzarella is made, the curd is added to hot water and sinks to the bottom. As it is stirred and then kneaded by the cheesemaker, its texture is developed. When it's ready, lumps of cheese are pulled and pinched off of the mass (the verb *mozzare* means to cut off), and the balls are dropped into cold water, either plain or salted. Although the texture would be affected by the saltwater because water (or whey) would be drawn out of the salted version, the additional flavor from the salted water is why it would be used. All fresh mozzarella is at its most elastic right from the *latticeria*, and should spring back when poked, although it should still be tender, not rubbery. As it ages, the consistency will become softer and creamier, which sounds good, but is not because the texture becomes mushy, losing its springy, toothsome quality. The best mozzarella, when sliced, should release some of its milky whey, and smell of fresh milk. There are three main styles: unsalted, salted, and smoked. Unsalted is quite bland, and is usually reserved for cooked preparations where the salt comes from some of the other ingredients. Salted mozzarella tastes better by itself and is often served with tomatoes and basil, or roasted sweet peppers. Smoked mozzarella has an added complexity that is welcome either when eaten by itself or as part of a dish.

WHEY CHEESES

RICOTTA

Although Little Miss Muffet might have enjoyed both curds *and* whey, many cheese producers need to dispose of the whey. If the cheese they produce yields a high-acid whey (as it would from whole milk cottage cheese or ricotta), it is almost unusable, and must be disposed of ecologically — not into a water supply of any sort. However, the "sweeter" whey can be used for a number of things. Many farmers feed whey to their pigs, and I can attest to the tastiness of whey-fed pork. There is, however, a traditional use of whey that benefits humans more directly, and that is traditional ricotta.

FIGURE **2.10** Ricotta

Ricotta was originally made by cooking the whey to aid in the coagulation of the many proteins not caught up in the coagulated casein proteins during the production of the primary cheese. The original ricotta was largely made from the whey left over after mozzarella was produced. Because it is coagulated largely by acid, rather than rennet, it is a non-melting cheese.

TYPES OF RICOTTA

The word *Ricotta* means "re-cooked" in Italian, and refers to a small family of cheeses that aren't technically cheese. The original ricotta is technically a whey cheese, that is, it is made from the main by-product of cheesemaking, whey. It was discovered that by heating and perhaps further acidifying the run-off from the cheese vat, a fresh, soft, non-melting "cheese" could be produced. From this initial product come a few spin-offs. The original ricotta is great for pasta stuffings and as a topping for some dishes, or even to be used with fresh fruit as is cottage cheese. But for desserts and finer applications, ricotta impastata is a smoother product that has been whipped to lighten it and remove the larger lumps. Lastly, as a fresh and high-moisture cheese, it doesn't keep very well. Hence ricotta salata was created, which is salted, pressed, and dried to increase shelf life. There are locally produced baked and smoked versions in southern Italy, but these products tend not to be available in the United States, and are also variants that were created to increase the shelf life of what is essentially a by-product of the cheesemaking process. Leave it to Italian ingenuity to make what used to be a troublesome waste product into a delicious ingredient.

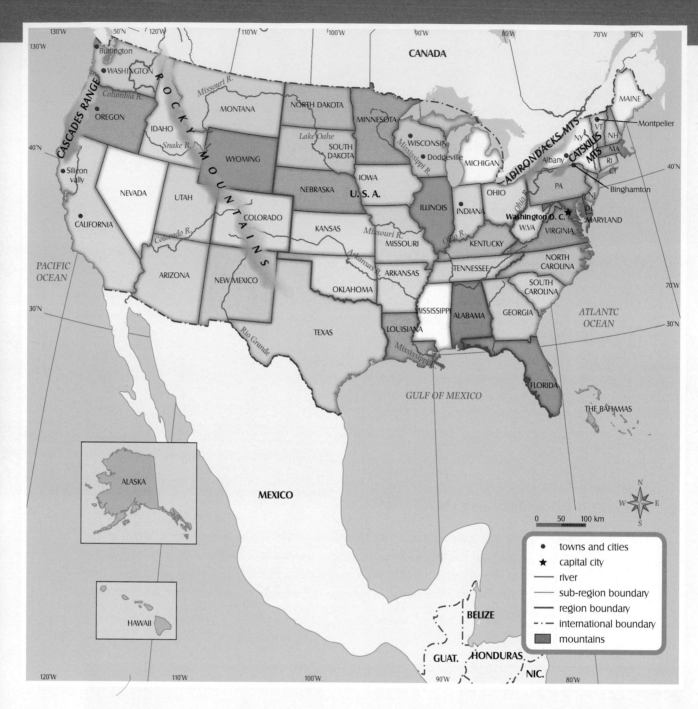

American Cheese. It's an evocative phrase that might not lead to thoughts of complex flavors. But in typical American fashion, we have made tremendous advancements in and contributions to the world of cheesemaking over the last few decades. We now have blues like Maytag Blue and Point Reyes Original Blue that can stand toe-to-toe with Roquefort and Gorgonzola. Washed-rind stinkers like Red Hawk from Cowgirl Creamery and Eden from Sprout Creek are more than capable of holding their own in the ring with Reblochon and Taleggio. Similarly, the wines of California, Oregon, and New York are now considered world-class and comparable to the wines of France, Italy, and Germany.

You may have noticed a trend forming there. The American versions of traditional cheese are from specific producers, whereas the European ones are regional cheeses made by more than one producer. This is largely due to passage of time and accumulated history. In Europe, specific styles of cheese have evolved over decades, even centuries, and reflect the slow process of trial and error, eventually resulting in a cheese that is unique to that region.

In the world of wine, it's called *terroir*, and essentially means that the product tastes like it does because of where it's from. This is determined by which animals (or grape varieties) will thrive there, what the climate is like, and both the topography and geology (soil) of the region. The finer points of *terroir* take generations to be uncovered.

Americans have little patience for such a thing. We decide what we want and then go for it. This opposite approach can result in fine products — it still involves trial and error, but tends to show its results sooner, for better or worse.

Tradition is the way of the old world. Over time, specific natural products have evolved into particularly fine examples of food and drink. Champagne and Brie were not created overnight and are very important products as well as objects of French pride. In the United States, however, tradition, though still revered, is not the blueprint. We tend to look at the circumstances (growing conditions, climate, etc.) and figure out what will work best given the conditions. Sometimes the product will mimic an old world paradigm, such as English Farmhouse Cheddar. However, Americans are just as likely to come up with something brand-new and fabulous like the Wabash Cannonball from Indiana or Humboldt Fog from California. These are unique cheeses that have no European counterparts. As truly American originals, they were arrived at through innovation and imagination. While the cheeses born of European tradition are still some of the best in the world, and deserve our respect, American cheese — *truly* American cheeses are fun, exciting and delicious, and bear the stamp of American ingenuity.

Wisconsin

More cheese is made in this state than any other in the United States, to the tune of 2.5 billion (yes, *billion*) pounds in 2007. Admittedly, the vast majority of the cheeses made there are of the industrial variety, with cheddar, Italian-style, and process cheeses making up the bulk. But highly individual cheeses are made as well, both in large- and smaller-production facilities.

Cheese production began in the 1840s, when European immigrants who had been living in the Northeast began to move west and settle in promising areas. Dairy farming was a good choice for agriculture because, while the soil was fertile, it was also quite rocky because of glacial activity in the past. Both dairy farming and cheesemaking exploded in popularity over the following decades, and soon even the University of Wisconsin was offering courses in both. By 1945, more than 500 million pounds of cheese were being produced annually. In that so much is produced there, it shouldn't be surprising that almost every type of cheese that Americans eat is well represented. From process American cheese to Auricchio Provolone — even the feared Limburger, they're all made in Wisconsin. So is Pleasant Ridge Reserve from the Uplands Cheese Company in Dodgeville. In a style similar to the French alpine Beaufort, Pleasant Ridge has won many awards, having been named the best cheese in America twice by the American Cheese Society. Even if it is the standout famous fine cheese from Wisconsin, there are many other artisanal cheeses produced there, in a broad array of styles. Whatever type of cheese you want, Wisconsin has it . . . lots of it.

California

There is a basic incongruity in the way many think about California. The Central Valley is one of the most important agricultural centers in the world, but then there's Hollywood, too, which is as far from agriculture as possible. California's dairy farmers produce more milk than any other state . . . but then there's Silicon Valley and an economy roughly the size of Italy's. Which California is the real California? Well, for the purposes of this book, it is a dominant cheese-producing region in the United States, rapidly approaching the annual production levels of Wisconsin. In fact, their production levels have almost doubled in just ten years. There were 1.17 billion pounds of cheese made in 1997, and 2.2 billion in 2006. The milk was already being produced at a high level, but now more of it is being made into cheese.

Even though a tremendous amount of industrial cheese is produced, the artisanal producers have a somewhat higher profile than those of other states. Just naming Cowgirl Creamery, Cypress Grove, and Point Reyes Farmstead Cheese Company, along with the venerable Laura Chenel's Chèvre (1970s) and Vella Cheese Company (1931), brings to mind specific fine cheeses that are available around the country. For whatever reason (maybe it's the talking cows on television), California's artisanal cheeses get attention. It might be California's reputation for modern and fresh food combined with the popularity of its wines, but at least in the food world, the name "California" confers status as well.

When it comes to the farming itself, the climates and soils of this third largest state are quite varied. From Mediterranean to sub-arctic, with mountain ranges, plains, and coastline, virtually any species of dairy animal can be raised in an environment that will result in high-quality milk. That said, most of the producers are in locations you might expect. For instance, the California Artisan Cheese Guild, with about twenty members, has eight producers in the Sonoma/Marin County area, and seven in the Central Valley. Both of these areas are lush agricultural regions and perfect for dairy cows. But in this state that has a culinary reputation for fresh food and access to great produce . . . and wine of course, perhaps it is expected to have great, artisanal cheese producers as well. Perhaps, then, it is also true that its huge volume of cheese production is a bit surprising.

New York

In some ways, the situation in New York is similar to that of in California. For most Americans the words "New York" conjures up either Times Square or the Yankees logo. There's more to this beautiful state north of Manhattan — like the Catskills, Buffalo, and the largest state park in the country, Adirondack State Park. There is a lot of agricultural history *and activity* in the Empire State. The apple industry is one of the largest in the country, and other prominent farm products include dairy, cherries, cabbage, and onions. In fact, the Black Dirt region in Orange County is one of the most important onion-growing regions in the country, and New York is the third-largest cabbage growing state in the United States.

Grapes are a major crop as well, for table grapes, jelly, juice, and wine. New York is the third-largest grape growing state after California and Washington. New York State wine has been garnering newfound praise from critics and wine drinkers alike,

and certain vinous icons seem to be emerging, such as Finger Lakes Riesling and Long Island Cabernet Franc. The Hudson Valley, the country's oldest wine region, is having great success with Cabernet Franc, Tocai Friulano, and the burgundian varieties.

The Hudson Valley is also home to some very successful goat farms, making it sort of an American "Loire Valley." They even have the mansions! Coach Farm and Sprout Creek Farm both make remarkable goat cheese, although the latter turns out great cow's milk cheeses as well. Other regions for good cheesemaking include the Finger Lakes, the New York border with Vermont, and even along the Route 88 corridor from Binghamton to Albany. And for some great fresh mozzarella, go to New York City and look for anything called a "latticeria" or with the word "latticini" in the name. Many old timers will bemoan the current situation, but it is still some of the best fresh mozzarella available in the country.

Luckily, New York City is also a great restaurant and food capital, and great cheese is appreciated by many local residents. In fact, two of the great cheese retailers in the country are there, Artisanal Premium Cheese and Murray's Cheese; and for great American farmstead cheeses, go to the tiny Saxelby Cheesemongers in the Essex Street Market. Many great restaurants have cheese programs now, and some (like Gramercy Tavern) have had serious cheese programs for many years. It's a good time to be a cheese lover in New York — great cheese is being made, sold, and eaten.

Vermont

The old saw about Vermont is that there are more cows than people. This is not true, although they have the largest number of cows per capita in the country . . . partly because the only state with fewer people is Wyoming. Still, it gives an idea that the dairy industry is an important one there — in fact, the most important form of agriculture in the state.

Vermont is pretty small in a number of ways. Its economy is one of the smallest in the nation, its state capital and largest city are the smallest in the country (respectively Montpelier, around 8,000 and Burlington about 39,000), and it ranks forty-third in area. There is nothing small, however, about the flavor of their cheeses.

No shortage exists of wonderful cheese producers in this beautiful state, and all you have to do is check with the Vermont Cheese Council's website to find thirty-nine producers on the Vermont Cheese Trail (twenty or so of whom are open to the public).

There are both very large producers like the Cabot Creamery Cooperative, owned by 1,400 farm families, as well as small farmsteads like Orb Weaver Farm with only seven cows (all named). Somewhere in the middle is Grafton Village Cheese Company, which makes one of the finest cheddars in the country. With such a seemingly small footprint, Vermont makes a huge contribution to the world of cheese, especially if you are concentrating on the northeast and New England. And even if the Green Mountain State's contribution to the cheese department doesn't impress, maybe you should go over to the frozen foods section and pick up some Chunky Monkey from Ben and Jerry's.

Other States

It would be unfair to stop here because truly great cheeses are made in most of the other states. However, it also does not make sense to cover all of them in depth because other countries also need to be included. Some cheeses in this book are from states that haven't been covered, but there is not enough critical mass of cheesemakers in that state to cover it here. That said, there are some great books on American cheese included in the appendix, and you will certainly find the information you are looking for in one (or more) of them.

GJETOST

The only other famous whey cheese is Gjetost, which is made by cooking down the whey of cow's or goat's milk until the lactose caramelizes, creating a cheese that might seem more like a slightly sour caramel fudge than like cheese. It is part of a traditional Norwegian breakfast, sliced paper-thin with a cheese slicer and served on bread.

FIGURE **2.11** Gjetost

MILD AGED CHEESES

Most of the cheeses in this chapter have not spent much more time aging than those in Chapter 2. A change has taken place, though. These no longer seem like a somewhat solid version of milk – they are definitely cheese. Their flavors tend toward the subtle and fresh. Also, their textures are varied, from chalky to buttery, dry to creamy. In general, the commonality of mild flavor is due to the limited aging they have undergone. The cheeses still retain a lot of their moisture, and so are not as intensely flavored – think of the difference in flavor between a stock and a sauce. But the bacteria and their leftover enzymes (even in pasteurized milk) have not had the time to break down the fats and proteins into their more intensely aromatic molecules. This means that, whereas the mild cheeses have more flavor than the fresh ones, they will still not have the kind of character and complexity found in cheeses that have been aged longer.

This chapter's cheeses are organized roughly by their intensity, with the mildest cheeses first. In fact, some examples toward the end of the chapter have a fair amount of intensity, but are the mildest versions of that category. For example, Fourme d'Ambert is quite mild for a blue cheese, but has a bit more lead in its pencil than Pierre Robert. Conceptually, these somewhat stronger cheeses belong together, because if you're looking for a mild blue, it makes sense to look in the mild chapter, not in the sharp chapter where many blues reside.

MILD CHEESES

VOLUME CHEESES

Most of the individual entries in this book are singular cheeses, often made by hand and in very small quantities. However, there are some cheeses made in huge quantities, usually in more industrial settings. Their production far outweighs that of the artisanal cheeses made in the United States, and by definition so does consumption of them.

Because this book is a reference for industry, it behooves us to include cheeses from this volume category in the appropriate chapters. But because they tend to be categorical rather than individual, their descriptions will be a bit more general and not refer to specific producers, or even the states they hail from.

With a total 9.7 billion pounds of cheese made in the United States in 2007, the most popular categories are so-called Italian-style and American-style cheeses. Mozzarella alone accounted for almost one third of that production, making it the most-produced cheese in the country.

These numbers come from the International Dairy Foods Association, a trade group based in the United States with some 530 member dairy companies.

FIGURE **3.1** Boursin

BOURSIN

François Boursin established the Boursin brand of flavored fresh cheeses in Normandy when he created his first garlic and herb spreadable cow's milk cheese. It earned *Appellation d'Origine Contrôlée* (A.O.C.) status (see sidebar on page 55) in 1963, and is now available in a few varieties, including its second flavor incarnation, cracked black pepper. Essentially it is a flavored cream cheese.

FIGURE **3.2** Domestic Brie

BRIE

The original and most traditional expressions of Brie come from the Île de France region, and are made from unpasteurized milk. But now that brie is so popular around the world, versions of this round, soft, bloomy cheese are being made in almost all dairy-producing regions. The domestic versions are almost all made from pasteurized milk and do not develop much beyond the state at which they are shipped. That is, they tend to be creamy and somewhat rich, with a clean white bloomed rind. There can be some mushroomy and earthy aromas but the flavors are usually clean and relatively simple.

FIGURE **3.3** Mild Cheddar

MILD CHEDDAR

For years, cheddar was the most popular cheese in the United States, and was only recently unseated by mozzarella (because of the popularity of pizza). The mild version of cheddar is often yellow (though sometimes not colored, thus white), with a semi-soft texture. The flavor is usually restrained, sometimes with a hint of tartness that could eventually become sharpness. It's fair to say that it has a little bit more bite than American Cheese, but is still rather tame.

FIGURE **3.4** Fresh Goat Cheese

FIGURE **3.5** Ashen Goat Cheese

FRESH DOMESTIC GOAT

Goat cheese is more popular than ever in this country. Although the Agriculture Marketing Resource Center estimates there are 350,000 goats in the United States, that number pales in comparison to the 9 million American dairy cows. Still, the proliferation of warm goat cheese salads and the increasingly popular combination of beets with goat cheese is bringing this tangy, usually fresh cheese to more tables.

MONTEREY JACK

The original version of this cheese was semi-firm and occasionally aged for up to a year to produce "Dry Jack," a hard and well-flavored cheese. The more common modern

FIGURE **3.6** Monterey Jack

FIGURE **3.7** Dry Jack

volume Monterey Jack is usually aged for less than a month and tends to be quite soft and mild, with a slight tang. It melts very well, and sometimes has chopped jalapeño peppers added to its curd early in the cheesemaking process, yielding Jalapeño Jack. This somewhat spicy and pepper-flavored cheese is used for eating on its own, and is often the cheese of choice for making quesadillas.

MOZZARELLA

Domestic mozzarella is now the most popular cheese in the land. It surpassed cheddar a few years ago because of its use on pizzas. The four major types of mozzarella produced in the United States are whole milk or part-skim, in either high- or low-moisture versions. The low-moisture types were created to increase shelf life. The different fat contents affect flavor and texture, but also the melting properties of the mozzarella when heated. Mozzarella with higher fat and/or moisture content melts and pools more readily, and browns more evenly on pizza. This is not a pizza book, however, so we'll leave it at the fact that there are many choices to be made regarding mozzarella (and other cheeses) choice if you make pizza professionally.

MOZZARELLA CURD

To make your own mozzarella, as shown on page 164, you will need to find a source of fresh cheese curd. It is almost always cow's milk, and will be either whole milk or part-skim. Freshness is of the utmost importance because the high-moisture curd will sour very quickly. The best places to look are Italian neighborhoods, or cities with large Italian populations. If you can't find curd, but there is a market that features fresh, hand made mozzarella, ask where they get their curd — and sometimes they will even sell some to you. The salting takes place later, so the

FIGURE **3.8** Jalapeño Jack

FIGURE **3.9** Mozzarella Loaf

FIGURE **3.10** Fresh Mozzarella Curd

FIGURE **3.11** Domestic Muenster

FIGURE **3.12** Domestic Gouda

biggest decisions are how much to buy and whether it's whole or part-skim.

DOMESTIC MUENSTER

Our Muenster is one of several global Muensters (or Munsters). The domestic version is modeled after the German and Dutch versions. Those two are different from ours in shape (usually round) and flavor (usually more). American Muensters are usually loaf shaped to make them deli slicing machine-friendly and are coated with paprika. Their texture tends to be very smooth and quite soft, with a very subtle flavor. The soft texture and very good melting quality are two of the reasons for this cheese's popularity. Now, the French Munster is a completely different animal, with a washed (hence, stinky) rind and creamy paste. Not exactly what the customer at the deli is expecting on a roast beef sandwich.

DOMESTIC GOUDA

This cheese is very similar to domestic Edam, and both are actually rather close in style to their Dutch counterparts – at least the less-aged versions of them. The American versions are usually made from partially skimmed cow's milk and are somewhere between semi-soft and semi-firm. Usually a noticeable saltiness and a slight tanginess are detectable in the finish, but not much complexity of flavor. Their red wax coatings are easy to recognize, and the cheeses are easy to enjoy.

SMALLER PRODUCTION CHEESES

LA TUR

Milk – Cow, sheep, and goat

Origin – Caseificio Dell'Alta Langa, Alta Lange, Piedmont, Italy

Rind – Natural, beginning to form bloom

Paste – Hedonistic velvety creamy mousse-like center, with just a hint of runny creaminess near the surface

Aging – 15 days at the caseificio. Should be eaten fresh

FIGURE **3.13** La Tur

This was described by a local cheesemonger as the "sexiest cheese in the world." In fact, she said that some of her customers (at the Cheese Plate in New Paltz, NY) will come by for a wheel if they've had a particularly bad day . . . and go home to eat the whole thing with a spoon. While cheese therapy is not normally recommended, it does provide an idea of how deeply satisfying La Tur can be. All three milks add to its broad balance of fresh flavors – each one adds some of its own character without being obvious. The most important thing to remember is to take this cheese out of the refrigerator at least a half hour before serving it. For the texture to be at its best, it should be closer to room temperature.

ROBIOLA

Milk – Cow, goat, or a blend of the two, sometimes with the addition of sheep's milk

Origin – Mostly from Lombardia and Piemonte, some from the Langhe, Northern Italy

Rind – Usually natural, acquiring bloom or mold with age. Some are wrapped in leaves, either chestnut or Savoy cabbage.

Paste – Depending on age, the texture is almost always moist, with varying degrees of creaminess

Aging – as little as 3 to 10 days, but the more complex versions are aged up to 3 months

D.O.P. – some members of the Robiola family have name protection

FIGURE **3.14** Robiola Bosina

The Robiola family is one of rich, luxurious cheeses from the north of Italy. The base milk is not a constant, but the general style is – whether young or aged for a few months, these cheeses are rich, moist, and not terribly challenging to the palate or beverage accompaniment. Small differences abound as you move from producer to producer, so it's worth being observant as you're shopping for Robiola. Aging brings complexity, of course, but rarely does it lead to funkiness. One exception would be the versions with washed rinds that can resemble Taleggio, meaning stinky. Still, versions like Robiola Bosina (pictured) are more representative of the bunch. It is a blend of cow's and sheep's milk, with a gentle bloomed rind. With just enough character from the sheep's milk to keep it from being boring, this is a true pleasure to eat while not having to think too much. It comes from a town (Bosia) just south of Alba in Piemonte; try pairing it with an Arneis (white) wine from the region, or a sparkling Franciacorta Brut from neighboring Lombardia.

COULOMMIERS

Milk – Cow (pasteurized)
Origin – Île-de-France, France
Rind – Bloomy
Paste – Light to bright yellow, creamy, sometimes with a chalky center
Aging – 1 to 4 weeks

FIGURE **3.15** Coulommiers

This is from the Seine-et-Marne Département in Île-de-France, the administrative region of France that includes Paris. Similar to Brie in several ways, it tends to be a bit smaller. The flavor is subtle, with a milky, nutty, earthy flavor and aroma. Its exterior should be white and velvety with mold. The main difference between this and a Brie or Camembert is that this smaller cheese is relatively thick, and the ripeness doesn't always reach the center of the cheese by the time of purchase. With one to four weeks of aging, younger ones might still have a small band of chalkiness in the center. There is nothing wrong with this, in fact, it adds textural interest, and is an indication that the flavor will be particularly fresh.

RITA

Milk – Cow (pasteurized)
Origin – Sprout Creek Farm, Poughkeepsie, NY
Rind – Bloomy
Paste – Creamy, pale yellow
Aging – 3 to 6 weeks

FIGURE **3.16** Rita

If you like Brie, and would prefer to go local, you might want to look for Rita from Sprout Creek. The cheese is rich, creamy and buttery, with just enough of an earthiness and acidic tang at the end to keep it from being boring. It is only available from October until March, and is one of only two bloomy cheeses made at the farm.

FOUGERUS

Milk – Cow (pasteurized)
Origin – Île-de-France, France
Rind – Bloomy, with a fern on top
Paste – Yellow-light gold, creamy
Aging – 4 weeks

FIGURE **3.17** Fougerus

Another brie-like cheese. It was originated by Robert Rouzaire, the producer of Pierre Robert. The fern on top is somewhat controversial. According to some, it was originally put there by Rouzaire to identify this Coulommiers-style cheese as one of his products. Some even say that he used it to hide defects in the original cheeses. There is also disagreement on both the edibility of the fern, as well as its effect on the cheese itself. Most say it is inedible and has no effect on the cheese. Technically, it is edible, and some reliable sources, such as Max McCalman, say that the fern "seems to tone down the soapiness" of this cheese.

Whatever you believe, it is a wonderful, creamy, earthy cheese that isn't too heavy on the salt. The original version was made with raw milk, but the version imported to the United States is made with pasteurized milk. Even so, it can easily surpass many so-called Brie and Camembert cheeses in quality.

EUROPEAN ALPHABET SOUP

The capsule descriptions of the cheeses, in some cases, will have an entry that might look like "A.O.C. – 1959." This indicates that the cheese received approval to be considered a product unique to a certain place, and is now protected by the French government. Essentially, this protection means that the name of the region can only be used for *that product*, and may not appear on the labels of any other. For instance, Champagne is a sparkling wine from the Champagne region in France, made under specific controls and from within a specific boundary. Sparkling wines from other regions in France may not (by law) use the term *Champagne* on their labels. Such wines are usually referred to as "Cremant de (region, e.g., Alsace)" and might even be made from the same grape varietals and in the exact same method as authentic Champagne.

This system protects the original producers of a particularly fine product from imitators who try to get in on the action by making a similar product in a different place. The systems, as you might imagine, are far from perfect – quality is not necessarily guaranteed, just provenance; and towns whose names appear in other A.O.C.s are not allowed to put the name of their own town on the label.

So why all the wine talk in a cheese book? Since 1990, A.O.C.s have been applied to more than wine. There are now cheeses, honey, even lentils and chickens with A.O.C. protection, and it therefore applies to some

(Continues)

products in this book. France isn't the only country with such controls. Italy, Spain, and Portugal have had them for many years, and the foundation of the European Union (E.U.) brought about the need for a more all-encompassing system. So under many of the cheeses' basic descriptions, you will see three letters and perhaps a date – the date that the cheese received legal protection from its home country or the European Union. Here's what the letters mean:

A.O.C. – *Appelation d'Origine Contrôlée* means "controlled name of origin." A system like this has been around in France for hundreds of years, but wasn't codified until 1919, and in 1925, Roquefort was given A.O.C. status. The creation of the INAO, the *Institut National des Appellations d'Origine* in 1935 led to a much more widespread use of the appellation system, because there was now a branch of the French ministry of Agriculture in charge of the proceedings. France has 48 A.O.C. cheeses, with more applying for the status all the time. Although the letters don't necessarily guarantee quality, you are at least assured that this *type* of cheese has been thoroughly vetted out by the French government, and that you can find out exactly how it was made.

D.O./D.O.P. – These are used in Spain as the *Denominación de Origen* for various foods and wine. It was based on the French system, although some parts of the system were in place (as in that of Rioja) earlier. As you may have guessed, the first one means "name of origin," and works in basically the same way as the French laws. D.O.P. stands for *Denominación de Origen Protegida*, and is explained below.

D.O./D.O.C./D.O.P – These acronyms stand for the Italian terms *Denominazione d'Origine, Denominazione d'Origine Controllata*, and *Denominazione d'Origine Protetta*, respectively. The first two were established in 1963, and largely modeled after the similar A.O.C. laws from France. There is one more term used for wine, D.O.C.G. that adds the word *garantita* to the term, meaning that the provenance of the wine is actually guaranteed by the government. You might be wondering about the "D.O.P.," though. Keep reading.

D.O.P. – In 1992, the European Union (E.U.) Agriculture and Rural Development department established laws to protect food products unique to certain locations. These "Protected Designation of Origin" or P.D.O. laws are now in place in most European countries, and in a few others who have made agreements with the E.U. The protected items include some fruits, vegetables, ham, meat, beer and, of course, cheese. When written in some languages, the P.D.O. moves around to become D.O.P., but it means the same thing. Also some items that have been registered for many years as A.O.C. or some other older designation may have also applied for the more wide-ranging P.D.O. designation that is valid in the whole E.U. and in associated countries. Some cheeses in this book will have both designations, and sometimes both years of certification will be listed.

Does all of this make a difference to you? Perhaps, because the approved versions of some cheeses will be made from the unpasteurized milk of a certain breed of animal – as controlled by *law*. This can have a very real (positive) effect on the complexity of flavor in the cheese, and even affect marketing and pricing of an item. That is, if you sell the product as "true A.O.C. Crottin de Chavignol," you can charge more for it, and if the guest is knowledgeable about such things, they will pay for it.

CHAOURCE

Milk – Cow (pasteurized)
Origin – Champagne, France
Rind – Bloomy
Paste – Chalky, velvet to creamy/
runny, depending on age
Aging – 2 to 4 weeks
A.O.C. – 1977

FIGURE **3.18** Chaource

In production for at least 600 years in its region, the size and shape of this cheese greatly affect its texture because of how it ripens. It is almost as tall as it is wide, so the ripening doesn't get to the center of the cheese as quickly as it might in a flatter cheese. Because of this, it can be served at a broad range of ages, at least for a bloomy, high-moisture cheese, a type that usually has a relatively short shelf-life. At its youngest, the paste has a velvety texture, and some say that it feels like snow melting on your tongue. As it ages, the creaminess creeps in, as does some flavor. At its ripest, the buttery texture will be accompanied by a slight tanginess, but the overall impression should still be rather mild, but very rich. If the cheese is runny, it is past its prime and will probably be unpleasantly strong in flavor.

CHABICHOU DE POITOU

Milk – Goat
Origin – Poitou-Charentes, France
Rind – Natural, off-white to beige
(can have blue-gray mold on the
exterior as it gets older)
Paste – Chalky, pure white when
young; acquires waxiness as it
ages
Aging – ≥ 10 days
A.O.C. – 1990

FIGURE **3.19** Chabichou de Poitou

This cute little cheese is a good representation of goat's milk. It is a little less salty and tangy than some of France's other famous goat cheeses. Its cylindrical shape and size (2 1/2 in/6.35 cm tall, about 2 in/5 cm wide) allow it to age quickly, yielding a nuttier, stronger cheese with a waxier texture. Most agree that it is at its best with just enough age to add some density to its texture while maintaining the flavor of sweet goat's milk. Signs of this stage are a beige exterior and a pure-white interior.

CABÉCOU DE ROCAMADOUR

Milk – Goat
Origin – Midi-Pyrénées (Quercy, historically), France
Rind – Natural, moldy with age
Paste – Chalky, creamy, tender
Aging – 1 to 2 weeks, up to 4 weeks
A.O.C. – 1996

FIGURE **3.20** Cabecou Feuille Eau de Vie

This is also a very cute little cheese. In fact, *cabécou* in the local dialect means "little goat." There are some cheeses that are cuter, but remember that the diminutive size can have a very real effect on the cheese during affinage. At 2 in/5 cm across and only a 1/2 to 2/3 in/1.25 to 1.7 cm high, this cheese has a very large surface area for only 1 1/2 oz/43 g of initial weight. Thus, it ages very quickly, losing moisture and developing a new texture. It is usually eaten fairly young, but for those who like their cheese a little funky and looking like a lichen-covered rock, this can be achieved with only four or five weeks of aging. Its A.O.C. status has led some producers to shorten the name to "Rocamadour" to differentiate it from the other, more generic "Cabecou" cheeses. This is because there are other "little goats" in France, but not all of them are of the same quality.

RICOTTA SALATA

Milk – Sheep
Origin – Originally Sicily and Lazio (Rome), Southern Italy
Rind – None
Paste – Chalky, smooth, crumbly, and firm with some moisture
Aging – 3 months

FIGURE **3.21** Ricotta Salata

This cheese was originally made from the whey left over after the production of Pecorino di Sicilia and Pecorino Romano. Pecorino is, of course, sheep's milk cheese, so the true Ricotta Salata is made from ewe's milk. It is, though, wholly different from what most Americans think of when they hear "ricotta." Pure white, very firm, and slightly salty, it's almost like an Italian version of Feta. Because of its sweet milky flavor and light saltiness (contrary to the *salata* part of its name), it is highly versatile, pairing well with olives and cured meats as an antipasto, grated over any number of pastas, or served with grilled and marinated vegetables. A slice of Ricotta Salata served with a perfectly ripe pear makes the perfect simple dessert.

HUMBOLDT FOG

Milk – Goat

Origin – Cypress Grove Chevre, Arcata, Humboldt County, California, United States

Rind – Bloomy over ash

Paste – Chalky, moist, and pure white when young, a line of ash through its center and a coating of ash under the bloom. Creaminess creeps in from the surface as it ages.

Aging – 4 weeks for 1 lb/454 g size, 8 weeks for 5 lb/2.27 kg, in both cases before cutting.

FIGURE **3.22** Humboldt Fog

Cypress Grove Chèvre is in *very* northern California, just off the Humboldt Bay in the town of Arcata. It is a region of rain, fog, and cool temperatures. This and the local vegetation lead to large amounts of flavorful milk from the herds of goats that supply the creamery. Of the eleven cheeses they produce, several are in this book.

The graphic appearance of Humboldt Fog is striking. Stark white paste with a thin stripe of ash down its center, then a thin line of ash around the perimeter with a fuzzy coating of mold over that. The more aged version is even more striking, with an ivory-colored layer of creaminess between the surface and the white interior. This cheese is at once light, creamy, tangy, rich, and earthy. It can last as long as six months if properly stored, however the desired level of creaminess for most people (about 3/8 inch/0.95 cm thick) is reached at about three weeks in the small version or four to five weeks in the big Humboldt Fog cheese. Cypress Grove said also that some people like the creaminess so much that they will let it go longer (sometimes as long as 8 weeks for the large cheese) to develop even more "goo" and complexity. It is past its prime when the ammonia aroma does not dissipate after having been unwrapped for an hour or more, or when a wedge of the cheese does not maintain its structure, that is, the fresh-looking center falls out of its creamy surroundings. As with other goat cheeses, it is lovely with fresh fruit as part of a light dessert.

WABASH CANNONBALL

Milk – Goat
Origin – Capriole, Inc., Indiana, United States
Rind – Bloomy over ash
Paste – Chalky but creamy and light, more crumbly as it ages
Aging – 3 weeks

FIGURE **3.23** Wabash Cannonball

Diminutive but profound, the beguiling appearance of this small sphere belies a depth of flavor and quality that result from very careful cheesemaking. The balls start out at 3 oz/85 g, with a wrinkled coating of *Geotrichum candidum* mold over ash. At three weeks, the flavor is mild and slightly tangy, with a creamy texture. With five weeks of age, the ash starts to show through the mold, and this is also when the paste of the cheese begins getting drier and more crumbly. At either stage, the Cannonball looks great on a cheese board, and is the perfect size to share with a few friends. An added convenience is that they are intact little cheeses, and don't dry out as quickly as a wedge of cut cheese will. Also, you use up one on the cheese board and, presto, put another new one out there, no cutting. Delicious and convenient, that's how we like 'em.

COUPOLE

Milk – Goat's (pasteurized)
Origin – Vermont Butter & Cheese Company, Websterville, Vermont, United States
Rind – Bloomy (geotricum mold) with a dusting of ash
Paste – White, slightly chalky but creamy
Aging – 45 days

Coupole is a goat cheese original from Vermont that relies on French tradition, but moves forward in a very American way. It comes in an interesting shape, like a small dome, and as it dries it forms its rind and a few wrinkles. As Coupole ages, the rind takes on a distinctly yeasty and slightly sweet flavor while the paste retains its freshness. It ages more slowly than the Bijou (just below) because of its size, around 6-1/2 ounces versus the 2 or 3 ounces of the Bijou. This reduced surface area helps Coupole to maintain more of a fresh flavor. So if you like more funk, buy an aged Bijou and if you like more fresh milk flavor, get a piece of Coupole.

BIJOU

Milk – Goat's (pasteurized)

Origin – Vermont Butter & Cheese Company, Websterville, Vermont, United States

Rind – Bloomy (geotricum mold)

Paste – White and fudgy textured but creamy, turning softer and smoother with age

Aging – 10 days upon release, viable through different stages until 75 days old

Bijou means "jewel" in French, and it is a French jewel of goat cheese that acted as the inspiration for this American version. If Crottin de Chavignol (below) is a classic, Bijou from Vermont Butter & Cheese is well on its way to becoming one, and is different from its forbearer in that the rind is intentionally bloomy. Because of this, it is somewhat subtle in its first weeks of aging, but even when aged longer it doesn't smell so much like goats that you think you're standing in a barn. It is delicious with a few weeks of age, and is thoughtfully packaged in what Vermont Butter & Cheese calls a "micro-cave" to promote aging. The challenge is to restrain oneself and not eat the whole thing.

CROTTIN DE CHAVIGNOL

Milk – Goat

Origin – Central Loire Valley, France

Rind – Natural, can form spots of (edible) mold if aged

Paste – Chalky and smooth when young, turning waxy as it ages, eventually to a grating-only texture

Aging – 10 days to 4 months

A.O.C. – 1976

FIGURE **3.24** Crottin de Chavignol

I have been told that the name of this cheese comes from its shape, in that it resembles a small horse, uh, apple. Admittedly, aged versions of Crottin do take on a somewhat earthy appearance. It comes from the section of the Loire Valley that is quite far inland, and happens to be very close to the important wine town of Sancerre. Conveniently enough, younger versions of the cheese get along famously with the well-known Sauvignon Blanc-based wine of that town. In a curious alchemy, the relatively high acid of the cheese and of the wine seem to cancel each other out to create a more pleasant flavor combination. At its best, Crottin smells like hay and goats.

This diminutive cheese is extremely popular with both consumers and professionals for slightly different reasons. For those selling it, Crottin is easy to handle and sell — it's almost always sold whole, and if the seller has proper storage, it is possible to sell it in several stages of ripeness, from very fresh to well aged and suitable for grating. This change also happens rather quickly – in weeks rather than months.

As for the consumer, it's the other side of those same factors. In buying a whole cheese, there's no cutting by the cheesemonger, so it doesn't dry out as quickly in the show-case. Its size makes it perfect for a cheeseboard at home, and Crottin is available (at least from larger retailers) in a range of ages. Fresh is great with fruit for dessert, or for heating up to put atop a salad, and well aged can be grated or shaved over the same salad, or used in recipes.

UP IN SMOKE, RIVER'S EDGE CHÈVRE

> **Milk** – Goat's (pasteurized)
> **Origin** – Three Ring Farm, Logsden, Oregon, United States
> **Rind** – Smoked, wrapped in smoked maple leaves
> **Paste** – Semi-soft, white, and slightly chalky
> **Aging** – 3 weeks

Pat Morsford tends and milks her herd of 60 goats in Logsden, Oregon, with many years of experience behind her. She has raised goats most of her life, starting when she was eight. These days, she makes sure that they are healthy, happy, and eat well so that their milk will turn into delicious cheese. One of the most unique cheeses she makes is called Up in Smoke, and is small and roughly spherical; it is smoked and then wrapped in maple leaves. Even though a number of other smoked cheeses are on the market, there really is nothing like Up in Smoke for the unique combination of a relatively young, fresh goat cheese with smoky flavor. Interestingly, some Pinot Noirs from Oregon wineries can have a slightly smoky character to their aromatics; a potential match made in . . . the Pacific Northwest.

TRIPLE-CRÈME CHEESES

Some of the most decadent food experiences in the culinary world lie within the moldy boundaries of these hedonistic cylinders of barely fermented dairy. In particular, the triple-crème cheeses are required (in France, at least) to have a minimum butterfat content of 75 percent. Now, before reaching for the cholesterol medicine, remember that the percentage is of *solids* and because of the high moisture content in these softer cheeses, the fat calories aren't as bad as one might think. Face it, though, this still isn't diet food.

It might not be surprising to learn that the richness is usually achieved by adding cream to the milk or curd before the cheese is formed. The various cheeses in this category do not vary much from each other in flavor profile. Basically, it's about rich, smooth texture with salty, earthy flavors. Think of a cross between whipped cream and cream cheese, with enough salt to season it well. Yes, it's decadent. Most of the well-known versions are made in Île-de-France, the region around Paris – indeed, the same region originally known as *Brie*. A few are famous, some of which are known by brand name. The slight differences are noted.

CONSTANT BLISS

Milk – Cow's (raw) evening milking, Ayrshire breed

Origin – Jasper Hill Farm, Greensboro, Vermont, United States

Rind – Bloomy, with a mottling of different-colored molds

Paste – Creamy, off-white to ivory (with age)

Aging – ≥ 60 days, acquiring character with more time

FIGURE **3.25** Constant Bliss

The Kehler brothers took over Jasper Hill Farm in Greensboro, Vermont in 1998 largely in an effort to restore farming in an area that had lost five dairy farms in just that one year. After having tried making farmstead beer and tofu from their own soybeans, Mateo and Andy Kehler settled on cheese. They bought their small herd of Ayrshire cows in 2002, and started making unique cheeses using (mostly) traditional methods. In 2004, the brothers were in need of additional help and got their wives to join in the operation.

This cheese is gentle and powerful at the same time. It is made from the evening milk of the Kehler's Ayrshire cows, a milk already richer than that of many other breeds. Evening milk is higher in fat than morning milk, so Constant Bliss starts out with more fat than many other bloomy cheeses, and does not need the addition of heavy cream that triple-crèmes rely on. In adherence to Jasper Hill Farm's insistence on using only raw milk, Constant Bliss is aged for 60 days to be within the law, and is ready when you get it. Some cheesemongers like to age it even longer, but the Kehler's refer to it as a "sell it or smell it" cheese. It's up to your own taste to decide how old it should be. And while you may assume it's name comes from the emotional state that eating it provides, Constant Bliss was the name of a settler who was killed while defending the Bayley Hazen Road, for which another cheese (see page 63) of theirs is named.

BRILLAT-SAVARIN

Milk – Cow (pasteurized if being sold in the United States)

Origin – Seine-et-Marne, Île-de-France, France

Rind – Bloomy

Paste – Rich, smooth, creamy, salty, earthy but with no obvious ammonia smell. Should bulge slightly when cut, but not be runny

Aging – 3 to 7 weeks

FIGURE **3.26** Brillat-Savarin

First alphabetically of the French triple-crèmes, and also in many cheese-lovers' hearts, this cheese was "invented" in the 1930s by Henri Androuët. It was named for the legendary French gastronome Jean Anthelme Brillat-Savarin, whose famous work, *The Physiology of Taste,* was published in 1825. This is one of the best of its class, and should be eaten before it gets runny – at that point, it is past its prime and may smell of ammonia.

EXPLORATEUR

FIGURE **3.27** Explorateur

Milk – Cow (pasteurized for the United States)
Origin – Île-de-France, Fromagerie Petit Morin, France
Rind – Bloomy
Paste – Rich, smooth, buttery, creamy, earthy
Aging – 3 weeks

This small, rich cheese is named for . . . well, various sources say that it was named for the French explorer Bertrand Flornoy (who apparently loved cheese); the first American satellite, Explorer 1; and for Sputnik, the infamous Russian satellite that shamed America. There is a picture of an early rocket ship on the label, so you can decide which story you want to believe. It might not be the best of this class, but Explorateur is readily available, and still rates near the top with regard to its overall quality.

PIERRE ROBERT

FIGURE **3.28** Pierre-Robert

Milk – Cow (pasteurized for the United States)
Origin – Fromagerie Rouzaire, Île-de-France, France
Rind – Bloomy
Paste – Light, creamy, mouth-coating, yet delicate; with an earthy/salty character
Aging – 3 weeks

Another brand-name cheese, this was "invented" by Robert Rouzaire, a famous *affineur* in the region known for its Brie and Brillat-Savarin cheeses. In fact, Robert and his pal Pierre were reportedly tiring of their Brillat-Savarin, and decided to let it age a bit longer and see what happened. The result was this earthy, salty, creamy cloud of a cheese. At optimal ripeness, the wedge of cheese removed from the whole wheel should droop slightly at the point, and from its middle, but not run all over the plate. Any overt ammonia smell also indicates that the cheese is past its prime and should be avoided. Usually, such smells are accompanied by a leathery or slightly gray rind. As marvelously rich as this cheese may be, the butterfat actually *lightens* the texture (fat is lighter than water), and a bite of it might actually have fewer calories than a bite of cheddar or gouda. So go ahead, order a glass of Champagne Doux or Demi-Sec to go with this and some lovely, ripe strawberries. And have a butter cookie, too.

HUDSON VALLEY CAMEMBERT

Milk – Sheep and Cow (BGH-free)

Origin – Old Chatham Sheep-herding Company, Old Chatham, NY, United States

Rind – Bloomy

Paste – Soft, creamy, buttery

Aging – 18 to 20 days

FIGURE **3.29** Hudson Valley Camembert

This is the most popular (and famous) cheese made by Old Chatham Sheep-herding Company. While rich and creamy, the presence of sheep's milk adds some flavors that all-cow versions of Camembert lack. It is available in a few different sizes, but the most recognizable is the 4 oz/113 g square – perfect for a restaurant's cheese cart, or for the cheese platter at a dinner or cocktail party. Most first-timers trying this cheese let out a low moan of pleasure after their first bite. In fact, this cheese with some ripe pears and a glass of Moscato d'Asti is a wholly satisfying dessert. Switch to a glass of Clinton Vineyards Sparkling Seyval Blanc, and you will be satisfying the locavore in you as well as the hedonist.

NANCY'S HUDSON VALLEY CAMEMBERT

Milk – Sheep and cow (pasteurized)

Origin – Old Chatham Sheep-herding Company, Old Chatham, New York, United States

Rind – Bloomy

Paste – Off-white, creamy

Aging – 2 to 4 weeks

FIGURE **3.30** Nancy's Hudson Valley Camembert

This is a large version of the Hudson Valley Camembert square. Its larger size means that there is a higher paste-to-rind ratio than is found in its smaller sibling. With a texture approaching that of a triple-crème French cheese like Pierre-Robert, Nancy's version is very rich and luxurious. It doesn't have the mushroomy or earthy aromas and flavors of its French relatives, though. This is just fine for many Americans, of course, and is not a negative point. The gentle nature of this "camembert" is delightful, and means that it should be paired with relatively calm counterparts, such as a gentle sparkling wine from the Finger Lakes and some juicy local apples. And if you're in a store that carries the cheeses of Old Chatham Sheepherding Company, they will be easy to find—just look for a round green label with a black sheep on it.

MARQUIS DE TÉMISCOUATA

Milk – Cow, Jersey breed
Origin – Fromagerie le Détour, Notre-Dame-du-Lac, Québec, Canada
Rind – Bloomy
Paste – White and chalky when young; ivory, creamy and bulging à point
Aging – 4 to 10 weeks

Among the artisanal Canadian cheesemakers whose products are available in the United States, a few names pop up more often than others. One of those is Fromagerie le Détour in the Témiscouata region of Québec. Mario and Ginette Quirion own and run the dairy, which has been making cheese since 1999. They are perhaps better known for their washed rind Le Clandestin, a mixed sheep and cow cheese that has won many awards, including first prize from the American Cheese Society in 2007. The Marquis de Témiscouata has also won awards, but sits in the shadow of its stinky sibling. The Marquis (a childhood nickname of the cheesemaker, Mario Quirion) is a rich Brie-style cheese that might present Americans with the closest experience to eating genuine Brie in France. It is elegant, creamy, rich, and buttery with just enough earthiness to keep it from being simple. It is worth seeking out.

FIGURE **3.31** Green Hill

GREEN HILL

Milk – Cow (pasteurized)
Origin – Sweet Grass Dairy, Thomasville, Georgia, United States
Rind – Bloomy
Paste – Ivory, thick and creamy
Aging – ≥ 4 weeks

The Wehner family had been part of a dairy partnership with 1,100 cows on concrete, but decided that there had to be a better way. In 1993 they created Green Hill Dairy, and later, Sweet Grass dairy. Both rely on traditional pasture rotation and sustainable practices, and the quality of the milk shows the dedication they have towards their cows and goats.

Green Hill is their flagship cheese and is a small camembert-style cow's milk round. In this country where such a cheese cannot be made with raw milk (it is aged less than 60 days), the quality of the not-so-raw product is what makes it especially good. Frankly, it is probably better to have excellent pasteurized milk than mediocre raw milk. In the case of Green Hill, the great milk is obvious in the final product.

CAMEMBERT DE NORMANDIE

Milk – Cow (unpasteurized)
Origin – Normandy, France
Rind – Bloomy, *Penicillium camemberti*
Paste – Creamy throughout, bulging when cut. Once it's runny, it has passed its peak
Aging – 3 to 4 weeks
A.O.C. – 1983

FIGURE **3.32** Camembert de Normandie

When most Americans hear "French cheese," they immediately think of Camembert or Brie. There is something iconic about these white wheels of sticky, gooey, sometimes runny (if so, they're overripe) cheese. The fact is that most Camemberts exported to the United States are factory-made and largely bereft of character. For a more genuine and unique experience, look for the A.O.C. version of Camembert de Normandie that was invented by Marie Harel in 1761, which is not available in the United States. The other big name in the history of this cheese is Monsieur Ridel who invented the round poplar-wood box container. Because of this development, Camemberts could be shipped all over France, and eventually the world.

It is a molded cheese – the curd is carefully ladled into forms where it drains and is salted with dry salt. The ladles fit perfectly inside the molds, and there must be a minimum of four ladling procedures for each cheese. They are aged for a minimum of twenty-one days, sixteen of which have to be in the place of manufacture. Unfortunately, the A.O.C. version is not available in the United States because it has to be made with unpasteurized milk. Pasteurized versions are available, but the label will read *fabriqué en Normandie,* which means "made in Normandy." Because it's made of the same basic stuff as Brie, it tastes much the same, although its smaller size allows it to achieve ripeness a little more quickly. Remember also that, the high moisture content means its shelf life is not very long – eat it before it gets runny and stinks of ammonia.

SAINT-MARCELLIN

Milk – Cow, but historically goat
Origin – Dauphiné Province (southeast, but north of Provence), France
Rind – Natural but sometimes comes in a ceramic crock; develops a light white mold with age
Paste – Soft, creamy, becomes spoonable with age
Aging – 2 to 6 weeks

Several cheese experts name this as one of their absolute favorite French cheeses. It is rich and tastes of lightly soured cream, but also has a degree of complexity. Rich, light, creamy, and delicate, but with a nutty complexity. It is made similarly to Banon, but without the chestnut leaf wrapping and dip in marc, and so is a bit subtler in overall character. It is often packed in a crock that keeps it from collapsing once it reaches service temperature. It should provide hedonistic pleasure on par with that of La Tur (earlier), but is a little creamier, though still not frighteningly high in butterfat – remember, the younger cheeses have higher water content, which adds to the creaminess. So enjoy it with somewhat diminished guilt.

FIGURE **3.34** Selles-sur-Cher

SELLES-SUR-CHER

Milk – Goat

Origin – Central Loire Valley, France

Rind – Ash that encourages bloomy

Paste – Chalky (but smooth) and dense when young, gaining creaminess with age

Aging – ≥ 8 days

A.O.C. – 1975

This cheese is the love child of Brie and Montrachet. It is a diminutive disk curdled from whole goat's milk, ladled into a form and allowed to drain, then salted and coated with ash. As the Selles-sur-Cher ages, it acquires a bloom of mold and the paste gets creamier. Its size allows it to ripen more quickly than many other goat cheeses, and because it happens fairly quickly, the flavors stay rather mild. There is still a characteristic tanginess, but the overall impression is still one of mildness. The rind is edible, and adds both texture and strength of flavor to the experience. Serve it with fresh fruit, by itself, and if you want to include wine, pick something from the region, such as a Sancerre or Vouvray.

POULIGNY-ST.-PIERRE

Milk – Goat

Origin – Berry, Loire Valley, France

Rind – Bloomy, eventually acquiring blue-gray mold with age

Paste – Pure white and semi-soft, with a texture that gets more clay-like with age

Aging – ≥ 10 days, most are aged 4 to 6 weeks

A.O.C. – 1976

FIGURE **3.35** Pouligny-St.-Pierre

Often called the Eiffel Tower or the Pyramid because of its shape, Pouligny-St.-Pierre is one of the famous goat cheeses of the Loire Valley. The usual goaty tartness is balanced by salty and sweet components, and complexity of flavor becomes more apparent after five weeks of aging. At this point, the cheeses usually have acquired a smattering of blue-gray mold on their surface, which is considered edible. As the blue mold arrives, the pH is actually increasing, so the cheeses are getting less tart with the arrival of blue mold, which makes the cheeses taste mellower.

GARROTXA

Milk – Goat (pasteurized)

Origin – Catalonia, Spain

Rind – Natural with a grayish-blue bloom

Paste – Stark white semi-soft to firm with a chalky appearance

It's funny how some products become lightning rods for artisanal production. This is a cheese that almost died out, but was brought back to a certain degree of prominence by young Spaniards who wanted to return to the land. It is a great vehicle for goat's milk, with a combination of dry but creamy texture, occasional resinous (pine) aromas, and

FIGURE **3.36** Garrotxa

a characteristic nuttiness described as resembling either hazelnuts or pine nuts. Its newfound popularity has invited imitation around the country, so some Catalonians are looking for D.O. status to protect their original product.

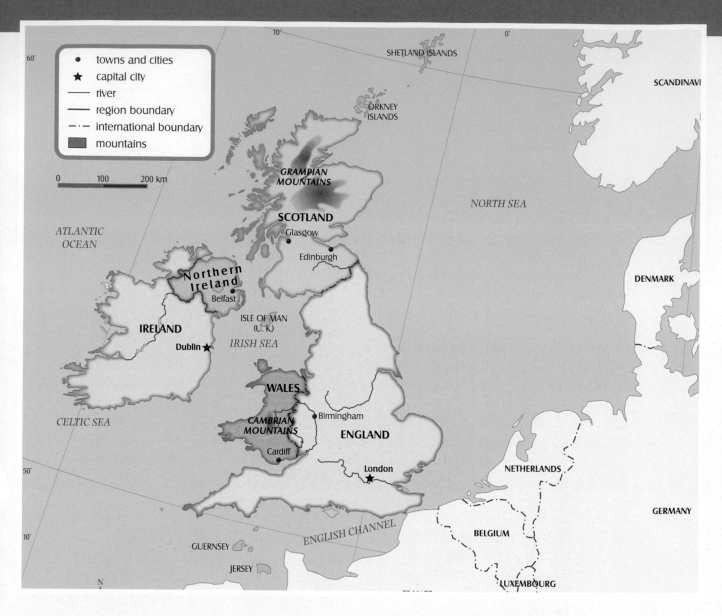

The British Isles and Ireland have been known for their dairy products for thousands of years — since the Romans "visited" in 43 C.E. Cheddar is a village in England. Jersey and Guernsey are islands in the English Channel, as well as two of the most important breeds of dairy cattle for cheesemaking. The rolling and lush hills, especially of southwest England, provide the perfect conditions for cows to produce rich, delicious milk and cream. In fact, Devonshire Cream and clotted cream are some of the most luxurious foods on the planet, best used in combination with jam on scones still warm from the oven.

The cheeses from these islands aren't quite as hedonistic, and in fact are mostly large, firm to hard cheeses whose best attribute (among others) is durability. Cheddar, Cheshire, and Wensleydale have

their positive flavor characteristics, though. At their best, there is a sharp complexity combined with an underlying sweetness. Along with the justifiably famous blue Stilton, they are the standard bearing cheeses and represent the English well.

There was a time, though, when all (or most) cheeses of character were leading endangered lives. Farmhouse producers had been trundling along, making their traditional cheeses for centuries, but a number of factors made survival difficult. The Industrial Revolution increased mechanization in dairies and made transportation more efficient, so farmers no longer needed to make cheese — they could just send their milk to London where it made instant cash. Then World War I devastated the entire country and made all forms of farming more difficult. In that war's wake, the Milk Marketing Boards were established in 1933; trade groups that were intended to centralize and control the quality of milk products in Britain. Although they were successful in some ways, cheese quality was almost *too* closely controlled, and individuality (i.e., character) was quashed. Farmhouse cheeses almost became extinct, in that milk from many dairies was being combined, and the artisanal making of unique cheeses was made virtually illegal because many of the traditional methods could lead to "inconsistencies" . . . like flavor.

Luckily, some traditional cheesemaking survived the era of regulation, and there is a number of cheeses from England that act as standard-bearers. The most famous is definitely Farmhouse Cheddar and these cheeses, such as those from Keen's and the Montgomery family at Manor Farm (both in Somerset), are real Cheddar. There is one other cheese, though, that could possibly dim the glow around these great handmade cheeses, and that is Stilton. From the outset, Stilton did not originate in the town of that name, but was sold in volume there. Sold in volume because it was and is one of the most important blue cheeses in the world — a member of the Four Big Blues (see page 131). In concert with a glass of vintage port and perhaps some crumbly graham crackers, it provides one of the most perfect flavor pairings on earth.

There are some other types of cheese surfacing as artisanal production methods become more popular, such as Berkswell, a firm sheep's milk cheese from Warwickshire, and some other fine blues. English affection for blue cheese actually manifests itself in an interesting practice that some turophiles there have adopted. Occasionally, a person who wants more blue in their lives will slightly break open a cylinder of cheddar just enough so that mold spores will be able to get down into the cheese and form some blue veins.

Ireland

Ireland is famous for being green. Its lush pastures are heaven for dairy animals, and the cows there produce a lot of milk. The major presence of Irish dairy products in the United States (and worldwide) belongs to the products of the Kerrygold brand of both butter and cheeses. They produce a range of high-quality, high-volume dairy products, most of which is exported.

There are a few smaller producers on the Emerald Isle, like the Grubb family of County Tipperary who have produced Cashel Blue since 1984. There is also a fine stinky cheese from County Cork called Ardrahan that the Burns family established that same year. Although these may be the best known by Americans, there is a group of farmhouse cheesemakers under the banner of CÁIS, the Irish Farmhouse Cheesemakers Association. The current membership of thirty-six farms might not be well represented in the United States yet, but considering the current interest in cheese here, maybe we'll be seeing more of them in the near future.

Scotland

There are fewer small production cheeses currently available from Scotland than England or Ireland, although there is a significant amount of good cheddar made there. Speaking of cheddar, a fine raw milk artisanal version comes from, and called Isle of Mull, and is also known as Reade's Cheddar. Scotland, like its neighbors, is well suited to pasturage because of the humid climate and geography, and some small cheese producers are beginning to emerge. As with Ireland, it is likely that the products of these artisanal producers will start showing up in the display cases of good cheesemongers in the United States.

It's not unreasonable to say that the United Kingdom and Ireland are at the same place on a somewhat parallel path with Americans. There has been a lot of high-quality industrial cheese produced for a long time, but the artisans are really starting to show the ability to produce excellent cheeses in reasonable quantities — and get them into the hands (and mouths) of appreciative cheese fans. There is absolutely nothing wrong with large-scale production of predictable cheeses; however you should also have the opportunity to partake of a handmade cheese that shows both the quality of the raw product and what it can be turned into by a craftsperson. Nothing wrong with the print of an original painting — but sometimes you want the original itself.

VALENÇAY

FIGURE **3.37** Valençay

Milk – Goat

Origin – Valençay (near the Touraine), Loire Valley, France

Rind – Bloomy, with a light layer of ash underneath

Paste – Pure white and chalky in the center, with a runny creaminess near the surface

Aging – 8 days to 1 month

A.O.C. – 1998

Famous cheese loved by famous Frenchmen. It is one of several cheeses that were "approved" by Napoléon Bonaparte. It was served to him by Talleyrand at the Château de Valençay in the Loire. The cheese originally came in a pyramid shape, but some say that Napoléon was so displeased by his Egyptian campaign that he personally lopped the top of the cheese off with his sword. Valençay now comes in the shape of a truncated pyramid. It's a mild-tasting cheese that still has some wherewithal; as it ages, it acquires a goaty nuttiness. This brings to mind an experience at Restaurant Paul Bocuse in Lyon. When the cheese board came out, most of the cheeses were in pristine, white condition. A few of us were surprised that there were no runny, scary, rotten-looking cheeses on the board, and we mentioned that to our French colleague. He said, "I always thought you Americans were crazy, waiting for the cheese to be old and nasty before you eat it!" Well, now it makes sense that these bloomed rind cheeses have a short period during which they are at their best – you should catch them at just the right time, after they've become creamy, before they're runny.

MORBIER

FIGURE **3.38** Morbier

Milk – Cow (pasteurized or unpasteurized)

Origin – Franche-Comté (just south of Alsace on the Swiss border), France

Rind – Natural, rubbed and washed with water

Paste – Semi-soft, creamy ivory, with a thin layer of ash separating the top from the bottom

Aging – 2 to 4 months

A.O.C. – 1990

This cheese is gaining some real popularity in the United States, certainly for its flavor, possibly because it's pretty easy to pick from a lineup. Its shape, a large wheel, is somewhat common, but there aren't many cheeses with a stripe of greenish-black ash running down their centers. Because this cheese is just on the cusp of having some funk, it satisfies some American's urge to try stinky cheese. It is not truly stinky, though, and you might notice that it has a slight aroma of peanut skins and shells. It is rich and creamy with some density, and the unpasteurized versions (aged at least 60 days) tend to be the best.

There is a story behind the ash, of course. Legend has it that the makers of the local favorite Comté cheese would often have some leftover curd from the morning milking, but not enough to make a whole cheese. So, they would put that curd in the bottom of a mold or barrel, and dust the curds with ash to protect it from vermin and from drying out. Evening milking would come along, and presto, there would be enough curd to finish off this "secondary" cheese, that was often taken home by the workers. There are still some truly artisanal producers, but sadly, some of the Morbiers these days only have food coloring running through their middles instead of ash. Even worse, the producers will sometimes mold the cheese, slice it in half and then add the coloring, only to slap the two halves together again. Ah, well, at least this now-popular cheese is inching the American public closer to the funk.

WENSLEYDALE

> **Milk** – Cow
> **Origin** – Yorkshire, England
> **Rind** – Natural, clothbound
> **Paste** – Slightly crumbly, fine, and a little dry
> **Aging** – 3 to 6 months

How can you not love a cheese whose existence was preserved by Wallace & Gromit? This is a relatively mild cheddar-style cheese that was about to go out of production when its name was used in the first few Wallace & Gromit shorts and movie. Wensleydale is mellow and a bit citrusy, with a slight lactic tang. The combination of this acidity and its inherent saltiness make it a good match for fruit that has the wherewithal to stand up to it, like apples, pears, or even some dried fruits. Frankly, a chunk of this is nice with some good ale, crusty bread, and hearty mustard. But then there has to be a dartboard somewhere nearby as well.

CAERPHILLY

> **Milk** – Cow
> **Origin** – Wales and nearby England
> **Rind** – Natural, medium brown brushed with some white mold
> **Paste** – Somewhat dry and crumbly at 3 weeks. Creamy halfway in at 3 months.
> **Aging** – 3 weeks to 3 months

This cheese leans toward the buttery side of the cheddar style. Farmhouse versions are superior to factory-made, but all should have a mild, lemony aroma, and should be creamier than some of their

FIGURE **3.39** Gorwydd Caerphilly

English counterparts like Wensleydale. There is occasionally creaminess close to the rind. It was a great "cash crop" in years past because it matured rapidly, being ready to eat in only three weeks. More complexity is evident at three months, however, with some genuine funk evident around four months. Perhaps the best example of this cheese is the Gorwydd Caerphilly from Wales.

FIGURE **3.40** Mrs. Kirkham's Lancashire

LANCASHIRE

Milk – Cow (unpasteurized)
Origin – Lancashire, England
Rind – Natural, clothbound
Paste – Crumbly but creamy
Aging – 6 weeks to 8 months

This cheese could have appeared in the Medium Strength and Nutty Cheeses chapter because it is full-flavored, but most describe it first as mild, with some power behind. The buttery flavor and lemony quality are underscored by a distinct lactic acidity, which is explained by the fact that two- to three-day-old curds are mixed together to make the cheese. This seemingly short time allows the development of lactic acid from bacterial activity. Several cheese experts recommend sticking to the version from Beesley Farm, made by the Kirkham family. The current Mrs. Kirkham is from a long line of Kirkham women producing the best version of this cheese.

FIGURE **3.41** Hooligan

HOOLIGAN

Milk – Cow (raw)
Origin – Cato Corner Farm, Colchester, Connecticut, United States
Rind – Washed with buttermilk and brine, orange in color, and a little sticky
Paste – Semi-soft to soft, creamy and a little shiny, bulging when cut and with a smattering of small, irregular holes
Aging – 60 days

This is a little stinker. At about one and a third pounds, it is barely legal with just 60 days of aging. It comes from Cato Corner Farm in Connecticut, about which you can read more on page 85, in the entry on their Brigid's Abbey cheese. It is made from cooked curds and is washed with both buttermilk and brine, which lead to its stinky orange rind. As stinky as it is, the flavor is rather mild and sweet, but with a very earthy and long finish. The folks at the farm think that Hooligan makes a rather fabulous, if attention-getting, grilled cheese sandwich.

LA COMTOMME

Milk – Cow (raw, organic)
Origin – Fromagerie la Station de Compton, Compton, Québec, Canada
Rind – Washed
Paste – Ivory to gold, semi-firm with small, irregularly sized round holes
Aging – 3 to 5 months

The Bolduc family is carrying on the family farming tradition begun by their great-grandfather Alfred Bolduc. Their closed herd of about 50 Holstein cows eats only from the organically farmed pastures of the Bolduc Farm. Their cheeses are all made from the raw milk of this herd, and each one shows the family's dedication to organic farming and scrupulous adherence to careful and clean production practices.

The name of this cheese is a subtle play on words—it is a Tomme-style cheese from Compton, Québec. It is similar in style to Tomme de Savoie (below), and is consistent in having just the right amount of stink and bitterness to give the cheese character without being out of balance. It is rich and buttery with an aroma of apples and a lovely sweetness. This, and their other products, shows the perfect combination of traditional methods (organic farming and use of raw milk) combined with the use of modern technology ("green" fertilizers and stainless steel). A little old with a little new seems to be a good approach to use on the farm.

TOMME DE SAVOIE

Milk – Cow
Origin – Savoie, France
Rind – Natural, brushed with various white, red, or yellow mold spots. Slightly cratered
Paste – Semi-firm; light yellow with small, randomly sized and placed holes
Aging – 2 to 6 months

FIGURE **3.42** Tomme de Savoie

Something of an enigma, Tomme de Savoie is considered mild while still having a lot of earthy flavor. Often described as "beefy" and "hazelnutty," it is still considered mild. Hundreds of this type of cheese are produced, and the authentic ones will have a label that states "made in Savoy" or "*fabriqué en Savoie.*" Avoid those that just say "*affiné en Savoie,*" because those will have only been aged in Savoy, having been made elsewhere. Because there are so many producers in different parts of Savoy, there will be differences in fat level (as low as 20 percent, as high as 40 percent), but it should always be semi-firm, with a creamy texture and mild flavor – but a barnyard aroma as well.

The last three cheeses in this chapter are significantly stronger than the others preceding them. But, as blue cheeses go, they are considered mild.

MILD BLUE CHEESES

FIGURE **3.43** Fourme d'Ambert

FOURME D'AMBERT

Milk – Cow
Origin – Auvergne, France
Rind – Natural, light brown
Paste – Creamy with abundant blue mold
Aging – ≥ 28 days
A.O.C. – Originally shared with its sister cheese, Fourme de Montbrison in 1972, on its own since 2002

This is a very good blue cheese for people who think they don't like blue cheese. Its creamy texture and relatively mild flavor are not as dominating as Roquefort, stinky as Gorgonzola, or sharp as the Danish blues that most Americans know. Having been made since at least the 800s, the "fourme" in its name refers to the form it has been made in through the ages. If you are on a crusade to change someone's mind about blue cheese, give them some of this with a perfectly ripe Comice pear and some Coteaux du Layon dessert wine. If that doesn't work, nothing will.

FIGURE **3.44** Point Reyes Farmstead Blue

POINT REYES FARMSTEAD BLUE

Milk – Cow (unpasteurized)
Origin – Point Reyes Station, California, United States
Rind – None, foil-wrapped
Paste – Ivory paste with well-distributed blue veining, more creamy than crumbly
Aging – 3 weeks curing, 6 months aging

Tomales Bay is a beautiful, ten-mile long estuary bay about forty miles northwest of San Francisco. It separates Point Reyes from the mainland and is a fine destination for food lovers. The Tomales Bay Oyster Company is one place to stop, but for our purposes there are two cheese producers there; the Cowgirl Creamery and the Point Reyes Farmstead Cheese Company that make this blue cheese.

The Giacomini family had been running their dairy there since 1959, but decided to start making a product from their milk in 2000. Since then, they have enjoyed both critical success and increased sales, with good availability around the United States.

The cheese is similar to Fourme d'Ambert and Bleu d'Auvergne, two blues from France that tend more toward the creamy than sharp and spicy. This style is a good one for those who aren't sure whether they like blue cheese – it's a great starting point.

You will find this cheese again with the other blues in the strong chapter, but because it is a rather mild one, it also belongs here.

BLEU D'AUVERGNE

Milk – Cow
Origin – Auvergne, France
Rind – None, foil-wrapped
Paste – Creamy with abundant
    dark blue marbling
Aging – 4 weeks
A.O.C. – 1975

FIGURE **3.45** Bleu d'Auvergne

This is blue cheese with training wheels. It lacks some of the subtlety of Fourme d'Ambert, but is a non-prepossessing, rather soft and buttery, relatively mild blue. It also tends to be a very good value because it is made in large quantities to satisfy the French and American grocery store demand, and is somewhat less well known than the (sometimes less characterful) Danish Blue, which was originally based on Bleu d'Auvergne after World War II.

4

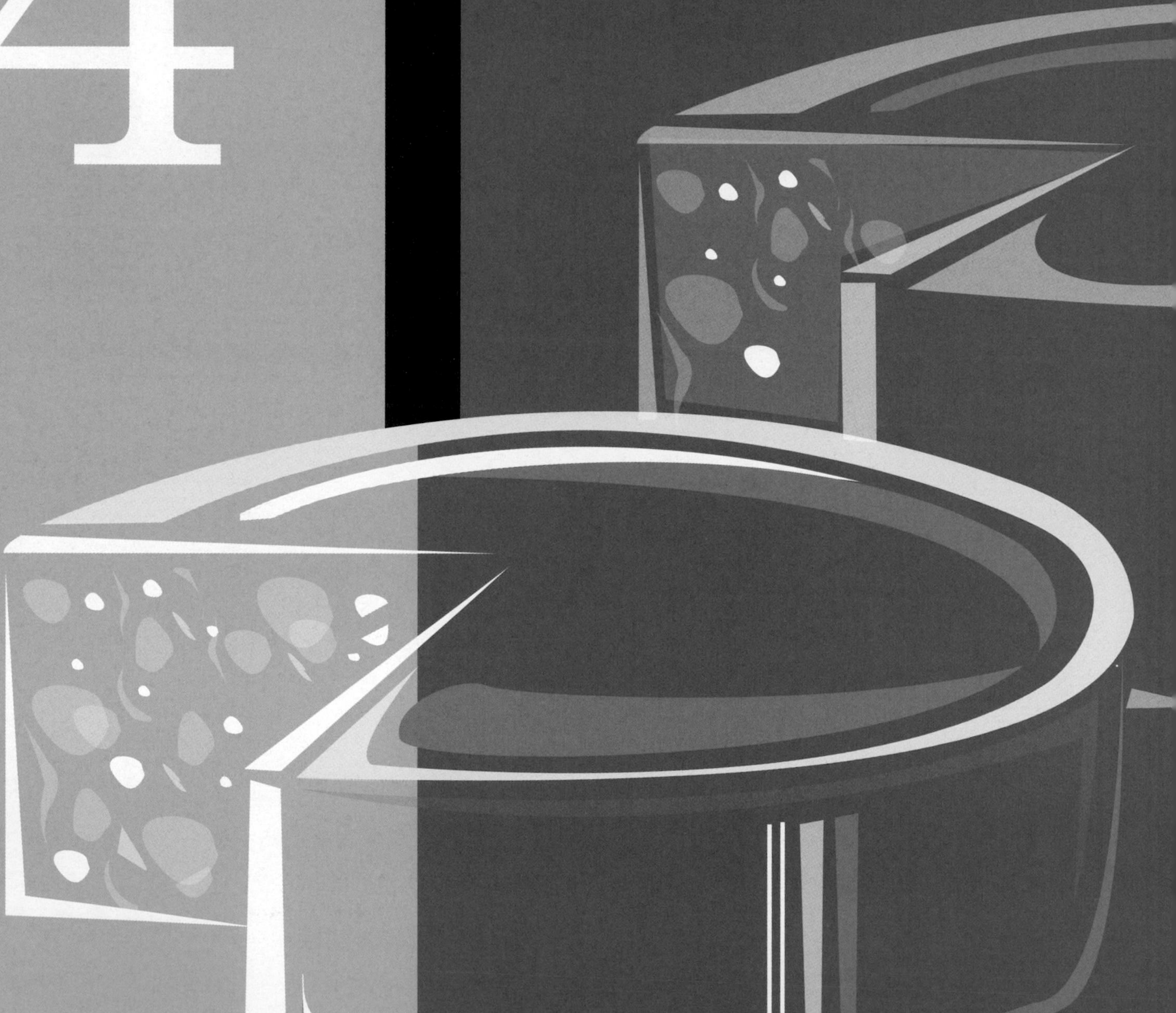

MEDIUM STRENGTH AND NUTTY CHEESES

For these cheeses, it's mostly about time. The cheeses of this chapter are a bit older than the mild cheeses in Chapter 3. The base milk and type of rind change the cheeses' flavor characteristics somewhat, but age is the major determinant of the overall flavor profile. As with the milder cheeses, evaporation of water increases the intensity of flavor. What's different now is that there has been more time for bacterial and fungal activity to create enzymes and other chemical by-products. These in turn have broken down some of the protein and fat molecules into aromatic, or flavor compounds. So, the intensity and complexity of flavor will both increase over time. This happens in most cheeses, whether made with raw milk in a traditional manner, or as a squeaky-clean factory cheese. Both will lose some of their water content through evaporation, and almost all have had some form of starter bacteria that helps to develop flavor with age. Of course, raw milk versions will have a lot more bacteria and more potential complexity of flavor. And although pasteurized milk cheeses will not develop as much complexity, they will still become more intense in flavor, and whatever bacteria were allowed to remain, or were inoculated into the cheese, will help to create aromatic elements in that cheese.

The use of raw milk in cheesemaking is limited by the United States Department of Agriculture (USDA) to cheeses that will be aged a minimum of 60 days. In most other countries, there is no such law, and so fresh and young cheeses can be made with raw milk—unless they are to be exported to the United States. The thing is, if the cheese is traditionally aged for longer than two months anyway, as in the cases of English farmhouse Cheddar and Italian Parmigiano-Reggiano, raw milk may be used, and Americans are getting the real deal . . . raw milk artisanally produced cheeses.

The other, and perhaps most noticeable, change in cheese as it ages is its increasing hardness. Although mentioned earlier in the book, cheese that is intended for longer aging usually begins its life somewhat differently. Reduced moisture in the paste will help the cheese to be less perishable, so getting moisture out of the curd at the beginning of the process helps produce a cheese that will last longer. Cutting the curd into smaller pieces allows more whey to escape the curd. Gravity is also used in several ways, the simplest of which is to allow the curd to drain naturally. But just as a sponge will still contain water if left to drain on its own, more moisture can be expelled from the curd by applying pressure. The simplest of these methods involves stacking curd or cheeses on top of each other. Usually, the pieces of curd will be rotated through so each one spends some time at the bottom, and the number of cheeses in a stack also can determine how much pressure is applied and how much whey will be removed. Curd and young cheeses will also often be turned over regularly to keep the moisture in the cheese evenly throughout. Many traditional producers use presses to remove whey from whole cheeses. Both single cheeses, as well as stacks of cheeses can be pressed to remove the whey more quickly than draining, or even stacking and draining will.

VOLUME CHEESES

DOMESTIC SHARP CHEDDAR

Cheddar is now playing second fiddle to mozzarella in the United States. As the base cheese for many "cheese foods," most Americans know the flavor of so-called sharp cheddar. The important point here, though, is that "sharpness" is a relative term, and is in the mouth of the taster. One person's "sharp" could be another's "boooooring" – whereas the intensity of a "sharp" English Cheddar might frighten people with more tender sensibilities.

The domestic cheddars are almost always made from pasteurized cow's milk and can be yellow, because of added annatto, or white. Unlike the smaller production artisanal cheddars in this country, higher volume versions tend to be a bit softer and less crumbly, but can still have a fairly high acid level, and thus sharpness. Still, the sharpness in the volume cheeses tends to be a bit simpler, which some might prefer for cooking applications. In other words, the subtlety of a farmhouse cheddar could be largely wasted in a cheddar-broccoli soup, or in white cheddar cornbread.

FIGURE **4.1** Sharp Cheddar

DOMESTIC BLUE CHEESE

There is a tremendous amount of blue cheese made in the United States, one Wisconsin manufacturer estimating an annual production of over 50 million pounds from that state alone. Most of that production used to go into salad dressings, but an increasing percentage is being packaged as wedges or crumbles, used mostly for salads and melting applications. In general, the quality is quite high, with most domestic blues having a fairly high saltiness and the requisite spicy and peppery characteristics that tend to come with the blue-green *Penicillium* molds. Some smaller American producers such as Maytag, Rogue Creamery, and Point Reyes Farmstead make truly world-class blue cheeses, but even the volume-oriented producers in major dairy states don't lag too far behind with the very high level of quality of their cheeses.

FIGURE **4.2** Domestic Blue Cheese

SPROUT CREEK FARM

Cheese is delicious, and a potentially profound and broad subject of study. As with wine, you can study the biology, history, chemistry, sociology . . . it goes on and on. But then you go to the farm. When you visit either a truly artisanal cheese producer or a farm where cheese is made, it changes your understanding of what cheese really is. The intellectual study of cheese is potentially endless, but being at the farm is more than absorbing, it is embracing. Meeting the animals, letting the goats and cows nuzzle your hand as you reach over the fence — it creates a living connection between you and the cheese you are either about to make or eventually eat.

Sprout Creek Farm in LaGrange, New York is a working farm that was originally founded as an educational farm for children. Its origins were in a smaller farm just north of Greenwich, Connecticut, that had been founded and was successful in the 1980s. In 1990, the farm moved to the Poughkeepsie area at the behest of Elise Kinkead who donated her Woodford Farm to the cause. Since then the educational programs have burgeoned, as has cheese production there.

Initially, the production of cheese from the milk of the farm's animals was intended to show the children that the grass grown on the farm and eaten by its cows and goats could be fashioned into a renewable food product other than meat.

Cheesemaking there has become more consistent over the years, and until recently, the important cheeses were their very consistent Toussaint, Ouray, and Barat. With these cheeses as dependable performers, a Culinary Institute of America bachelor's student named Colin McGrath, who had been working part-time at the farm, started taking cheese seriously. He is now the head cheesemaker at Sprout Creek and is making more than fourteen different cheeses, including fresh, bloomy, and washed-rind versions, and a room was built recently in which to age blue cheeses. Demand for these artisanal, farmhouse cheeses has been increasing rapidly in the Northeast, especially in the fine cheese shops and restaurants of New York City and the nearby Hudson Valley. Having made cheese at the farm with Colin, I can tell you that these cheeses are made with intelligence, care, precision, and a lot of heart.

FIGURE 4.3 Cotija

COTIJA

Milk – Cow
Origin – Cotija, Michoacán, Mexico
Rind – None (young), Natural (aged)
Paste – White and crumbly (young), Pale yellow and semi-hard (aged)
Aging – Fresh: no aging, Aged: 3 to 12 months

Sometimes referred to as "Mexican Parmesan," Cotija is actually used in similar ways, being grated and added to soups and other dishes. The fresh version is very similar to feta and is used similarly to that cheese as well — being crumbled over salads, and even as a filling for quesadillas and the like.

DRUNKEN GOAT (QUESO DE CABRA AL VINO)

Milk – Goat (pasteurized)
Origin – Murcia, Spain
Rind – Natural, but soaked in red wine
Paste – Very white, semi-soft, and more pliable than most goat's cheeses
Aging – ≥ 45 days

FIGURE 4.4 Drunken Goat

This cheese has become very popular over the past few years. Part of the popularity is undoubtedly due to the name and novelty aspect of its wine-soaked exterior, but the cheese has undeniable high quality and an approachable nature. Each cheese spends from 48 to 72 hours soaking in Doble Pasta wines, a concentrated wine made in the Jumilla region in Murcia, Spain. The wine is made with a second dose (hence *doble*) of grapes to intensify its richness. As rich as the wine may be, the cheese is rather calm, with a creamy texture and light grapy fruitiness.

WINNEMERE

Milk – Cow's (raw) evening milking, Ayrshire breed
Origin – Jasper Hill Farm, Greensboro, Vermont, United States
Rind – Washed with raspberry lambic beer, wrapped with a strip of spruce bark
Paste – Soft, sticky, and bulging when cut
Aging – ≥ 60 days

This interesting and novel cheese is only available for six months each year, from November through April. If it's not enough to have a ripe cheese made from the milk of happy Ayrshire cows, the addition of regular washings with raspberry lambic beer and a strip of spruce bark around the cheese might tip the balance for you. Winnemere is a seductive cheese with a highly complex set of aromatics; the flavor of the paste gets stronger the closer it is to the rind. Piney and woodsy, with a hint of raspberry and some funk from the wild yeast collected at the farm on its exterior, Winnemere keeps calling you back until the piece you bought is gone. *Caveat emptor*, it is hard to resist.

COMTÉ (GRUYÈRE DE COMTÉ)

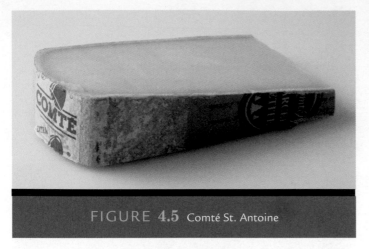

FIGURE **4.5** Comté St. Antoine

Milk – Cow
Origin – Franche-Comté, Jura, Lorraine, Champagne, Rhône-Alps, and Burgundy (Eastern), France
Rind – Brine-washed and rubbed with *morge*
Paste – Firm but supple
Aging – 90 days to 1 year
A.O.C. –1958, with an update (stricter regulations) in 1976

This is the most popular cheese in France, to the tune of 40,000 metric tons (about 88 million pounds) made each year. It is big in almost every way — flavor, size (up to 110 lbs/49.9 kg each), quality, and its area of production. A.O.C. laws are quite strict for such a high-production cheese; milk must be renneted from 14 to 36 hours after milking, depending on its refrigerated temperature. Although it can be heated to 104°F/40°C right before renneting, no further cooking is allowed, which adds to the smooth texture of the cheese. During affinage, it is kept at a rather warm 66°F/19°C and high humidity, and both washed with brine and rubbed with *morge*, which is brown scrapings from the rinds of older cheeses mixed with brine. As a result of tight A.O.C. regulations, about 5% of the annual production is actually rejected — but it is then allowed to be sold as Gruyère. Also, no grated cheese is allowed to be sold as Comté.

The firm paste occasionally has holes, from pea-sized to the size of a cherry, and the flavor is sweet, salty, nutty, and profound. This is a highly versatile cheese, going well with fruit, wine, and salads, and is remarkably tasty when used in a Croque-Monsieur sandwich or in fondue.

GRAND CRU GRUYÈRE SURCHOIX

FIGURE **4.6** Grand Cru Gruyère Surchoix

Milk – Cow (pasteurized)
Origin – Roth Käse USA Ltd., Monroe, Wisconsin, United States
Rind – Natural
Paste – Firm, ivory with a random placement of different sized holes
Aging – 9 months

The best way to explain this cheese is that it is a swiss-style cheese made by Swiss cheesemakers who had moved to Wisconsin and started Roth Käse USA Limited. They make a range of cheeses beyond this gruyère style, but the Grand Cru Surchoix is selected from the maturing gruyère cheeses to be the longest aged of the lot. It acquires a caramel-type sweetness along with a distinct nuttiness and a firm handshake of flavor from the onset.

The cheese itself is quite a bit smaller than traditional Gruyère from the founders' homeland, but beyond that, it is a fine substitute for the original. Great for eating and use in other traditional recipes, it makes a darned good fondue.

BRIGID'S ABBEY

Milk – Cow (raw)
Origin – Cato Corner Farm, Colchester, Connecticut, United States
Rind – Natural, medium tan, occasionally with a light bloom of mold
Paste – Semi-firm, ivory with a creamy texture
Aging – 2 to 4 months

A mother and son team runs Cato Corner Farms in Colchester, Connecticut. Elizabeth MacAlister and her son, Mark Gillman, share the cow-based and cheese-based responsibilities (respectively) at this relatively small farm of 40 or so cows. With a dedication to sustainable and healthy production values, they help the cows lead healthy and happy lives, which results in lovely milk for their cheeses.

Brigid's Abbey is their most popular cheese, and is similar to some of the Trappist cheeses from Belgium, such as Chimay. It is creamy, rich, and full of flavor but is still relatively mild. It is an excellent "second cheese" for a cheese board — after the fresh cheese, but before the stronger firm cheese. It is also excellent on a hamburger, or in calmer recipes, such as quiche. Frankly, it is great with just about everything . . . which is probably why it's their most popular cheese.

IDIAZÁBAL

Milk – Latxa Sheep (raw)
Origin – Basque country and Navarre, Spain
Rind – Natural, sometimes smoked
Paste – Firm, with some elasticity. Very small holes, and beige to pale yellow color.
Aging – ≥ 2 months, as much as 4 to 8 months
D.O.P. – 1987

FIGURE **4.7** Idiazábal

Idiazábal is to Basque country as Manchego is to La Mancha. It is similar in style to its cousin, although its somewhat more rustic upbringing is apparent in its overall flavor profile. Even the unsmoked versions are described as "smoky." But the cheeses that are to receive the smoking treatment go through the complete aging process, whereupon they spend about ten days over wood fires of cherry or beech wood. The smoked versions show a brown edging close to the rind, and have a gentle whiff of smoke rather than a heavy-handed smoke-house aroma. The best way to think of this cheese is as the outdoorsman's version of Manchego.

COACH FARM GREEN PEPPERCORN AGED GOAT

FIGURE **4.8** Coach Farm Green Peppercorn Aged Goat

Milk – Goat (pasteurized)

Origin – Coach Farm, Pine Plains, New York, United States

Rind – Bloomy

Paste – Chalky white and dry looking, studded with green peppercorns

Aging – 3 to 5 weeks at farm, 5 to 7 weeks for most, but will age to a more intense, even grating consistency eventually (3 months)

Coach Farm is one of the best-known sources of goat's milk products in the Northeast. Having been founded by the Cahn family (Miles, Lillian, and daughter Susi) who had previously owned Coach Leather, it went from pastime to all-consuming business. In fact, Miles Cahn would often say that they were being held hostage by 1,000 goats. The cheese production and distribution parts of the business are owned by Best Cheese Corporation, an importer of European cheeses. The cheeses have shown no appreciable change, that is to say, they are still excellent and very consistent. The aged peppercorn cheese has a lovely herbal spiciness that nicely complements the slightly tart, clay-textured paste that is wrapped in a bloomed rind.

MIMOLETTE AND BOULE DE LILLE

FIGURE **4.9** Mimolette

Milk – Cow

Origin – Normandy and Lille, France

Rind – Natural, beige with pock-marks, looking somewhat like a cantaloupe

Paste – From semi-firm to hard, depending on age

Aging – 3 months to 2 years, up to 4 years for a very hard cheese

This cheese could have a place in the mild chapter as well, but most agree that it is at its best after at least one year's aging and perhaps two. At 18 months to two years, Mimolette acquires a semi-hard, but still somewhat plastic texture as well as a sweet nuttiness with caramel overtones. I often describe it as being a cross between Parmigiano-Reggiano and Sharp Cheddar. The orange color comes from *roucou*, the French word for annatto seed (also called *achiote* in Spanish). This is the same coloring agent used in most yellow/orange cheddars. Legend has it that King Louis XIV had the cheese made to resemble Edam, and that Mimolette was colored orange to distinguish it from that Dutch cheese. One fun fact is that it takes 42 qt/40 L of milk to make one 6 lb, 9 oz/3 kg boule of Mimolette — roughly the output of one cow in one day.

Another curiosity is that, as Mimolette ages, cheese mites are introduced to the surface of the cheese. They bore tiny holes in the surface that allow the aging cheese to breathe and develop its characteristic flavors. Their presence on the rind gives the impression of a dusty surface.

BREBIS DES PYRÉNÉES

This phrase means "ewes from the Pyrenees," but it refers to a whole family of sheep's milk cheeses from the western Pyrenees. An A.O.C. was created in 1980 for Ossau-Iraty-Brébis Pyrénées, and a number of cheeses belong to it. Most A.O.C. laws for cheese control the shape and size of the product, but there are so many small producers of *Brebis* that variation is allowed. Most of the cheeses are quite large and in the classic squat drum shape. One notable exception to both size and shape is Tourmalet, a farm-made drum 3 by 4 in/7.5 by 10 cm, that tends to be both high quality and easier to sell because of its convenient size. As a family, Brebis tend to have a slightly granular yet creamy texture, and a sweet, nutty flavor. These cheeses are easy to like, with a combination of savory and sweet flavors, and perhaps a slight perfume from the wild herbs and mountain flowers that the sheep eat. To meet the criteria for A.O.C., the milk is not viable until at least 20 days after lambing and must be renneted within two days. Also, the word *montagne* cannot be used unless the ewes had been grazing in mountain pastures between May 10 and September 15. Any cheeses not fitting the A.O.C. have to be sold as, simply, *fromage de brebis* or "sheep's cheese."

FIGURE **4.10** Tourmalet

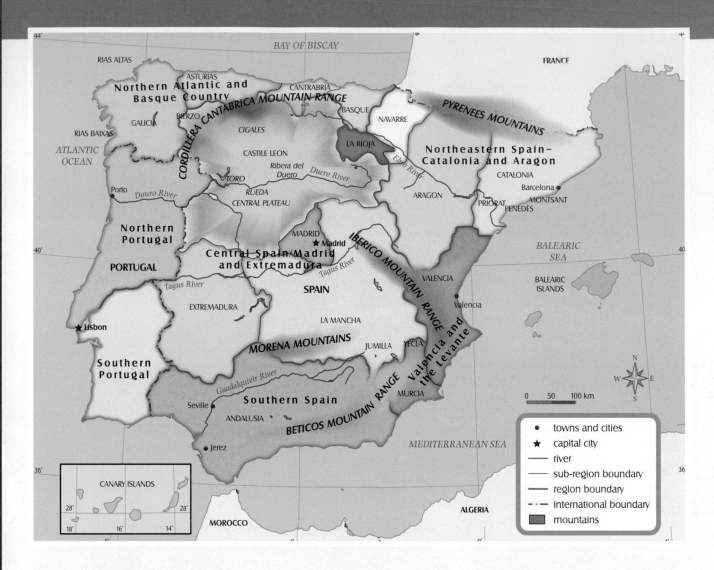

Spain has a surprisingly small footprint in the United States with regard to its cuisine, especially its food and wine products. This has positive and negative aspects, though — the positive being that, because of relatively low demand, some very fine products are available for less money than their French and Italian counterparts. The bad part is that it's a shame these delicious products are not as readily available because of that same relatively low demand. There has been a shift in the wind lately, though, and we are becoming more familiar with the *comidas y vinos de España*. Some items are familiar already, like the wines of Rioja and Manchego cheese. There is also the pricey but mind-numbingly delicious Iberico Ham (and its less-expensive cousin, Serrano Ham). But more and more Americans are trying and enjoying other products from Spain, some traditional, some modern. There are great value wines (mostly red) from regions like Yecla, Jumilla, and Toro; but the classic Priorat and Cava wines can still offer great value. Similarly, there are newer cheeses such as Cabra Romero, with its coating of rosemary leaves, but also some classics like Garrotxa that have been around long enough to acquire D.O. status.

Because there is such an amalgam, the foods and wines of Spain make for somewhat of a moving target — at one moment you're drinking a pedigreed Rioja from a winery with centuries of experience, and the next glass you lift is filled with a boisterous red from Cigales in Castilla y León made by a former banker. The good news is that the current body of knowledge (in the United States, at least) regarding Spanish food and drink is small enough that almost any product you try will be a novel experience, and will enhance your awareness. So the best approach is to go in with your eyes wide open, ready for anything. Here's a tour of the regions of Spain, starting in the northeast and moving in a largely counter clockwise direction around the country.

North Coast (Asturias and Cantabria)

The northern coast of Spain is lovely, with a combination of rugged as well as sandy beaches for the many tourists (both Spanish and foreign) who visit there. Fish and seafood dominate the local cuisine and are plentiful. Grilled anchovies, langoustines, gooseneck barnacles (called *percebes* there), tuna, and hake are all very popular, and most of the traditional dishes, at least from the coast, are filled with them. As you move south, mountains rise up and create a natural barrier between these two regions and Castilla y León. It is the pastures in the northern foothills of these mountains that are home to the cows that produce two of the finest blue cheeses made anywhere, Picón and Cabrales.

Galicia

This is the upper-left (northwestern) corner of Spain, and sits atop Portugal. Nicknames vary from the "green corner" to "the seafood coast," and its mild, maritime climate is pleasant and nurturing year-round. Much of its cultural heritage is Celtic, and you can even find bagpipers there. The coast of Galicia is ringed by a series of *rias* that are basically flooded river valleys and resemble small fjords. Two regions of these *rias* are divided into Rias Altas and Rias Baixas or upper and lower *rias*. Simple seafood preparations are complemented by simple country food from the interior — dishes like *Caldo Gallego*, a stew of beans and potatoes or turnips with chorizo and greens. The local bitter green *grelo* is basically broccoli rabe. The region is also known for its empanadas with meat or fish fillings, as well as one of the most famous Spanish cheeses, *Tetilla*. This is the cheese whose name tells you what it's shaped like, a woman's breast. The cheese is made from pasteurized cow's milk and is rather mild, and is more famous for its appearance than its flavor. Luckily, its novelty is usually surpassed by high quality, and it pairs nicely with some of the white wines of the region.

Those wines are some of the finest whites produced in Spain, and the best-known region for wine production in Galicia is Rias Baixas — and the best-known grape is Albariño. There are other wines produced there, but Albariño can yield a complex, crisp, and herbal mouthful of wine that is just perfect for a range of fish and seafood dishes.

In all, it is a rather rural region, with the fishing and agricultural (including lumber) industries, along with increasing tourism, as the main economic contributors. Galicia is a region with a seemingly low profile that just happens to be the place where two of the most famous Spanish exports originate, Tetilla and Albariño.

Castilla y León

"Old Castile" is the largest region in Spain and makes up a large portion of the interior northwestern part of the country. It is largely a dry basin surrounded by mountains, with a number of important rivers and roads running through. Castilla y León is also the historical home of royalty and religious leadership in Spain and is often referred to as the "land of castles." The "old" part of its name refers both to its history as a center of political and religious power, but also to differentiate it from the "New Castile" region to the south, around Madrid and *its* mountains. As such a venerable region, there is a tremendous amount of tradition and dignity within its inhabitants. As the source of the Castilian dialect of Spanish, it is spoken best there, and regional pride extends to their food and wine.

While the Duero River is a large and important waterway that cuts through Castilla y León, it does not provide a majority of the region's protein. Pork is the primary meat source here, and lamb comes in at a close second. In fact, because of the relatively meager growing conditions, sheep are the main dairy animal and supply most of the milk for cheeses. The two most famous cheeses made here are Castellano and Zamorano, the latter having much smaller production levels, but usually more distinctive flavor. They are very similar to the famous Manchego from farther south, and sometimes, because they're not as well known, offer a better value. Sheep and pig will occasionally lie down together . . . on a serving platter. The local cheeses are often served with thin slices of the famous hams from the region. The recommended beverage pairing is, of course, local wine.

Some of the most important regions in the world of modern Spanish wine are here. Rueda and Ribera del Duero produce some of the biggest, baddest, and most attention-getting red wines in the world. The dry, hot conditions there are similar to those in parts of California (Napa Valley) and Australia, so it is not surprising that the wines are big with lots of dark red fruit flavors. Their European provenance, however, does lend them a bit more of an acidic backbone and tannin structure, so the wines are well built for aging. One of the most famous producers is Vega Sicilia, which has been making Unico for many years. They release each vintage when it's ready to drink, which is sometimes decades after the wine was made. There are other producers of course, such as Tinto Pesquera, Dominio de Pingus, and Bodegas Alion, as well as a few more noteworthy wine-producing regions. Especially for value seekers, Toro, Cigales, and Bierzo are place names worth remembering.

Altogether, Castilla y León may not be the most famous tourist destination in Spain, but it holds a wealth of history and simple beauty. More importantly for us, the ham, lamb, cheese, and wine from there are some of the best in the world.

Castilla-La Mancha

This region is a largely barren plain in the center of Spain. The continental climate goes to extremes here — with very hot, dry summers and fiercely cold winters. And the wind hardly ever stops blowing. Under such conditions, the few who survive are tough; sheep, shepherds, and grapevines. There are a lot of sheep and vines here, and they each produce large volumes of important products.

The sheep provide milk for the most important cheese of Spain, Manchego. Just as, for many people, "Wisconsin" means "cheddar," if you mention cheese and Spain in the same sentence, many Americans will immediately think of Manchego. Most won't, however, know that it is made from sheep's milk, or know that there are very similar cheeses made in other parts of Spain. Manchego's dominance in the market virtually guarantees that the "smaller" cheeses will be a better value because of the relative lack of demand for them. Still, if you've never had a Spanish cheese, try Manchego (preferably an aged

version), and have it with *membrillo*, the local quince paste. It is a combination you will not soon forget.

As for the grapevines, there is a surprising statistic related to this region. The most popular grape grown here is the Airen variety. Until recently, it was used almost exclusively to make wine that was distilled into brandies, such as Cardinal Mendoza and Carlos I. Because the region is so dry, the vines are spaced widely apart, giving each plant access to more area and therefore more rainwater. Because of this, the Airen grape variety covers more area, worldwide, than any other variety. More than Chardonnay, Merlot, Cabernet Sauvignon . . . even Thompson Seedless. Modern winemaking techniques (mostly, refrigeration) are now being used to produce dry white wines from Airen, but its importance is still based in brandy production.

This seemingly barren landscape is more abundant than appearances would suggest. You might not want to *go* there, but you will want products that *come* from there.

Mediterranean Coast

It is pretty hot down in Andalusia, the southern tip of the Iberian Peninsula, and there aren't very many famous cheeses made there; many are made, but they are mostly eaten locally. This does not make the region unimportant to the food world, though. Gazpacho (the cold, raw, delicious tomato and vegetable soup) comes from there, and Jerez is where Sherry is made, one of the most important fortified wines in the world. Andalucia might not be big on the cheese map, but it holds its own in the food world.

The regions that creep up around the eastern Mediterranean coast, however, produce some important cheeses. Murcia is the source of some well-known goat cheeses, particularly Drunken Goat, a relatively mild, semi-soft cheese that spends some time floating in red wine from the region. The wines from there are notable, particularly those from Jumilla, a source of affordable and robust reds. There is also some good wine produced in the province of Valencia, to the north, but this region is much more famous as the home of paella. The rice in this region has its own D.O. of *Arroz de Valencia*, so you know that they take their grains seriously here.

Catalonia does produce a famous, and currently very popular cheese, Garrotxa. This is a goat cheese with a lot of personality and has taken American cheese counters by storm. It is just powerful enough without being overbearing and has shown many people that goat cheese isn't always that innocuous creamy white log. Goats can have personality. Catalonia is also very famous in food and wine circles for a number of reasons. First, there is easy access to fine ingredients. Perhaps more importantly, Barcelona is home to several great chefs, with Ferran Adrià to the north at El Bulli restaurant. He is thought by many to be the greatest chef alive, and has brought a tremendous amount of attention to Spanish cuisine. In fact, his friend and fellow chef José Andrés is now living and cooking in the United States, in Washington, D.C., and has introduced many Americans to the avant-garde cuisine of Spain. Not to leave out the wine, some of the best wines made in Spain are from Catalonia, including Cava (sparkling), Penedès, Priorat, Costers del Segre, and Montsant. Great food, great wine, and some great cheese, all from along the Mediterranean coast. Sounds like a visit is in order.

Pyrénées (Aragon, Navarre, and Basque Country)

The border Spain shares with France runs through the Pyrénées Mountains. For most of its length (even near the coasts), it is a rugged terrain that determines the kind of life that its inhabitants will lead.

Starting in the west, the Basques are an ancient and proud race with their own unique language. Their economy is largely agrarian, and the cuisine is a fine combination of its products. There is a combination of wonderful seafood from the coast, peppers, pork, and other produce from the nearby interior, and they all merge to form an exciting, vibrant group of flavors. Geological and political borders have had a profound effect on their food as well; the mountains that separate the maritime regions have helped to create two different groupings of dishes, and the French influence from across the Pyrénées is also seen in some dishes, like Pipérade.

Because of the topography, dairy comes mostly from goats and sheep, and the most famous cheeses of the area are from sheep's milk. Basques use cheese in cooking, but it is mostly eaten on its own, very often as a *pintxo*, which is a Basque *tapa*, or bar snack eaten before dinner. The most famous Basque cheese is Idiazábal (see page 85). The wines of the area are almost all white and fairly simple, but good. They tend to be crisp and acidic (especially from the coastal vineyards) and are made from grapes that most people probably never heard of. A glass of Ondarribi Beltza before dinner, anyone?

The Basques are a very proud people and enjoy their food as much, if not more so than any other European race. There is an intensity to their cuisine, but more importantly, their food is alive; it's vibrant — it's joyous.

Moving east along the mountains, we pass through Navarre and Aragon, which are more Spanish than Basque. Their cuisines tend to be soil rather than water based, with meat the dominant animal protein, although some freshwater fish are popular. There are great wines from both regions, Navarre known for its rosés and Aragon especially for its Somontano region. Rioja lies just to the south of these regions and is the most famous wine region in Spain. Produce is excellent in all of these regions and while the cuisine is landlocked, there is still great food to go with the justly famous wines.

Although Spain might not have as much of a presence in America as France and Italy, it is the source of varied and charismatic cuisines, first-class wines, and top-notch cheeses. With the influence of its current chefs (such as Adrià and Andrés) and the increasing recognition of cheeses like Manchego and Garrotxa, it is possible that there will be a rise of American awareness regarding the products of Spain. Whether this happens (or not), there is some great Spanish food and wine in this country *right now*, and there is no better time to get acquainted with them. If nothing else, have some Manchego with a little quince paste — that'll get you started.

EDEN

FIGURE 4.11 Eden

Milk – Cow (raw)
Origin – Sprout Creek Farm,
Poughkeepsie, New York,
United States
Rind – Smear-ripened (washed)
Paste – Semi-soft, pale gold
Aging – ≥ 60 days

As you might expect from its ripening method, this is a stinky cheese, but subtly so. In fact, this would be a great first experience for someone who is scared of stinkers and wants to start slowly. A butterscotchy-sweetness and some apple aromas underlie the pungent aroma caused by the bacterial coating. When asked whether the rind was edible, Colin McGrath, the cheesemaker said, "Heck I eat it, but that's because I know how much work went into making it in the first place."

SARABANDE

Milk – Cow (raw)
Origin – Dancing Cow Farm, Bridport, Vermont, United States
Rind – Washed with brine
Paste – Golden, silky, and semi-soft with some chalkiness in the center
when young
Aging – 60 days

There is a certain joy available to those who have no need to follow the rules. American cheesemakers are largely unaffected by laws governing their production methods. This allows them to make cheeses like Sarabande, a washed-rind, raw cow's milk truncated pyramid that is aged for 60 days. In fact, that last bit is some of the only rule-following that Karen and Steve Getz adhere to. The milk goes straight from the cows into the cheesemaking vat and is never cooled. Such a practice might sound scary to some, but it is more likely to result in highly flavorful cheeses. This is partly because the extant bacteria in the milk are all still alive, and the chemicals they produce help to create more aromatic molecules during the aging process. We're lucky that this simplicity of method can lead to such complexity of flavor. Because of the Getz' adherence to such traditional methods, this cheese was a Slow Foods American Raw Milk Cheese Presidium selection.

PECORINO FRESCO

Milk – Sheep (raw)
Origin – Dancing Ewe Farm, Granville, New York, United States
Rind – Natural, with some brine-washing
Paste – Semi-soft, off-white to bone color
Aging – ≥ 60 days

Once upon a time, Jody Somers was studying veterinary medicine in England. He also had been training sheepdogs as a hobby, but realized that there was another path that lay ahead for him. Jody decided that he wanted to make cheese and went to Tuscany to learn from the master producers of Pecorino Toscano, one of the most celebrated sheep's milk cheeses in the world. While there in Maremma, he also became friends with Luisa Scivola, who is now Luisa Somers — they are now partners in business as well as in life. The couple can be seen at green markets around New York, at Union Square, in Troy, and Rhinebeck.

Their cheeses have both rusticity and sophistication and show that the animals producing the base milk are cared for very well. The Pecorino Fresco could technically be called a "pecorino seco," because it is aged longer than the Italian version. This longer aging is only done to allow the use of raw milk, which we know produces a more flavorful cheese. Jody says that, were it not for the law, a 40-day version of this cheese would be optimal — an Italian "fresco" is usually aged 20 to 30 days. Dancing Ewe Farm's Pecorino Fresco is clean but earthy tasting with a milky sweetness and lovely texture. Do as in Tuscany and serve it with some fresh, raw fava beans, and a drizzle of very good olive oil. Also keep in mind that they produce a lovely ricotta from the whey of their sheep and cow cheeses. This is as would be in Italy, where nothing goes to waste. We can be thankful that there is now a farm in Granville, New York, where the spirit of Italy is leading to the production of cheeses that can bring back memories of the Tuscan countryside.

PECORINO TOSCANO

Milk – Sheep
Origin – Tuscany, Italy
Rind – Natural, sometimes rubbed with olive oil or tomato paste
Paste – Depends on age, with younger versions showing plasticity and pale yellow color. Older cheeses will be firm to hard, with an almost flaky appearance and darker yellow color.
Aging – 1 month to 2 years
D.O.C. and D.O.P. – 1986 and 1996, respectively

FIGURE **4.12** Pecorino Toscano

Sheep's milk cheeses are made in many regions of Italy, including Sardinia (Sardo), Rome (Romano), and Sicily (Siciliano). However, many Italians will agree that the best come from Tuscany (Toscano), and even from a smaller sub-region around the village of Pienza. Pecorino di Pienza is a much sought-after cheese largely because it has the expected savory sweetness of a good sheep's milk cheese. There isn't a tremendous amount of it made, though, and because the real thing is rarely inexpensive, counterfeit cheeses abound. This is definitely a case where you get what you pay for; a cheap "tuscan pecorino" is probably not the genuine article. To get the real thing, expect to pay more than $20 for a pound of this precious little cheese. And if you're wary of using Pecorino Toscano as an eating cheese because you know what Pecorino Romano tastes like (sharp and salty), the Tuscan versions are much calmer and noticeably sweeter than the Roman versions.

FIGURE 4.13 Ossau-Iraty

OSSAU-IRATY BRÉBIS

Milk –Sheep's milk (raw), from Basco-Bearnaise or Manech ewes

Origin – From a number of small producers in the Pyrénées Mountains, Southwest France

Rind – Natural, light brown

Paste – Semi-hard with a slightly granular texture; but with a soft, creamy mouthfeel

Aging – Minimum of 60 days for the smallest cheeses, 80 days for larger, but perhaps at its best after about 5 months of age

A.O.C. – 1980

FIGURE 4.14 Abbaye de Belloc

Ossau-Iraty bears some resemblance to the cow's milk mountain cheeses such as Gruyère and Emmenthal, but has a sweetness and pleasing nuttiness that seems to make it more delicate. This is one of the tastiest, most satisfying cheeses on the planet. Like some great wines or pieces of music, it is approachable and easy to enjoy without any thought or analysis; but if you decide to examine it closely, the cheese reveals a depth of complexity and uncanny balance that is difficult to find in any food product. So chow down on a chunk or sit and contemplate a small bite — Ossau-Iraty will be happy to oblige either way. One of the finest examples is produced by the Abbaye de Nôtre Dame de Belloc in Aquitaine. They age it for six months so that it acquires a lovely caramel aroma and flavor. The name of the cheese is usually shortened to Abbaye de Belloc.

GOAT TOMME

Milk – Goat (raw)
Origin – Twig Farm, West Cornwall, Vermont, United States
Rind – Natural, with a mottled gray-white bloom
Paste – Semi-hard, off-white
Aging – 80 days

FIGURE **4.15** Goat Tomme

Michael Lee and Ellen Sunderman own Twig Farm in West Cornwall, Vermont, where they take care of their thirty or so goats and make cheese. There are four varieties that they produce regularly, and the one that has received the most attention is this one, the Goat Tomme. It seems that most of the goat cheeses made in this country are consumed young, so it's nice to find one that has acquired the complexity that can only come with aging. This little drum ages for at least 80 days, and is rich, tangy, floral, and grassy all at the same time. The texture is thick, a little dry, and a little creamy at the same time. It would be lovely with some fresh fruit but if you serve it with a glass of Coteaux du Layon dessert wine from the Loire Valley, the pleasure may induce short-term memory loss.

MADELEINE

Milk –Goat's milk (raw)
Origin – Sprout Creek Farm, Poughkeepsie, New York, United States
Rind – Mold-ripened
Paste – Sweet, floral, grassy flavors. Firmer and somewhat dry texture.
Aging – 7 months

FIGURE **4.16** Madeleine

This is a cheese that makes you wonder why there aren't more like it. The combination of its characteristics seems unlikely, but it is a truly harmonious cheese. Made from raw goat's milk and aged for 7 months, the bloomy rind conceals a fascinating interior. The relatively long aging gives Madeleine a complex grassy sweetness as well as a dry but still rich texture. And there is still a little bit of that characteristic tanginess from the goat's milk. Since there is a season for goat's milk in the Hudson Valley in New York (March through October), Madeleine is not available year-round. Judging by the aging period, its availability would be from October to April.

PRIMA CACIOTTA

FIGURE 4.17 Prima Caciotta

Milk – Cow (raw)
Origin – Dancing Ewe Farm, Granville, New York, United States
Rind – Natural, but rubbed with tomato paste and olive oil
Paste – Semi-firm, yellowish (Spring/Summer milk), off-white (Fall/Winter milk)
Aging – 10 months

For information on Dancing Ewe Farm, see their Pecorino Fresco entry on page 93.

This is a non-traditional Caciotta from a great Italian-style farmstead cheesemaker in upstate New York. The treatment of the rind with tomato paste and olive oil is usually reserved for pecorino (sheep) cheeses in Tuscany, but it works very well on this American Caciotta to keep the cheese's exterior from drying out as it ages. Jody Somers has arrived at a cheese that is perfectly balanced between power, sweetness, clean flavor, and rusticity. It also happens to be a beautiful cheese with its ruddy exterior. They make a similar cheese in the spring with the addition of sheep's milk from the herd as they come up to speed in the beginning of their milking season. This cheese is called Misto, referring to the mixed milks, and is a little bit sweeter than the Prima Caciotta. Both are delicious and pair well with the Sangiovese-based red wines of Tuscany.

MIDNIGHT MOON

Milk – Goat
Origin – Cypress Grove Chevre, Arcata, Humboldt County, California, United States
Rind – Natural/black wax
Paste – Firm, with some granular texture
Aging – ≥ 6 months

In 1983, Mary Keehn, a successful breeder of Alpine goats, founded Cypress Grove Chevre after she found herself with a lot of milk one day. Amateur home cheesemaking led to another business, and eventually to some of the most recognized (and awarded) goat cheeses made in the United States. Another of their products is in the mild chapter, and that's their somewhat more famous Humboldt Fog. It is fantastic but the Midnight Moon takes my breath away. It is at once sweet, salty, granular, creamy, and has notes of caramel and beurre noisette as well.

CANTAL/FOURME DE CANTAL (A.O.C.), SALERS

Milk – Cow (pasteurized or raw)
Origin – Cantal and surrounding towns, Auvergne, France
Rind – Natural
Paste – Semi-hard, smooth ivory-colored, getting darker with age
Aging – 30 days to 6 months
A.O.C. – 1956 (Salers received its own in 1961)

FIGURE **4.18** Cantalet

Cantal is a town in south-central France, in the Auvergne region. It is one of the oldest known cheeses in France, having been written about by Pliny the Elder in the first century. It is a pressed, uncooked cheese with a pleasant, straightforward flavor that belies the complex process of making it. After renneting, the curd is gathered into a relatively small mass of from 77 to 220 pounds (the equivalent of 1 to 3 completed cheeses), wrapped in cloth and pressed to create the *tome*, a thick slice of curd. The tome is broken up and pressed a few more times, then allowed to rest for eight hours to allow the lactic acid level to rise, which helps to form the proper protein structure. The tome at this point is milled, salted, and allowed to cure. When ready, it is poured into a cloth-lined mold and pressed for 48 hours. This is repeated a few more times, and when considered the correct size and shape, the cheese is moved to the aging room for affinage, where it is turned and rubbed clean twice a week until release. Thirty days of this process yields a young, pale, simple cheese. The cheese starts to noticeably change in 2 to 6 months (*entre-deux* or *doré*), and in the cheeses older than 6 months (*vieux* or *charactère*). As it gets older, the paste turns from ivory to a medium-yellow, and the flavor becomes more intense. The cheese never loses its classic, straightforward buttery/nutty flavor. For the most complexity, stick to the Salers versions of this cheese that must be made from raw milk. Also, there is a smaller, factory-made version of this cheese called Cantalet that offers many of the same pleasures (though with somewhat less complex flavor) in a more convenient size.

EMMENTAL GRAND CRU

Milk – Cow (raw)
Origin – Franche-Comté, Alsace, Savoie, Haute-Savoie, and Burgundy, France
Rind – Lightly washed
Paste – Firm but supple with large circular holes
Aging – 10 weeks

This is not the easiest "Swiss"-type cheese to come by in the United States but if you find some, it will probably outshine the actual Swiss version. It's made with raw cow's milk in a fairly large area that includes Franche-Comté, Burgundy, Champagne, Lorraine, and even down into the Rhône Alps. Authentic cheeses will have a red stamp that includes information like fat content and where the cheese was made. Look also for the phrase "Emmental Français Grand Cru." There is a prevalent sweetness to both the aroma and flavor of the cheese. This, in combination with the chewy, giving texture make it a very toothsome cheese — one that's great for snacking or even as a before-dinner choice. It is one of the classic choices with which to make fondue, and makes a great presentation on your cheese board because of its sheer scale. The holes can be as large as ping-pong balls, and the cheese itself can be three feet in diameter, ten inches high, and weigh over 200 pounds. The Swiss versions are not bad; they just lack some of the intensity/complexity of the French. Just remember to look for the real *Grand Cru* versions with the characteristic Emmental Grand Cru stamped in red, and not the ubiquitous mass-produced, pasteurized versions.

5

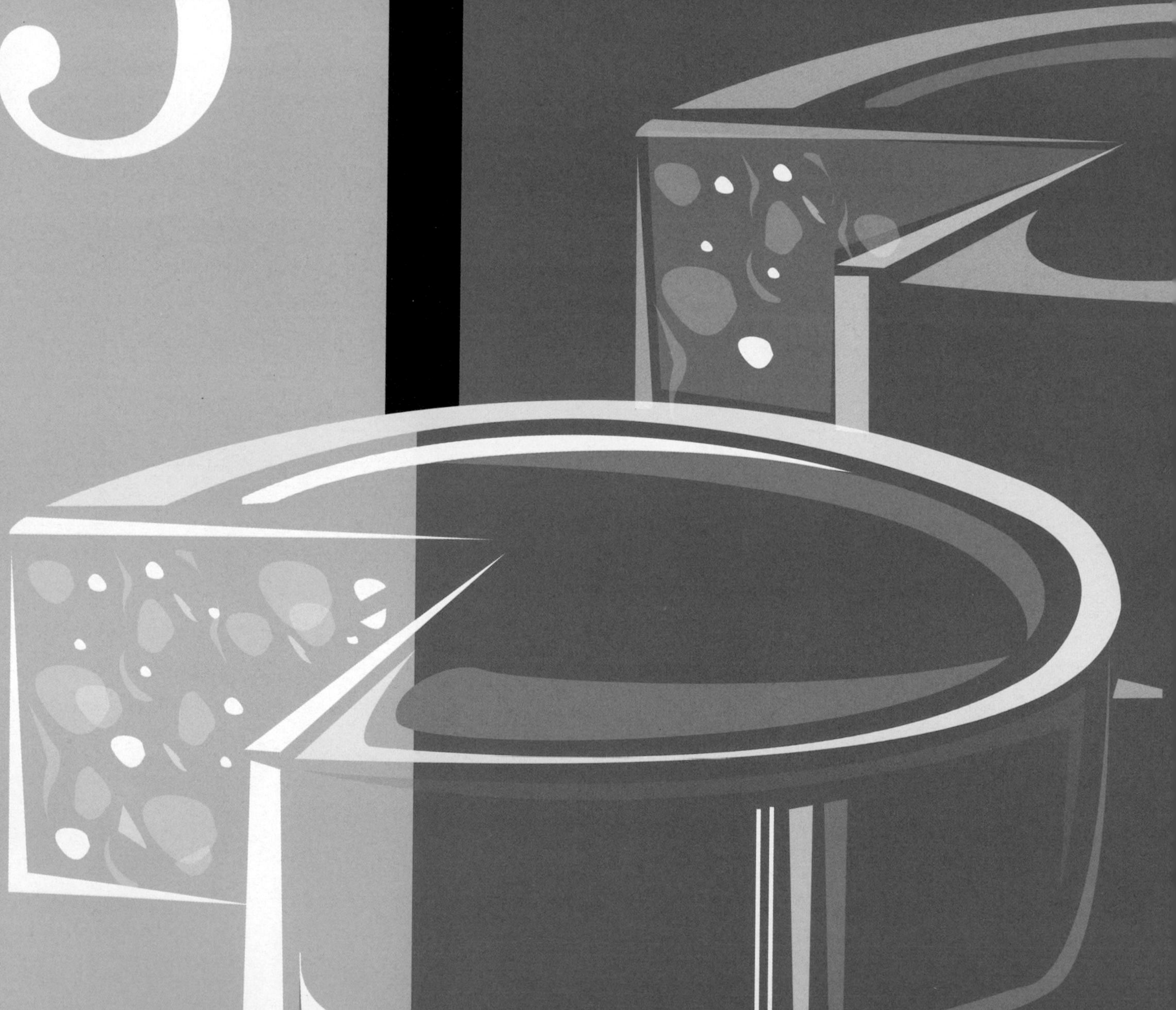

STRONG AND STINKY CHEESES

As food lovers in the United States have become more interested in new cuisines and flavors, they have also become more accepting of and even interested in some stronger flavors. Along the way, the word *stinky* has become acceptable in polite company, at least when it's used in reference to cheese. In fact, the term has become a badge of honor for some who like to show their preference for the odiferous. "The stinkier, the better" they'll say, usually loud enough to be heard by other diners nearby. The interesting thing is that the strong smell can belie more subtle flavors of some washed-rind cheeses. In fact, most of these cheeses are fairly high in moisture, and have a similar life cycle to many of their bloomy cousins. That is to say, they are meant to be eaten fairly young, before they turn runny and putrid-smelling. There's a difference between stinky and *stinky*. Still, washed-rind cheeses will always have some form of *odeur* — it's the nature of the beast.

Strong cheese is a somewhat different story. Stink is a form of strength, but so are sharpness, earthiness, and salty moldiness. A fine Roquefort will have salt, pepperiness, and moldy funk, but not that bacterial funk. A small piece of well-aged cheddar will fill your mouth with powerful flavors and make you wish for a piece of bread or sip of beer. And not to be left out, a washed-rind cheese can be strong enough (in scent *and* flavor) to steal the show. In general, when eaten during a cheese course, you should eat the strongest ones last or you won't be able to taste the tamer cheeses on the plate.

The sharpness of cheese usually depends on its age and seems to be a combination of intensified flavors because there's less water and increased acidity. Also, the term *sharp* is imprecise in that there are many flavors that it connotes. To some, it is indeed acidity, but can also be a reaction to salt or bitterness levels. *Sharp* also happens to be a relative term, even in its familiar surroundings of cheddar. There is some so-called "sharp cheddar" that has about as much flavor as a loaf of process American cheese food product. However, there are other handmade cheddars with both a power and subtlety, even though they're just called "cheddar." Let's not get caught up in semantics, though. For us, "strength" and "sharpness" will mean intensity and pronounced flavors.

Another aspect of these cheeses that should be mentioned is the presence of glutamates or glutamic acid. These are the main providers of the so-called "fifth taste," *umami*. As proteins are broken down during the aging process, glutamate can increase in concentration, especially in cheeses like Parmigiano-Reggiano and Roquefort, which have some of the highest glutamate levels of any foodstuff on the planet. This taste is sometimes described as "meaty" or "hearty." Other foods with lots of glutamic acid (one form of which is known as MSG or monosodium glutamate) are soy sauce, fish sauce, seaweed, shiitake mushrooms, vine-ripened tomatoes, and anchovies. This savory taste was proven to have its own receptors (on human and other animals' tongues) by California scientist Charles Zuker in 2001. Coupled with aromas, MSG does indeed make food taste better, and so cheese with lots of it can seem more satisfying.

With this in mind, the following cheeses vary widely in styles and flavors, everywhere from the stinky but somewhat mild Reblochon, to attention-grabbing aged cheddars, to blues that will singe your nose hairs.

CHEDDARING

This verb form has only been seen in print since 1909 (according to the *Oxford English Dictionary*), but it describes a cheesemaking activity that has been used for at least a few hundred years. In the process, the curd is soured and renneted, then cut into approximately one-inch cubes. These cubes are then usually cooked gently and stirred, removing more whey, but also tightening the protein structure. The curd is then allowed to form a single, thick mat that is cut into slabs and stacked up. Each slab moves through the stack in a programmed way and is occasionally flipped over. The weight of the slabs squeezes out more whey, but more importantly; rising acidity from the lactic acid bacteria (which are still consuming lactose) causes the casein to form longer strands that help give cheddar its characteristic "flaky" texture once aged. Another notable feature caused by the acid is the characteristic tanginess of cheddar-style cheeses. While it isn't immediately obvious to the taster, "sharpness" in cheddar is closely related to the acid level, higher acid being sharper. After pressing, the curd slabs are usually ground up, and the process can be repeated to produce an even drier cheese.

FIGURE **5.1a** Gruyère

FIGURE **5.1b** Swiss Emmentaler

VOLUME CHEESES

DOMESTIC GRUYÈRE/EMMENTAL

Made mostly in Wisconsin and New York, the "Swiss"-style domestic cheeses might not have as much intensity of flavor as their role models, but they can still be very high quality. Mostly made from pasteurized, part-skim cow's milk, they tend to be a bit sweet and mild, with the characteristic holes created by propionic bacteria releasing carbon dioxide. The characteristic Swiss cheese flavor of propionic acid is created by the same bacteria.

DOMESTIC ROMANO

Made with part-skim cow's milk in the United States, domestic Romano cheese is usually higher in fat and sharper than its Parmesan sister. Usually aged from 5 to 12 months, it bears little resemblance to the Pecorino Romano of Italy. It is useful, though, as an ingredient in dishes with bolder flavors than the ones complemented by Parmesan. For instance, a fresh tomato sauce with onion and basil would be better off with Parmesan. Long-cooked tomato sauce with garlic and oregano would do better with Romano as a partner.

SMALLER PRODUCTION CHEESES

PROVOLONE VAL PADANA

Milk – Cow
Origin – various provinces of Northern Italy
Rind – Natural, smooth
Paste – Pale yellow, darkening with age
Aging – 3 to 18 months
D.O.P. – 1996, with some regulation going back to 1938

Essentially, if you hang fresh mozzarella in an aging room and rub it occasionally with an oiled, brined cloth, you end up with Provolone. It is a *pasta filata*, or spun-curd cheese, and begins to acquire character after about four months of aging. The real fun starts after about a year of aging, when the cheese has acquired a level of sharpness not unlike that of good cheddar. There is a bit more depth and breadth of flavor than in average-quality cheddars, though, and the texture is quite different. It has a certain oiliness to it, and starts to show fissures in its paste, whereas cheddars become more crumbly and granular. This cheese, and other provolone from Italy, bears little resemblance to the American-manufactured provolones that adorn Philly Cheesesteaks and Italian combo heroes. To obtain the real thing, either ask for the namesake Provolone Val Padana, or for Provolone Piccante (spicy). Of course, it will also help if you are in a good cheese store.

FIGURE 5.2 Brin d'Amour

BRIN D'AMOUR

Milk – Sheep
Origin – Corsica, France
Rind – Natural, but coated with dried herbs
Paste – Pale ivory, softish, with a creamy chalkiness
Aging – 1 to 3 months

This is essentially a medium-strength cheese that is transformed into a fuller-flavored one by its coating of dried herbs. Its name means "breath of love," but this is from the same country where you call your sweetheart "my little cabbage" (*mon petit chou*). The paste is slightly creamy, with a light sourness to it, and on its own might be considered mild. But the coating of rosemary, savory, and sometimes juniper berries and small hot peppers makes quite the olfactory impression. So, Brin d'Amour could find a home in an earlier chapter, but the overall effect of this little beauty from the islands is a rather powerful one. As it is a younger cheese — kind of a sheep in wolf's clothing — Brin d'Amour does not have the shelf life of older, harder cheeses and should be served or eaten soon after purchase.

JULIANNA

Milk – Goat (raw)
Origin – Capriole Farmstead Goat Cheeses, Greenville, Indiana, United States
Rind – Natural, with some bloomy mold and coated with dried herbs
Paste – Firm and just off-white, with a fudgy consistency
Aging – 4 to 8 months

Judy Schad is well known in the cheese world for producing great goat's milk cheeses on her farm in Indiana. Though she might receive more notoriety for her Wabash Cannonball, there is a great cheese made there that takes a cue from the Corsican curiosity, Brin d'Amour. Judy's version, Julianna, is made with raw goat's milk and is coated with dried herbs during aging. It has a slightly nutty richness to it, and the herbs are a nice accent to the goaty tang; the flavor of the cheese becomes more intense as it ages. Pair a white wine with it — something that has enough power to stand up to it, but some herbal aromas to match the cheese's coating. An American Sauvignon Blanc or Fumé Blanc would do nicely.

AGED GOUDA

Milk – Cow
Origin – Southern Holland
Rind – Natural, sometimes coated with wax (red, yellow, and black are most popular)
Paste – Pale caramel color with a flaky but organized structure, sometimes with crunchy crystals
Aging – 1 to 6 years

FIGURE **5.3** Aged Gouda

Most Americans know a version of this cheese — red wax-coated ovoids of mild, semi-soft cheese that were always on the holiday appetizer table. The real thing bears very little resemblance to the supermarket cheese of our youth. When aged for at least two years, Gouda (properly pronounced "HOW-duh") acquires a flaky and crystalline, but still creamy texture, along with a lovely sweetness reminiscent of caramel or butterscotch. It has a powerful, intense flavor that easily overshadows the flavor of the young, mild gouda that most people have in mind. But because the name is not currently protected, it is up to you and your supplier to determine which version you are buying.

MANCHEGO

Milk – Sheep
Origin – La Mancha, Spain
Rind – Natural, oil-rubbed, with cross-hatch pattern from the grass aging basket
Paste – Off-white to ivory, firm, dense, and slightly flaky, with a few small holes
Aging – It is sold in a broad range of ages, from 2 months to 2 years. Real character begins to show after a year, but it is perhaps best after 2 years.
D.O.P. – 1984

FIGURE **5.4** Manchego

This is the most famous and popular Spanish cheese in the world. That is both good and bad, as a large number of manufactured versions of this cheese flood both the world market and Spain itself. Raw milk cheeses will obviously have more complexity, and those from responsible, artisanal producers will have the most potential for basic quality. This leads to the other factor that will determine your Manchego experience — age. At two months, it is an inoffensive, slightly sweet, and bland cheese that is just fine and is easy to cook with, but somewhat boring. To find real character, look for a cheese that is at least a year old, up to two. At this point, the sharpness will provide a nice counterpoint to the sheepy sweetness. One of the most famous combinations in the food world is that of Manchego with *membrillo*, a Spanish quince paste. The age of the cheese almost doesn't matter — the combination is truly magical, almost to the point that either product won't taste right by itself, at least once you've tried them together.

ZAMORANO

Milk – Sheep, Churra breed (raw)
Origin – Zamora, Spain
Rind – Natural, oil-rubbed, with a herringbone pattern from the woven grass forms. Acquires a white mold that turns brown with age.
Paste – Pale gold, dense, with very small holes
Aging – ≥ 100 days
D.O.P. – 1988

If you have tried Manchego and enjoyed it, this cheese will make you even happier. It is much smaller in volume of production, and the Churra sheep's milk is higher in fat than that of the *oveja manchega* breed used for Manchego. Zamorano has more complexity and depth than its famous cousin because of the higher fat content and the more traditional production methods used. Actually, it is not far from the style of Parmigiano-Reggiano. Its flavor is nutty, has a subtle caramel sweetness, and is creamy even when flaky in texture. An added benefit is that it keeps very well — it's a sturdy cheese that can survive less-than-perfect storage conditions. It pairs very well with the same things Manchego does, good ham, fresh fruit, and *membrillo*, the famous Spanish sweet quince paste.

FIGURE **5.5** Asiago d'Allevo

ASIAGO D'ALLEVO

Milk – Cow
Origin – Especially in the Veneto, Northern Italy
Rind – Natural, oil-rubbed
Paste – Hard with a deep ivory color and a granular flakiness. Young versions are off-white and supple.
Aging – Greater than 9 months (*vecchio* [most character]); 3 to 5 months (*mezzano*); 2 to 3 months (*fresco*)
D.O.C./D.O.P. – 1978/1996

There are some who fail to be won over by this cheese because of its subtlety. It is available in a range of ages, and at its youngest can be a fairly uncomplicated semi-soft eating cheese. Good for sandwiches and antipasto platters, it is creamy, satisfying, and uncomplicated. But age can do good things to it, and the *vecchio* (old) versions take on some of the characteristics of the great Parmigiano-Reggiano and aged pecorino cheeses of Italy, such as the flavor and the crumbly structure laden with tyrosine crystals. Although it will never reach the levels of complexity of the other two, it does have its own, rather simple, charm. Essentially, aged versions have a slight sweetness that complements the inherent nutty sharpness. It can be used on or in pastas, and is a nice eating cheese as well. The best versions come from the town of Asiago in the Veneto region of northern Italy.

CABOT CLOTHBOUND CHEDDAR

Milk – Cow (pasteurized)

Origin – Cabot Creamery, Montpelier, Vermont, United States

Rind – Natural, clothbound, brushed

Paste – Firm, a little flaky but not dry, ivory/beige

Aging – 10 to 14 months

FIGURE **5.6** Cabot Clothbound Cheddar

The Cabot Creamery Cooperative is a Vermont-based cheese producer. With about 1,350 farm members in New England and Upstate New York, you can figure they make a lot of cheese. They do, and almost all of it is cheddar of different styles and ages. Their consistently high-quality products are available nationwide, from Anchorage to Miami and most places in between.

Sometimes, large-volume producers get an idea in their head to make a lower production item that follows more traditional methods. The folks at Cabot wanted to make a traditional, English-style bandaged cheddar, but realized that such a cheese would require a type of affinage that they were not set up to provide. Enter the Kehler brothers of Jasper Hill farm. The young cheeses are sent from Cabot to Jasper Hill, where they are wrapped in cloth then coated with liquid lard, which seals the cheese to protect it from oxidation, but also helps to form a stronger rind. The cheeses are turned regularly, and eventually are brushed to keep mold to a minimum.

The finished product is one of the best cheddars made in the United States, and even won the gold medal at the World Cheese Awards in 2004 in London — not bad for an American in the home of Cheddar.

FLAGSHIP RESERVE CHEDDAR

Milk – Cow (pasteurized)
Origin – Beecher's Handmade Cheese, Seattle, Washington, United States
Rind – Natural, clothbound, rubbed with butter
Paste – Pale yellow, slightly crumbly but still creamy
Aging – ≥ 1 year

Pike's Place Market is a tourist destination for all food lovers who visit Seattle. It is home to many fine produce and dry good markets as well as the first Starbucks coffee shop and the Pike's Place Fish Market where they throw fish around.

It is also where Kurt Dammeier, the scion of a family with success in the printing business, opened an artisanal cheesemaking company in a storefront that faces the main market. Passersby can see cheese being made from the sidewalk, which often pulls them inside to taste and buy either some Beecher's Handmade Cheese, or one of the other products available, which includes their excellent "World's Best" Mac & Cheese.

Cheddar is their strength, and the most impressive is the Flagship Reserve. It is made only when the base milk is good enough, and is made differently than their regular Flagship Cheddar. The curd used is lower in moisture and higher in salt than the regular version, and is aged in a more traditional method, bound with cloth, and air-aged. It acquires a crumbly richness as well as a nutty, sharp complexity that earned it a "best aged cheddar" award from the American Cheese Society in 2007; their four-year aged Flagship Cheddar was named "best mature cheddar" in 2009. As with other cheddars, beer is the best beverage pairing, in particular a good pilsner or blonde Belgian ale.

FIGURE **5.7** Fiscalini Bandaged Cheddar

FISCALINI BANDAGED CHEDDAR

Milk – Cow (raw)
Origin – Modesto, California, United States
Rind – Natural, bandage-wrapped
Paste – Firm, creamy yellow with a few small irregular holes
Aging – 16 to 18 months

This is a world-class cheddar. It has won awards from the American Cheese Society, and even won the "best cheddar" award at the World Cheese Awards, held in England. Yes, it bettered the cheddars from Cheddar.

It is made by cheesemaker Mariano Gonzales, who was born in Paraguay, but learned how to make cheddar at Shelburne Farms in Vermont. He now works with the raw milk that comes from the cows of Fiscalini Farms to produce a sharp but buttery and complex aged cheddar. Fiscalini Farms has 530 acres devoted to the 1,500 cows and is run in a sustainable fashion. In fact, they even biologically recycle the whey and cow manure to produce methane, which is used to power generators that supply power to the dairy shed. With 46 million pounds of milk flowing through that barn every year, environmental savings are great — as is the cheese.

BOBOLINK FARMS CAVE-RIPENED CHEDDAR

Milk – Cow (raw)
Origin – Vernon, New Jersey, United States
Rind – Natural, bloomy
Paste – Semi-hard, ivory, but simultaneously creamy
Aging – 1 to 3 years

FIGURE **5.8** Bobolink Farms Cheddar

Jonathan and Nina White are the owners of and most dedicated workers at Bobolink Farms in Sussex County, New Jersey. In addition to this traditionally made cheddar, Jonathan makes a range of cheeses from their grass-fed herd of mixed-breed cows. They have been working with this herd to create their own breed of Bobolink Blacks, bred from some modern breeds crossed with the Kerry cattle of Ireland. The cheeses range from bloomy-rind Baudolino, to the big Drumm, to a large wheel named for the late, great chef Jean-Louis Palladin (they leave the "Palladin" off the cheese's name). All of their cheeses are full of flavor and character, are made in a very traditional manner, and go superbly with the breads that they bake on site.

TILLAMOOK SHARP CHEDDAR

Milk – Cow
Origin – Tillamook, Oregon, United States
Paste – Firm, pale orange (some of their cheddars are white)
Aging – 9 months

FIGURE **5.9** Tillamook Sharp Cheddar

This cheddar comes from a century-old cooperative that now includes 130 family farms. They use as much as 1 million pounds of milk a day to produce ice cream, butter, yogurt, sour cream, and more than a dozen cheeses. All of their products are very consistent and high quality. I have a particular fondness for their Vintage White Extra Sharp Cheddar, which is aged for more than two years.

GRAFTON VILLAGE CHEESE COMPANY CHEDDAR

Milk – Cow (raw)
Origin – Grafton Village, Vermont, United States
Rind – Natural, wax-coated
Paste – Ivory, with a little flakiness
Aging – 1 to 4 years

The Grafton Village Cheese Cooperative was originally founded in the late 1800s and was meant to take the excess milk of local farmers and make it into cheese that would then be returned to the farmers. The building it was in burned down less than thirty years later. Cheesemaking stopped until the cooperative was resurrected by the Windham Foundation, whose main purpose in 1963 was to restore Grafton Village and make it a viable community. In addition to restoring a number of buildings, including The Old Tavern at Grafton, the foundation reestablished the cheese cooperative. At that time, they pledged to use only the raw milk of Jersey cows, which has higher fat than Holsteins, and to age the cheese for at least one year.

All of their cheeses are delicious, but it might be best to start with the two-year aged cheddar to experience complexity without the extra-sharpness of the four-year aged cheddar. Their smoked cheddar is also excellent and makes a fine topping for your best burger. It is worth mentioning that availability of these cheeses is very good. Grafton opened another factory and store in Brattleboro, Vermont, in 2008. Even before the expansion, Grafton Cheddar was widely available, even in popular grocery store chains.

BARELY BUZZED

Milk – Cow
Origin – Beehive Cheese Company, Uintah, Utah, United States
Rind – Rubbed with coffee and lavender
Paste – Semi-firm with a few irregularly shaped holes and a few fissures
Aging – 5 to 8 months

Hail the innovation of American cheesemakers. Two brothers-in-law and lifelong friends, Tim Welsh and Pat Ford, decided to leave the worlds of real estate and software to try a slower, if more physically demanding life making cheese in Utah. There aren't many dairies in Utah, but this one makes some very good cheese including a cheddar, a jack, and even a parmesan style. Barely Buzzed is considered a flavored cheddar and has won first place awards in that category from the American Cheese Society in 2007, 2008, and 2009. It's rubbed with a combination of ground coffee and lavender buds which, oddly enough, impart a caramel or butterscotch-like sweetness to the paste just under the rind, although some of the aromatics from the rub do sink in to the paste as well. It is well regarded by the industry, and is a real attention-getter because of its quirky affinage.

GRANA PADANO

Milk – Cow (raw), partially skimmed
Origin – Specifically the Paduan
   Plain, Northern Italy
Rind – Natural
Paste – Ivory to pale yellow,
   granular; sometimes with visible
   tyrosine (an amino acid) crystals
Aging – ≥ 9 months, usually
   1 to 2 years
D.O.P. – 1996, with protection
   dating back to 1955

FIGURE **5.11** Grana Padano

This incredibly popular cheese lives in the comparatively small shadow of the legend-ary Parmigiano-Reggiano, much less of which is produced. With more than 4 million wheels a year, Grana Padano is one of the most popular cheeses in the world. *Grana* means "grainy" and refers to the granular nature of this cheese from the *Padana* val-ley. Parmigiano belongs to this family as well, but the higher volume and still-high-quality Grana Padano is a little bit milder and, because of the amount produced, a little bit less expensive. Both are excellent eating cheeses as well as being good for grating, their better-known use. Frankly, Grana Padano is so close in quality to its more famous cousin that they can be difficult to distinguish from each other in blind taste tests. So it's up to you to decide which product to use — if it's a matter of cost but you still want quality, use Grana Padano. If, however, you need the cachet of a more luxurious brand name, go for the Parmigiano-Reggiano.

PARMIGIANO-REGGIANO

Milk – Cow (raw)
Origin – Emilia-Romagna (primar-ily the cities of Parma, Modena,
   and Mantua), Italy
Rind – Natural, oiled and brushed
   regularly. Has dimpled impres-
   sions that spell out the name of
   the cheese as well as showing the
   date of production.
Paste – When freshly broken open, it
   is semi-hard, but has an engaging
   toothsome quality. It also has small,
   crunchy crystals of calcium lactate
   or tyrosine – they lend a character-

FIGURE **5.12** Parmigiano-Reggiano

istic surprise crunch from time to time. The older, the harder, of course.
Aging – Minimum 1 year (*giovane*, young), 2 years (*vecchio*, old), 3 years (*stravec-chio*, extra old), and 4 years (*stravecchione*, you guessed it, extra <u>extra</u> old).
D.O.C./D.O.P. – 1955/1996

This is one of the most important and influential cheeses of Italy, if not the world. Important because the genuine article is incredibly delicious and balanced in flavor; it works perfectly as a grating cheese but also provides a tremendous amount of pleasure when served as an eating cheese. It is influential because there are hundreds, if not thousands of imitations produced around the world, from wedges of "parmesan" to green cylindrical boxes containing a grated substance that resembles sawdust, although it still bears the name on its label.

The real thing is a legally protected cheese in the European Union (EU), made from raw cow's milk in a delineated area in northern Italy. Other than its remarkable flavor and texture, it also happens to be one of the most easily digested forms of animal protein available. This is because, at its advanced age, many of the complex molecules have been broken down into more easily digestible pieces. Also, there is not much lactose present.

It is made from a mixture of the whole morning milk and the previous night's milk that has been allowed to settle and has been skimmed. It is cooked, drained, and placed in its mold, just inside of which is a sheet of plastic with little bumps on it that imprint the name of the cheese on its rind along with the date and producer's number. Once the shape is set, the wheels go into a brine bath for about three weeks to toughen the rind and season the cheese. Then it's out of the bath and onto a shelf in the aging room where they are flipped regularly, brushed, and rubbed with an oiled cloth. There can be four seasons of this cheese. For instance, the cheeses made in spring are a bit more yellow (paste, not rind) because the cows are eating green young plants and more beta-carotene ends up in the milk. Also, the flavor can be subtly different. (herbal in spring, richer in winter), recent attempts by the Consorzio del Formaggio Parmigiano-Reggiano to reduce variation by controlling the cows' food supply has been successful, at least in making the cheeses more consistent. Some bemoan this homogenization in that the truly great cheeses are now harder to find, but the good news is that so are the bad ones.

If you've never eaten Parmesan (the French term, legal in the EU), do yourself a favor and get a chunk from a good cheesemonger, telling them that you are using it for a cheese board, not for grating. This should get you a fresher piece. Then, get a piece of good bread and some balsamic vinegar (also from Modena) or good honey. Oh, and a glass of Tuscan red wine.

MAHÓN

Milk – Cow (sometimes raw)

Origin – Menorca, Balearic Islands, Spain (in the Mediterranean)

Rind – Natural, rubbed with paprika or oil (the color will tell you which)

Paste – Yellowish, getting harder with age. Eventually it acquires a crumbly texture but should never be dried out

Aging – 9 to 12 months (*añejo* [the best]), 3 to 6 months (*curado*), 2 months (*semi-curado*); and 15 to 30 days (*tierno*)

FIGURE **5.13** Mahón

This flavorful cheese hails from Menorca, one of Spain's Balearic Islands in the Mediterranean. Mallorca might be bigger and more popular with the jet set, but Menorca has been known for its cheese and dairy products for centuries. Mahón is similar in style to high-quality cheddars or an aged gouda, but with a bit more subtle complexity. The younger cheeses are perfectly fine, but true character starts to show around the 10-month mark. The youngest cheeses are smooth and elastic with a simple sweetness — just fine for a snack or on a sandwich. As they age, the cheeses become harder and more granular, like aged Manchego or the *grana* cheeses of Italy. The raw milk versions show the most character (of course), but are also very rare in the United States.

SBRINZ

Milk – Cow (raw)

Origin – Lucerne, Switzerland

Rind – Washed, brushed, and oiled

Paste – Slightly golden yellow

Aging – Minimum 18 months, but will do well past 2 years, and even up to 4 years

A.O.C. – 2002

FIGURE **5.14** Sbrinz

The Italians have their noble Parmigiano-Reggiano, but the Swiss have this remarkable and impressive cheese, also based on raw cow's milk. In fact, it's possible that Sbrinz was the blueprint for its Italian counterpart. This cheese was being made in Switzerland at the time that Romans were in control there, and it is possible that the recipe was brought back to Italy by Roman soldiers.

The main difference between Sbrinz and Parmigiano-Reggiano is in the deeper color of the Swiss cheese, and in that it has a little more butterscotch flavor, as well as a less obvious level of salt. The lower salt level is explained by the shorter brining process than that of Parmigiano-Reggiano, 18 days versus 3 weeks.

As with Parmesan, Sbrinz can be served in a number of ways, either in slivers, chunks, or grated into or on top of pastas and gratins. In fact, a presentation that Italians are known for is also used in Switzerland, where the wheel of cheese is hollowed out and risotto is served inside the edible bowl.

PECORINO STAGIONATO

Milk – Sheep (raw)
Origin – Dancing Ewe Farm, Granville, New York, United States
Rind – Natural, brushed
Paste – Semi-hard, bone colored
Aging – 9 to 12 months

This cheese has some subtle power to it. Its sheep's milk origins come through, with a subtle sweetness and pleasing richness, but the extra aging gives it a little bit of a bite. This isn't the kind of sharpness that grabs the back of your throat as you swallow; it's just a nice (if firm) contrast to the sweet, slightly oily foundational flavor of the cheese. While still a great eating cheese, it has enough intensity of flavor to work well as a grated cheese in recipes that call for other hard Italian cheeses. For more information on Dancing Ewe Farm and its owners, see the Pecorino Fresco entry on page 93.

FIGURE **5.15** Pecorino Romano

PECORINO ROMANO

Milk – Sheep
Origin – Originally around Rome, Southern Italy
Rind – Natural, sometimes painted black with a food dye
Paste – Hard and off-white to ivory
Aging – ≥ 8 months

This is often thought of as the *other* grating cheese, opposite Parmigiano-Reggiano. It's a very different cheese, though, and has qualities that make it distinct. *Pecorino* is the general term for sheep's milk cheeses, and the *Romano* tells you where it's from. Most cheeses made by members of its trade consortium will emboss their cheeses with the image of a sheep's head underlined by the words *pecorino romano*. Also, they sometimes paint the exterior with a black food dye. During the aging process, the whole cheeses are salted by hand over a 70-day period, so this is a *very* salty and intense cheese. It is used almost exclusively as a grating cheese for pasta and vegetable dishes, especially those containing fava beans. Its use as an eating cheese is local to southern Italy, and even then it is served sparingly with salamis and olives, as well as other antipasti. While much of this name-protected cheese is made on the island of Sardinia (and therefore is technically Pecorino Sardo), there is still some produced in its original region, the area around Rome. Pecorino Romano is far from interchangeable with Parmigiano-Reggiano, which is quite a bit mellower and sweeter. Pecorino Romano is traditionally used on the stronger flavored dishes of the south, such as *Bucatini all'Amatriciana*, in which it is indispensable.

SCHABZIGER OR SAPSAGO

Milk – Cow, skimmed
Origin – Glarus, Switzerland
Rind – Natural, foil-wrapped
Paste – Hard, pale green
Aging – Unknown

FIGURE **5.16** Schabziger

This strange, green cheese is used only for grating as it is too strong to eat by itself. It comes in 3 oz/85 g truncated, pale-green cones. Its unique color is caused by the addition of melilot clover and/or fenugreek, which has a strong aroma and supposed medicinal properties. The cheese is often grated over vegetable dishes, into soups, and even onto buttered bread. It keeps very well because of its dry nature, so it can be a convenient and quick way to season and brighten up the flavors for a range of dishes.

MONT ST. FRANCIS

Milk – Goat (raw)
Origin – Capriole Goat Cheeses, Greenville, Indiana, United States
Rind – Washed with brine
Paste – Semi-hard, softening with age, but never runny
Aging – 4 to 8 months

Home to other great goat cheeses like the Wabash Cannonball on page 104, Capriole is thoughtfully run by Judith Schad and her family. This is one of her favorites, and was described by one of their customers as "a cheese you would not want to eat on a first date, but maybe on the second if the first one went well." It is definitely stinky, but has a firmer texture than many other washed-rind cheeses. If it has an ammonia smell and is runny, it is past its prime. Because of its inherent power, Schad actually recommends fortified and dessert wines, even Bourbon whiskey as an accompaniment. Its individuality is, of course, due to the base milk, in that there are not as many washed-rind goat's milk cheeses as there are from cow's milk. Goat's milk has a higher acid content and contributes more of an herbal characteristic to the finished cheese. It definitely deserves its place in this chapter for that reason, because as a washed-rind goat cheese, it is both stinky and tangy.

MT. TAM

Milk – Cow (pasteurized)
Origin – Cowgirl Creamery, Point Reyes Station, California, United States
Rind – Bloomy
Paste – Ivory, soft, and creamy with some irregular small holes
Aging – 3 weeks

FIGURE **5.17** Mt. Tam

This is a rich, triple-cream cheese from the Cowgirl Creamery. It has a lovely aroma of fresh mushrooms, and is a great American alternative to Explorateur or St. André. Each half-pound wheel is rich and gentle, but with enough character to be *present*. It can age to a creamier and more complex state if taken care of properly, but is better than okay upon arrival from the creamery. Mt. Tam is earthier in flavor that some of the other triple-crèmes, and so sits here above its sibling Red Hawk. For the slightly more adventurous, move ahead one space to the slightly stinky Red Hawk.

RED HAWK

Milk – Cow (organic) with the addition of heavy cream
Origin – Point Reyes Station, California, United States
Rind – Washed with brine
Paste – Soft and deep ivory to pale yellow with occasional small holes
Aging – 6 weeks

FIGURE **5.18** The Cowgirl Creamery's Red Hawk

The Cowgirl Creamery is a growing, successful, medal-winning company that was started in 1997. They make only four aged cheeses and three fresh (like Mt. Tam), but all of them are made to the highest standards of quality and sustainability. Having visited their store, many more cheeses are available there, including a cheese from the Hudson Valley, Sprout Creek Barat.

Red Hawk is, indeed, stinky, but is also a triple-cream which mitigates the stinkiness somewhat. The rind is reminiscent of real Munster, with its reddish-orange coating, but richness and relatively short affinage keep it from being overpowering. Its earthy aromas recall a *clean* barnyard, with the smells of hay and paddock dirt, but avoiding the deep funk. It's a good first-timer's stinky cheese and could be served with some chestnut or buckwheat honey, which have more complexity. It shouldn't be runny or smell like ammonia.

PLEASANT RIDGE RESERVE

Milk – Cow (raw)

Origin – Uplands Cheese Company, Dodgeville, Wisconsin, United States

Rind – Washed, brine and *B. linens* bacteria for 4 months

Paste – Semi-firm but supple with some small holes in an irregular pattern

Aging – ≥ 4 months

FIGURE **5.19** Pleasant Ridge Reserve

This is one of the most admired cheeses currently being made in the United States. I had heard much about it from a variety of sources, both friends and professionals (and professional friends). So, it was time to buy some. The young woman behind the counter nodded with approval upon hearing the order, and when I told her that I had never tasted it before, her face registered both disbelief and sadness. She immediately sliced off a sliver for me to taste, and watched carefully as I ate it. I must have displayed the proper combination of awe and pleasure because she smiled and went back to cutting my half pound.

Pleasant Ridge Reserve is based on the famous Alpine cheeses of France, the easiest variety of which to point to is Beaufort. This American version, however, has risen to the category of American original, and rarely fails to impress. The depth and length of flavor can be attributed to the care with which the cheese is made, but more importantly, the milk. Mike and Carol Gingrich and Dan and Jeanne Patenaude have farmed together since 1994, and own the cheese company together. Their cows are rotated through different sections of pasture during the spring, summer, and early fall to keep both cows and pastures healthy. The cows are allowed to follow their natural feeding/milking cycle which begins in the spring with the birth of the calves, and ends in the fall when the pastures go dormant. The cows are left "dry" for the winter, and the cycle begins again in the spring.

There is no doubting the quality of this cheese. It is sweet, nutty, and salty, but has just a little bit of funk to it from the washing with smear bacteria. They've won many awards, but the *reward* will be yours when you try it for the first time.

TARENTAISE

Milk – Cow (raw), Jersey breed
Origin – Thistle Hill Farm, North Pomfret, Vermont, United States
Rind – Natural, scrubbed, with concave sides
Paste – Semi-firm, yellowish-ivory
Aging – 6 months

FIGURE **5.20** Tarentaise

John Putnam was doing well in a Boston law firm and on the way to becoming a partner when he had a revelation. He realized that he did not want to spend most of his adult life working to become an established member of his firm; he wanted to "do something."

For the last fifteen years John, his wife Janine, and their four children have been tending to their organic farm in North Pomfret, Vermont. Thistle Hill Farm initially produced beef and vegetables, but the Putnams found cheesemaking to be more rewarding, and now produce one of the finest Alpine-style cheeses made in the United States.

Tarentaise has won a number of first and second place awards from the American Cheese Society at its national conferences. It is modeled after Beaufort (page 117), a cow's milk cheese from the Savoie region in the French Alps. It is made from the raw milk of their Jersey cows in a copper vat custom-made in Switzerland. There aren't many similar vats in this country, but the Putnams deemed it necessary for the style they wanted to produce. Most of the process is done by hand with very little mechanization. The result is a very complex, firm but supple cheese filled with the flavors of the farm. There is a nutty sweetness followed by the type of complex finish that can only be achieved with great milk. And great milk comes from happy cows that are usually tended by thoughtful and hard-working, but happy farmers.

REBLOCHON

Milk – Cow
Origin – Savoie/Rhône Alps, France
Rind – Washed with brine
Paste – Ivory, semi-soft to soft, with a slight stickiness
Aging – 2 to 5 weeks
A.O.C. – 1976

Technically a stinky cheese, Reblochon is one of the least offensive. That may sound like faint praise, but it's good for cheese neophytes who might want to gain a taste for washed-rind cheeses — this is a good starting point for them. It is from the mountains of Savoie, and has a slightly meaty, earthy quality that is boosted by a noticeable, but not overpowering saltiness. The name is said to come from the word *reblocher*, a local term for second milking, or "pinching the udder again." Supposedly, farmers paid taxes or tithes with the milk of their cows, and would prematurely stop the milking process, give the first milk to the boss and send them on their way. Then, the farmer would finish the milking, and this second milking had a higher fat content, making the subsequent cheese richer. There is also a Swiss version of this cheese named Kuntener, although its not as readily available. It is an important ingredient in *Tartiflette*, a traditional dish from the area that also has potatoes, bacon, and béchamel sauce . . . and is utterly addicting. A more complete recipe for an American version can be found in the cooking chapter on page 151.

FIGURE **5.21** Kuntener

PONT L'ÉVÊQUE

Milk – Cow
Origin – Pays d'Auge, Normandy, France
Rind – Washed with brine
Paste – Ivory/creamy-white with small holes of different sizes throughout, soft but not runny at room temperature
Aging – 40 to 45 days
A.O.C. – 1972, full status in 1976

One of the most famous cheeses from Normandy is Pont l'Évêque, named for its town of origin. It is justifiably popular with

FIGURE **5.22** Pont l'Évêque

the French, as well as abroad, and is many Americans' first stinky cheese. This is a good thing, because the smell, while apparent, conceals a more subtle, slightly salty, and moderately earthy flavor. Its history dates back to the 1200s, and it has been made in basically the same method since that time. When ripe, the exterior should be slightly sticky with a pink or orange tinge. At room temperature, the cut cheese should bulge or ooze out a bit, but not be runny. If the cheese looks dried out, has cracks in the rind, or has a pronounced (and I mean pronounced) scent of ammonia, the cheese is shot. For a more rustic, and sometimes more authentic experience, try Pavé d'Auge which is a very similar cheese from the same region — only it's more likely to have been made at a farmhouse or creamery than Pont l'Évêque. About 98% of those cheeses are made at a cooperative or *industriel* level.

NORMAN BOUNTY

Normandy is famous for more than its beauty — the regional cuisine is rife with long-standing traditions, most involving the natural bounty of the area. The two most famous agricultural products are apples and dairy. Seafood and fish run a close third, as you might expect, but apples and dairy dominate. Beyond the standard uses of apples for eating and cooking, the region produces a lot of hard cider that is sometimes distilled into apple brandy, including the justly famous Calvados. As for excess milk, Normandy is one of the most important cheese producing regions in France, naming Camembert, Livarot, Brillat-Savarin, and Pont l'Évêque as its native sons (daughters?). Frankly, the butter is quite something, too. So if you see a dish with the descriptor *à la Normande*, expect apples, butter, or cream . . . or maybe all three.

FIGURE **5.23** Époisses de Bourgogne

ÉPOISSES DE BOURGOGNE

Milk – Cow
Origin – Burgundy, France
Rind – Washed both with brine and Marc (pomace brandy), which is like French grappa
Paste – Soft to runny, ivory to pale yellow
Aging – 5 to 6 weeks
A.O.C. – 1991

This was Napoleon's favorite cheese. At least that's what every book entry, pamphlet, and cheese Web site says. Frankly, this is one of the stinkiest cheeses around, but its aroma is succeeded by a subtle complexity of flavor and texture in the mouth that is difficult to find anywhere else. It is, at once, rich, salty, and possessing of voluptuous flavor as well as mouthfeel. Époisses (as it is most often referred to) becomes runny, even spoonable at room temperature, at which point it shows best. The paradox of such a strong-smelling cheese being so subtle with its pleasures is surely what makes it one of the most-requested cheeses at restaurants and shops. The key is to get it *à point*, at the perfect level of ripeness, and to let it warm up to room temperature. To obtain a properly ripened cheese, it is best to deal with a good monger or affineur — the cheese should give a little when pressed, but not be at all mushy. Although it is a venerable cheese, it was on the endangered cheeses list during World War II, but became widely available again in the 1950s. Many are glad that it did.

GRAYSON

Milk – Cow (raw)
Origin – Meadow Creek Dairy, Virginia, United States
Rind – Washed, orangey-brown, and slightly sticky
Paste – Semi-soft and also a little sticky; bulges when cut, and with small irregular holes
Aging – 60 to 75 days

FIGURE **5.24** Grayson

If you are a fan of Taleggio, that famed Italian stinker, but have made a pledge to "'Buy American!," there is some good news for you. The folks at Meadow Creek Dairy have not only taken this style (also similar to Livarot) and run with it, they are making the best version of it possible in the United States. The raw milk comes from Jersey cows that are pastured on fresh-grown grass which has never been touched by herbicides or pesticides. The cows are also allowed to work in the natural milking cycle, beginning in the spring when calves are born, and winding down as the grass growth slows. With the milking season ending in the end of December, the cows and farmers take a two-month break.

The cheese itself has won many awards, including a number from the American Cheese Society. Flavors are rich, a little sweet, nutty, and beefy. Its powerful aroma fades a bit after unwrapping and resting a bit, but never goes away. In fact, while buying another cheese from Murray's counter in Grand Central Station one day, the young saleswoman apparently felt the need to tell me, "The Grayson is really *stinky* today!" This was meant, of course, as a compliment.

TALEGGIO

Milk – Cow
Origin – Lombardia, Italy
Rind – Washed with brine
Paste – Semi-soft to soft with age
Aging – 35 to 40 days
D.O.C./D.O.P. – 1988/1996

The French might be more famous for stinky cheese, but the Italians produce one of the best. Taleggio was originally made in the *Val Taleggio* in Lombardy, east of Milan and in the mountains, whence the best-quality milk comes. As the cheese has gained in popularity, its production has

FIGURE **5.25** Taleggio

moved down into the plain regions of Lombardy, where milk is more plentiful and production quite a bit easier. The best still come from the alpine valley, and are made from raw milk.

Once it has aged a bit, Taleggio can be salty, sweet, meaty, and fruity all at once. Look for cheeses that have turned a light reddish-brown, and are bulging a little at the sides. In cooking, it melts beautifully (if stinkily), and can be used in risotto as well as polenta — both dishes that can be found in the North.

APPENZELLER

Milk – Cow (both raw and pasteurized)
Origin – Appenzell, Switzerland
Rind – Washed
Paste – Smooth and creamy, becoming granular with age, showing pea-sized holes
Aging – Minimum 3 months, with real character arriving in 7 to 9 months

FIGURE **5.26** Appenzeller

This is Swiss Cheese. While some are pasteurized and produced in large quantity, the real versions made from raw cow's milk are washed with an herb brine, the recipe for which is considered a vital secret by each producer. The flavor is a bit sharper than that of Gruyère, but less so than of Tête de Moine. It is often used for fondue.

TÊTE DE MOINE

Milk – Cow
Origin – Jura, Switzerland
Rind – Washed with brine and brushed to prevent mold
Paste – Firm, ivory
Aging – ≥ 3 months, on pine boards

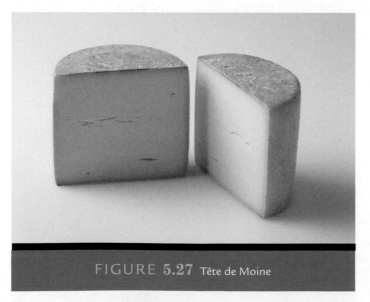

FIGURE **5.27** Tête de Moine

First made by monks at the abbey of Bellelay more than 800 years ago, this is the strongest of the Swiss cheeses. Gruyère and Emmenthaler will give you an idea of where you're going, but the final destination might surprise you. The cheese is much smaller than its cousins, and therefore can age more quickly. The flavor profile is often described as nutty, sweet, and beefy. In that it is such a strong cheese, it is usually consumed in small amounts. For many years, one would cut the top off of the cheese, or cut it in half, and then scrape off curls with a flat-edged, sharp knife.

In 1981, an ingenious device called a Girolle was invented to help make it easier to serve Tête de Moine. The gizmo consists of a metal rod that is shoved down the center point of the cheese; then a horizontal blade fits over the rod, and is turned with a small handle. The resulting action scrapes off florets of the cheese that are so delicate that they almost melt on your tongue. These rosettes form most easily when the cheese is somewhat cold, but they are so thin that they warm up to room temperature quickly. It can be served with grapes or other fresh fruit as part of a platter, or it can be used in any recipe that calls for Gruyère . . . just remember that it is a stronger cheese.

LIVAROT

Milk – Cow
Origin – Calvados, Normandy, France
Rind – Washed with brine
Paste – Soft to runny with age, and at room temperature. Small holes visible throughout
Aging – 3 weeks to 3 months
A.O.C. – 1975

FIGURE **5.28** Livarot

What is it with monks and stinky cheese? This cheese was originally made in abbeys more than 700 years ago, and became such a popular cheese that more of it was eaten than any other cheese from Normandy. As with other stinky cheeses, the aroma is much stronger than its flavor, but it is important that it have the right kind of stink. Too much ammonia is a bad thing, as it is the smell of decay rather than that of a clean barnyard. Also, the texture should be neither too hard nor too soft. Think of the way a ripe pear or tomato has a little give when squeezed or prodded. The best thing to do is to leave the decision up to a *maître fromager*, and ask for a Livarot that's ready to go. These, more than many other cheeses, have a narrow window of opportunity . . . if you have no other choice, buy one that's young and allow it to ripen in the warmest part of your refrigerator such as the top shelf.

MAROILLE

Milk – Cow (raw if *fermier*)
Origin – Maroilles, Nord-Pas de Calais region near the Belgian border, France
Rind – Washed with brine
Paste – Ivory to pale yellow with some small holes. Soft, oily texture.
Aging – 2 weeks to 5 months
A.O.C./A.O.P. – 1976/1996

This stinky nugget goes back to the tenth century, when it was made by monks. Available in three sizes: *Quart*: 3 1/2 in/8.9 cm square, about 12 oz/340 g, *Mignon*: 4 1/2 in/11.5 cm square, almost 13 oz/369 g, and *Sorbais*: 5 in/12.7 cm square and about 1 lb/454 g. They are aged for two, three, and four weeks, respectively. During its affinage, it acquires a red bacterial coating, as well as its prodigious aroma and flavors. Both salty and strong, the texture is the only yielding thing about it. At this level of strength, any accompaniments will have to be powerful, with a high funk-factor. As it ages, it will show bulging and/or drooping sides which is expected, but cracking and crumbling edges usually mean that it is past its peak.

FIGURE **5.29** Munster-Géromé

MUNSTER-GÉROMÉ

Milk – Cow
Origin – Alsace (Munster)-Lorraine (Géromé)
Rind – Washed with brine
Paste – Semi-soft to runny when ripe, ivory to pale gold
Aging – ≥ 3 weeks, but 2 to 3 months is more often the case
A.O.C. – 1978 (combined, but Munster had its own as of 1969)

What's that orange-painted soft white cheese in the deli case? The color of the mass-produced innocuous Munster cheese is merely a nod to the ruddy orange-red coating on the real thing. Munster and Géromé are essentially the same cheese from two sides of the Vosges Mountains. If you are lucky enough to find the real thing (which shouldn't be too difficult), expect an experience close to that of eating a fine Époisses, with all the requisite stinkiness, but also a broader richness of flavor. One big difference is that, in this case, the local wines pair marvelously with the cheese, especially some of the *vendange tardive* (late-harvest) Pinot Gris, Gewürztraminers, and Rieslings. Incidentally, since the two names were united in 1978, Géromé has been eclipsed by Munster.

WHEN YOU GOT DA BLUES

While it seems that many people are scared, or at least wary, of blue cheese, there is also the ubiquitous blue cheese dressing that drenches steakhouse salads and is served with Buffalo chicken wings. You would think that this familiarity would lead to a greater popularity of blue cheese in general, but it is one of the perennial challenges to sell blue cheese from the cheese board. Perhaps it's because it has a pungent smell all its own (volatile aromatics are created by the mold), or because they are often salty and strong in flavor.

The common thread among most blue cheeses is that the mold is usually a *Penicillium* type. For instance, the mold used in the production of Roquefort is *Penicillium roqueforti*. These cheeses were not so much invented as they were initially tolerated. Signs of mold in cheese would have first been seen as an indication of the cheese going bad. However, some brave soul tasted the moldy cheese and realized that a whole new set of flavors was present. The flavors unique to blue cheeses are there mostly because the *Penicillium* molds metabolize milk fat and break it into fatty acid chains, further breaking some of them down into flavor compounds. Because of this, most blues have a rather strong aroma that is quite different than what you will smell coming from a washed-rind (smear bacteria) coated cheese. The pungency of the blue cheeses can have a peppery component, and sometimes a whiff of ammonia. Most of all, they just smell moldy — in a good way. As you might imagine, there is a range of flavors available in the blue family, and although some are rather calm for a blue cheese, they're still blue. That's why they're in this chapter. The first two cheeses in this chapter also appear in Chapter 3. In that chapter, I said that you wouldn't look for a mild blue cheese in the strong chapter . . . but they also belong with their blue brethren, so here's a repeat.

HOW'D THAT BLUE GET IN THERE?

For the first blue cheeses, mold spores were living in the environment where the cheese was made and aged, like the caves in Roquefort-sur-Soulzon. The spores were incorporated during the cheesemaking process, and sprouted in the relatively low-oxygen environment of the cheeses' interiors. When cheesemakers wanted to take it from accidental to intentional, they did things like mixing the crumbs of a moldy loaf of bread into the milk or curds or aging the cheese in specific caves. Now that the strains of these molds have been identified and isolated, the molds themselves (or their spores) are added. Another traditional method is to poke narrow holes in the cheese to let air in. This does two things; the instrument that makes the holes will drag some mold spores into the cheese from the surface, and the holes allow air in so the mold can breathe. You can sometimes see evidence of this in a blue cheese, as it looks like the cheese was injected with mold spores. In a way, it was. So, one way or another, either by mixing mold into the cheese while it's being made, or introducing the spores to the whole cheese's interior later on, they get in there and give us the blues.

POINT REYES FARMSTEAD BLUE

Milk – Cow (raw)
Origin – Point Reyes Station, California, United States
Rind – None, foil-wrapped
Paste – Ivory paste with well-distributed blue veining, more creamy than crumbly
Aging – 3 weeks curing, 6 months aging

Tomales Bay is a beautiful, ten-mile long estuary bay about 40 miles northwest of San Francisco. It separates Point Reyes from the mainland, and is a fine destination for food lovers. The Tomales Bay Oyster Company is one place to stop, but for our purposes there are the Cowgirl Creamery and the Point Reyes Farmstead Cheese Company that makes this blue cheese.

The Giacomini family had been running their dairy in Point Reyes Station since 1959, but decided to start making a product from their milk in 2000. Since then, they have enjoyed both critical success and increased sales, with good availability around the United States. The cheese is similar to Fourme d'Ambert and Bleu d'Auvergne, two blues from France that tend more toward the creamy than sharp and spicy. This style is a good one for those who aren't sure whether they like blue cheese . . . it's a good starting point. See photo on page 76.

BLEU D'AUVERGNE

Milk – Cow
Origin – Auvergne, France
Rind – None, foil-wrapped
Paste – Creamy with abundant dark blue marbling
Aging – 4 weeks
A.O.C. – 1975

This is blue cheese with training wheels. It lacks some of the subtlety of Fourme d'Ambert, but is a non-prepossessing, rather soft and buttery, relatively mild blue that can be served with ripe pears or dessert wine. It also tends to be a very good value because it is made in large quantities to satisfy the French and American grocery store demand, and is somewhat less well known than the (usually somewhat inferior) Danish Blue, which was originally based on Bleu d'Auvergne after World War II. See photo on page 77.

FOURME D'AMBERT

Milk – Cow
Origin – Auvergne, France
Rind – Natural, light brown
Paste – Creamy with abundant blue mold
Aging – ≥ 28 days
A.O.C. – Originally shared with its sister cheese, Fourme de Montbrison in 1972, on its own since 2002

This is a very good blue cheese for people who think they don't like blue cheese. It has a creamy texture and relatively mild flavor and is not as spicy as Roquefort, stinky as Gorgonzola, or sharp as the Danish blues that most Americans know. Having been made since at least the 800s, the *fourme* in its name refers to the form it has been made in through the ages. If you are on a crusade to change someone's mind about blue cheese, give them some of this with a perfectly ripe pear and some Coteaux du Layon dessert wine. If that doesn't work, nothing will. See photo on page 76.

BAYLEY HAZEN BLUE

Milk – Cow's (raw) morning
   milking, Ayrshire breed
Origin – Jasper Hill Farm,
   Greensboro, Vermont, United States
Rind – Natural, beige/tan with a
   light bloom of white mold
Paste – Firm and seemingly dry,
   but with a buttery fudge-like texture. The interior is peppered with
   various-sized flecks of grayish-blue
   mold.
Aging – 4 to 6 months

FIGURE **5.30** Bayley Hazen Blue

For information on the Jasper Hill Farm,
see the Constant Bliss cheese entry on
page 63.

Bayley Hazen is a top-notch blue named for a military supply road in Vermont that
was commissioned by George Washington in 1776. The cheese's shape is that of a tall
cylinder, weighing roughly 7 pounds. The Ayrshire cows provide a particularly rich
milk, with very small fat globules, which the Kehler's say is especially beneficial for
the making of this cheese. Morning milk is used, though, which has lower fat content
than evening milk, and is better for Bayley Hazen (evening milk is used for Constant
Bliss). The cheese's flavor profile includes nutty and grassy notes, and more than one
taster has mentioned a hint of licorice. It is one of Vermont's great blues, and is feisty
enough to please even the most devoted Roquefort fan.

GREAT HILL BLUE

Milk – Cow (raw)
Origin – Marion, Massachusetts,
   United States
Rind – None (foil-wrapped)
Paste – Pale yellow with abundant
   blue veining, firm but creamy
Aging – ≥ 6 months

FIGURE **5.31** Great Hill Blue

This cheese was originally produced as a
way for the Stone family to survive financially at their dairy farm some 50 miles
south of Boston. With dairy farming becoming more expensive in their Buzzard's
Bay location, Tim Stone started thinking
about how they could make more money
with what they had, and cheesemaking struck the right chord. As for what kind of
cheese to make, he listened to the opinions of potential customers, many of whom said
that there wasn't a local cow's milk blue, and that it would fill a niche. So, in 1996,

they started producing a blue cheese from raw milk (another distinction). The cheese itself is creamy and rich while still having a good bite. It is similar in style to both Fourme d'Ambert and Bleu d'Auvergne, and that is very good company.

ROARING FORTIES BLUE

Milk – Cow (pasteurized)
Origin – King Island, Australia
Rind – Dark blue wax coating
Paste – Firm but smooth and creamy; can have a yellowish tinge because of beta-carotene from fresh grass
Aging – 4 to 5 weeks for blue mold development, coated with wax, and then aged 2 to 3 more weeks at creamery

King Island is a small, lush island between mainland Australia and Tasmania that was originally part of a land bridge between the two. The climate is rather mild, and allows for year-round production of both dairy and beef. Legend has it that the verdant pastures originated when grass-filled mattresses from French and British shipwrecks washed onto the shores of this fertile island and the grass spread inward.

The cheese has a sweet nuttiness, and retains a creamy, moist texture because of the wax coating. The wax also slows the development of blue mold to a crawl — keeping it where it should be for best eating.

FIGURE **5.32** Shropshire Blue

SHROPSHIRE BLUE

Milk – Cow (pasteurized)
Origin – Created in Scotland, now made in Nottinghamshire, England
Rind – Natural, browning and turning rough with age
Paste – Orange with green-blue veining
Aging – 3 months

Essentially, this cheese is a cross between Cheshire and Stilton. It is colored orange-yellow with annatto, like English Farmhouse Cheddar, but has blue veining throughout, like Stilton, because it uses the same *Penicillium roqueforti* mold. Although invented in Scotland in the 1970s, and thus a relatively young cheese, it is extremely popular both in England and abroad. Its flavor is not unlike Stilton, but it is sold younger, and so has a slightly creamier, moist texture. And while it may have a less meaty flavor, it can be stronger and more rustic than Stilton. In that it is so powerful, it tends to go best with richer beers (such as English Stout) or, as with Stilton, fortified dessert wines.

BLEU L'ERMITE AND BLEU BÉNÉDICTIN

Milk – Cow (pasteurized)
Origin – Abbaye du Saint-Benoît-du-Lac, Québec, Canada
Rind – L'Ermite, no rind; Bénédictin, a crusty natural rind
Paste – L'Ermite, ivory and creamy-crumbly with ample bluing; Bénédictin, dark ivory, semi-firm and crumbly with ample bluing

These are two of the most highly respected blue cheeses produced in Canada. The monks of Abbaye du Saint-Benoît-du-Lac make a number of agricultural products on the Canadian side of Lake Memphremagog (Vermont is on the other side). These blues are their best known products in the United States, but other cheeses are made, including goat ricotta, aged goat, gruyere, and fontina styles. All of the cheeses, honey, jams, jellies, and other agricultural products are available at their store, but few of their products are shipped across the border. Luckily, these blue cheeses are two of them.

BLEU DES CAUSSES

Milk – Cow (raw)
Origin – Aveyron, South-Central France
Rind – Natural, moist in summer; drier in winter
Paste – Firm but creamy, with moderate bluing. Winter cheeses tend to be drier.
Aging – ≥ 70 days; usually 3 to 4 months
A.O.C. – 1979

Bleu des Causses is from the same general area as Roquefort and is essentially a cow's milk version of that most famous French blue. It walks the line between being spicy and pungent, while still leaving a somewhat delicate final impression, probably because its saltiness is well controlled. Perhaps the best way to think of Bleu des Causses is as a halfway point between the calmer Fourme d'Ambert and peppery Roquefort. The fact that Bleu des Causses is made from unpasteurized milk lends it more complexity than Fourme; it is less spicy than its sheep's milk cousin, Roquefort.

PERSILLÉ

Milk – Goat
Origin – Savoie, Rhône-Alpes, France
Rind – Natural
Paste – Soft and dry to hard and very dry, depending on age
Aging – 1 to 3 months, with further affinage of 1 to 4 months (4 to 7 total)

This is actually a category of naturally blue goat's cheeses from the alpine region of the Rhône. They include Persillé de la

FIGURE **5.33** Persillé

Tarentaise, de Tignes, and du Semnoz (which sometimes has cow's milk also). The blue veining is hard to find in the younger cheeses, but tends to become more apparent after about three months of age. The word *persillé* means "parsleyed," and describes quite well the green-flecked exterior. These small cheeses age rather quickly because of their surface area, and acquire a complex spiciness after only four or five months. The tradeoff is that they are also drying out, and can become crumbly and tough. Really, it is up to your personal taste — try a few at different stages and see what you like.

MAYTAG BLUE

Milk – Cow (raw)
Origin – Newton, Iowa, United States
Rind – Natural, foil-wrapped
Paste – White to ivory paste with prominent blue veining
Aging – 6 months

The Maytag family had been manufacturing home appliances in Iowa since 1907, and started their own herd of show cattle in 1919. On October 11, 1941, they used the milk of their prize-winning herd of Holsteins to start making one of the finest blue cheeses produced in the United States, using a method developed at Iowa State University. They made the cheese by hand, incorporating *Penicillium roqueforti* mold, and then aged them for six months, which is now about twice as long as do many other American producers. The cheese is creamy, with a pleasing density and intriguing, but not overpowering spiciness. Its forthright style is somehow very American — and it's not a surprise that the chairman of Maytag Dairy Farms is Fritz Maytag. He is also the owner of Anchor Brewing Company, maker of the great Anchor Steam Beer (among other fine brews). Having met Fritz (who is Frederick Louis Maytag III), it is easy to see why the family has such a great legacy regarding all of its products. Fiercely intelligent, a stickler for detail, and possessor of a highly trained palate, Fritz knows when something is good, and why.

FIGURE 5.34 Rogue River Blue

ROGUE RIVER BLUE

Milk – Cow (raw)
Origin – Rogue Creamery, Central Point, Oregon, United States
Rind – Natural, wrapped with grape leaves
Paste – Ivory with moderate gray-blue veining
Aging – 8 to 12 months

This cheese recently won Best of Show at the 26th American Cheese Society conference. It triumphed over 1,326 other American entries, and was named the best blue cheese in the world at the World Cheese Awards in London in 2004, pushing aside both Roquefort and Stilton.

Unlike many of the other well-known specialty cheesemakers who are somewhat new to the industry, Rogue Creamery has been making cheese since 1935, and blues based on the methods used for Roquefort since 1957. The business was started by Tom Vella, known as creator of California Dry Jack (page 50). He, and then his family, ran dairy operations in both Sonoma and Oregon for decades, and when his son Ignazio sold their Oregon creamery, it was to the current owners, David Gremmels and Cary Bryan, who have maintained the level of quality originally demanded by Tom Vella.

The cheese is allowed to form a natural rind, but before sale is wrapped in Syrah grape leaves that have been soaked in Pear Brandy from Clear Creek Distillery, one of the best eau de vie makers in the United States. The wrapping is tied up with raffia, and the limited-production cheese makes its way to stores and cheese lovers. Rogue River Blue is known for its rich creaminess, but still retains a complexity of flavor that can be nutty (hazelnuts), fruity, and mushroomy at the same time. Not surprisingly, there is often a noticeable scent of fresh pears.

THE BIG FOUR

The next four cheeses are referred to by many in the food world as "The Big Four Blues." Their combined history, popularity, and overall quality put them in a place of prominence not only among other cheeses, but all foods. They are listed in increasing order of their relative power; Stilton, Roquefort, Gorgonzola, and Cabrales. As the most famous blue cheeses in the world, and representing four great Old World nations, they are readily available almost everywhere.

STILTON

> **Milk** – Cow
> **Origin** – Leicester, England
> **Rind** – Natural, with a reddish mold forming
> **Paste** – Ivory with substantial blue-green veining
> **Aging** – 9 to 14 weeks

FIGURE **5.35** Stilton

This is the King of English Cheeses. It's also the only legally protected cheese in England. Surprising to find, therefore, that there is virtually no farmhouse Stilton made anymore. Still, some of the creameries are quite small by factory standards, and a quality product is still available. In fact, the Stilton Cheese Makers Association (1936) licenses only six producers who all must use the same recipe.

It is the creamiest of the big four blues, and its readiness for eating is determined by texture, not degree of bluing. Along with the creaminess, the flavor profile is one of a controlled salt level with minerality and sweetness as well as both fruity and meaty flavors. The classic pairing for Stilton is vintage port. There are few greater pleasures in life than this combination, and it's one of those experiences that is worth both the effort (somewhat minimal) and expense (not minimal) to provide for your guests.

FIGURE **5.36** Roquefort

ROQUEFORT

Milk – Sheep (raw), mostly Lacaune sheep

Origin – Roquefort-sur-Soulzon, France (south-central)

Rind – Natural, foil-wrapped

Paste – Ivory with deep blue mold, with some holes of varying size

Aging – 3 to 9 months, with at least 3 months in limestone caverns

A.O.C. – 1925 (the first cheese to receive the designation)

Don't just listen to me; Charlemagne, Napoleon, Brillat-Savarin, and any number of other popes, celebrities, and kings have named this among their favorite cheeses. As the first cheese to receive A.O.C. protection, it must be aged for at least three months in the Combalou caves in the town of Roquefort-sur-Soulzon. The natural mold found in those caves is the *Penicillium roqueforti* that can now legally be used to inoculate the cheeses.

The cheese itself is a powerful one, with spicy, piquant flavors and aromas, as well as a pleasingly powerful saltiness. The salt level should not be the only thing you notice, and the overall balance should be between sweet, salty, spicy, buttery, and meaty components. Speaking of which, Roquefort has one of the highest levels of glutamate of any food. This is the stuff of MSG, and brings with it the taste of umami. With all its power, Roquefort is elegant as well — a balancing act that is very hard to pull off in the food world. To really experience this cheese at its best, let it approach room temperature and then serve it with a glass of Sauternes from the nearby Bordeaux. In a practical sense, the sweet wine offers a nice balance to the salty cheese. From perhaps a more poetic viewpoint, the moldy Roquefort is lovely with Sauternes, a wine made from grapes that have been affected by *Botrytis cinerea*, the "noble rot" that happens to be another form of mold. Moldy cheese with moldy wine — a match made in fungus heaven.

FIGURE **5.37** Gorgonzola

GORGONZOLA

Milk – Cow (pasteurized)

Origin – Lombardia and Piemonte, Italy

Rind – Natural

Paste – Ivory with plentiful veining, turning more yellow with age

Aging – 2 to 4 months

D.O.C./D.O.P. – 1955/1996

Gorgonzola is one of the great blues. It, or a cheese like it, has been made in northern Italy for more than a thousand years. Its modern history, though, started in the 1900s, when its production method became more consistent from producer to producer.

The youngest and creamiest of these cheeses is *Gorgonzola Dolce* (sweet), which is a luxurious cheese that unfortunately, because of its high moisture content, can be variable in quality. The most popular stage for this cheese is *Gorgonzola Piccante*, which still has a buttery texture, but is a bit firmer and spicier. The key to Gorgonzola is that its inherent sweetness provides a lovely balance to the spicy "blue-ness" that becomes more aggressive with age. As a side note, the punctures visible in the paste are not from the cheese having been inoculated with mold by syringe — the holes come from metal rods used to poke holes to allow air *and* mold spores into the interior of the cheese. Gorgonzola is used in a number of ways at home in Italy. As with the other blue cheeses, pears are a lovely accompaniment, but Italians also use polenta, risotto, and some pastas as a vehicle for both Piccante and Dolce versions of the cheese.

CABRALES

Milk – Cow (raw), traditionally with the addition of sheep and goat

Origin – Asturias, Spain (northwest)

Rind – Natural, foil-wrapped. Sometimes available wrapped in leaves.

Paste – Creamy but granular, off-white with a lot of blue veining

Aging – 3 months

FIGURE **5.38** Cabrales

Of the Big Four, Cabrales is perhaps the biggest. It has a strikingly sharp aroma and flavor that is perhaps driven by its saltiness and blue mold together. Yet the rich, creamy density keeps up with its power, resulting in a very powerful tasting experience. In fact, Cabrales should probably be served last if part of a cheese tasting . . . at which point it should be served with a sweet Spanish wine, like a Moscatel Sherry from producer Emilio Lustau, or perhaps some dried fruit.

Cabrales was originally made by small farmhouse producers and aged in the local caves. Luckily, the production is still done on a rather small scale in family-owned dairies around Asturias. While methods have been somewhat modernized, especially with regard to sanitary practices, most producers adhere to tradition in the most influential parts of the cheesemaking process. Also, whereas many of the cheeses are made with cow milk only, the addition of the other milks (sometimes from mixed herds) adds complexity. The sheep's milk adds a warm sweetness while the goat's milk adds a nice acidic tang, making for a more complex flavor profile. This really is one of the most important cheeses in the world, and if you are serious about learning all things casein, it should be on your short list.

COOKING WITH CHEESE

In that this book comes from The Culinary Institute of America, it would not be complete without at least a few recipes and tips on how to cook with cheese. There are standard recipes as well as some that take advantage of some cheeses' specific properties. Take note that all of these recipes involve heat application — for information on combining cheese with other uncooked ingredients, look to Chapter 7 on pairing (page 193).

CHEESE BEHAVIOR

The way various cheeses react when heated depends on a few simple conditions. Easiest to ascertain are the amount of moisture, fat content, and age of the cheese. Less obvious, unless you know what to look for, is whether the cheese was made with acid and rennet, or acid alone. The following information will help you figure out what to do with the cheese on hand, as well as how to pick a cheese to use when you have a specific final product in mind.

- Moisture level and fat content — Basically, the higher the moisture, the lower each cheese's melting point. Soft cheeses begin to melt at around 130°F/54°C, harder cheeses like Cheddar at around 150°F/66°C, and harder, aged cheese like Parmigiano-Reggiano won't give until around 180°F/82°C. This is largely because fewer water molecules surround the proteins of drier cheeses, so the proteins bind to each other more tightly. Another factor comes into play when the temperature gets even higher — that the moisture will eventually be driven out of the cheese, whereupon it becomes firmer again, and then solid. It is at this point that high-fat cheeses will leak fat and look oily. The proteins are now damaged enough to accentuate this, especially in those high-fat cheeses.

- Age of the cheese — The older the cheese, the more its proteins have been broken into smaller pieces by the ripening enzymes. This means a hard grating cheese will be much less likely to form long strings when melted. Younger cheeses with more moisture, such as Mozzarella and mild Cheddars, will be much more likely to be stringy when melted, which is obvious to anyone who has burnt their chin eating pizza or nachos. Other factors that reduce stringiness (or abet it) are acidity and salt content, both of which keep the melted cheese looser. This is used to an advantage in the making of fondue, which is usually based on the relatively salty Gruyère and has white wine as one of its ingredients. In fact, if you find that a cheese sauce or dish is seizing up in an unwanted way, the acidity from the quick addition of wine or lemon juice will often save the day.

- Why won't this cheese melt? — Here is where rennet use comes into play. Rather than going into the chemistry (McGee, pp 64–65), suffice it to say that cheeses that have been curdled exclusively with acid will not melt — at least not the way you think of cheese melting — into strings. Because of their molecular structure, Ricotta, Paneer, fresh goat cheese, and Halloumi will get somewhat softer as they're heated, but won't melt into a puddle or form strings. This leads us to an understanding of the preparation methods for which many of these cheeses are used. Ricotta in ravioli will stay put when you break it open with your fork; goat cheese will maintain its disk-shape when broiled for a salad, and paneer will stay in chunks when cooked with spinach. Don't confuse this with the property that allows you to make Parmigiano crisps—that cheese *did* actually melt first, before it was browned. But a piece of grilled Halloumi mostly keeps to its original form ... and happens to be delicious.

In general, understanding how different cheeses behave under different conditions will help you to cook better with cheese. If you want a smooth sauce, high heat will cause protein molecules to tighten up, congeal, and squeeze out fat and water, leading to a gritty mouthfeel and oily appearance — so don't overheat the cheese sauce. Extra agitation will make a stringy melted cheese even stringier, for better or worse. Acid-curdled cheeses won't melt, so don't try to make a fresh goat cheese fondue. For a simpler guideline, look at traditional recipes for individual cheeses, especially from the Old World where they've had hundreds of years to figure things out. If the cheese you're using is relatively new to the scene, pick an established cheese that it resembles and look up its traditional uses.

CROQUE MONSIEUR

YIELD: 2 PORTIONS

This sandwich is a great example of how American and French opinions differ on food. An American's idea of the grilled cheese sandwich involves *very* white bread and American cheese. Don't get me wrong ... this exact sandwich is a guilty pleasure for many at the CIA (myself included). But, the French grilled cheese uses more flavorful ingredients, and, in some cases, Béchamel sauce. What we end up with here is a fork-and-knife sandwich that transcends the American version. Serve with a simple green salad.

Béchamel Sauce

Unsalted butter	1 Tbsp	15 mL
All-purpose flour	1 Tbsp	15 mL
Whole milk	1 cup	240 mL

Sandwiches

Rustic white bread, slices	4	4
Spicy mustard, or as needed	1 Tbsp	15 mL
Gruyère slices, 1/8-inch thick	4	4
Country ham or Cure 81 ham slices (about 4)	4 oz	113 g
Unsalted butter, soft	3 Tbsp	45 mL
Grated Gruyère	1/4 cup	60 mL

METHOD

1. Make the béchamel in a small saucepan. Melt the butter over medium heat and stir or whisk in the flour. Cook the flour over medium heat until the raw smell is gone, about 2 minutes. Whisk the milk into the roux and cook, stirring, over low heat until the sauce has thickened, about 5 minutes. Remove from the heat and allow to cool to room temperature.
2. Preheat the broiler and place a rack at the highest position.
3. Lightly coat one side of each bread slice with mustard and place a slice of cheese on each. Top each piece of cheese with a slice of ham.
4. Close the sandwiches and butter the outsides with the softened butter. Cook in a broiler-safe skillet over medium heat until the bread is well browned on both sides and the cheese is melting, about 10 minutes.
5. Divide the béchamel in half and spread on the tops of the sandwiches. Sprinkle the grated Gruyère evenly over the sauce and place the sandwiches under the broiler until lightly browned on top, 4 to 5 minutes.
6. Remove from the broiler and allow to sit for a minute before cutting in half.

GRILLED HALLOUMI

YIELD: 4 APPETIZER OR 2 MAIN COURSE PORTIONS

Many folks are surprised to find out that the country with the highest per capita cheese consumption is not France, or Italy, or even the United States — it's Greece. Although fish is an important protein there, the sheep and goats running around provide a sustainable source of milk that can be converted into cheese. Halloumi is an acid-curdled cheese, usually made from a combination of sheep and goat's milk. It is wonderful fried or grilled (or raw), and in combination with salad ingredients. I'm not sure why, but when you eat Halloumi, it squeaks against your teeth. I find it charming, some find it annoying, but I'm sure that people who grew up on this cheese find the squeaking somehow comforting.

Halloumi cheese	8 oz	227 g
Pure olive oil	2 Tbsp	30 mL
Ground black pepper	as needed	as needed
Oregano sprigs	2	2
White Wine Vinaigrette (page 142)	1 cup	240 mL
Arugula, washed and dried	1 bunch	1 bunch
Kosher salt	as needed	as needed
Freshly ground black pepper	as needed	as needed

METHOD

1. Preheat the grill over medium-high heat. Once hot, clean the grill with a brush and oil the grates.
2. Slice the Halloumi carefully (it crumbles) into four appetizer or two main course rectangular pieces. Drizzle both sides of each piece with olive oil and grind black pepper onto all sides as well. It's a salty cheese, so no added salt is necessary.
3. Chop the oregano leaves and whisk into the vinaigrette. Place the arugula in a bowl, season with salt and pepper, and toss with one third of the vinaigrette. Divide the dressed arugula between the desired number of plates.
4. Place the Halloumi on the grill. If you want crosshatched grill marks, place them at a diagonal first. When you see that the edge where the cheese touches the grill is well browned, about 4 to 5 minutes, turn the piece over, keeping it at the same angle. For the next turn, flip the cheese over and place it at about a 90° angle from the first position. Continue on and grill the other side until the cheese is softened and heated through, about 8 minutes.
5. Place the grilled Halloumi on the plated arugula and drizzle the remaining vinaigrette over the cheese. This is complete as an appetizer, but for a main course, serve with a good, crusty loaf of bread.

WHITE WINE VINAIGRETTE

YIELD: 1 CUP

White wine vinegar	1/4 cup	60 mL
Dijon-style mustard	1/2 tsp	2.5 mL
Salt	as needed	as needed
Freshly ground black pepper	as needed	as needed
Extra-virgin olive oil	6 Tbsp	90 mL
Vegetable oil or safflower oil	6 Tbsp	90 mL
Minced herbs (optional)	1 to 1 1/2 Tbsp	15 to 22.5 mL

METHOD

1. Whisk together the vinegar, mustard, salt, and pepper.
2. Gradually whisk in the oils until they are incorporated and the vinaigrette is smooth and lightly thickened (as the vinaigrette sits, it will start to separate).
3. Season with minced herbs, if using, and additional salt and pepper, as needed.

MACARONI AND CHEESE WITH BACON

YIELD: 6 SIDE DISH PORTIONS

The popularity of this dish in the United States is undeniable. I've heard recently of the phenomenon of Lobster Mac 'n' Cheese in many American restaurants. I don't get it. Great macaroni and cheese is completely satisfying on its own. Adding lobster is what my mom would call "gilding the lily." The key is to use cheese that has enough flavor to compensate for the plain pasta. The top should be crunchy. There should be a creamy texture. And you should not eat the whole thing by yourself.

Smoked slab bacon	1 lb	454 g
Dried penne pasta	1 lb	454 g
Béchamel Sauce (page 139) (about 2 cups)	1 lb	454 g
Grafton 2-year aged Cheddar	1 lb	454 g
Coarsely ground black pepper	as needed	as needed
Butter as needed	as needed	

METHOD

1. Cut the bacon into lardons (1/4 by 1/4 by 1 in/6 mm by 6 mm by 3 cm). Cook over low to medium heat in a sauté pan until rendered and well browned, about 6 minutes. Drain and reserve the fat for another use.
2. Preheat the oven to 400°F/204°C.
3. Cook the pasta according to package directions until al dente; drain.
4. Place the béchamel in a large stainless steel bowl and grate the cheese into the sauce. Add the cooked pasta and bacon to the bowl and season with ground black pepper. Toss the ingredients until evenly coated.
5. Lightly butter a 2-qt/1.92-L oven-safe dish and pour in the macaroni mixture. Place in the oven and wait for it to be bubbling hot with a well-browned top.

Chef's Note: For a creamier version, increase the amount of béchamel sauce to 3 cups. Season the béchamel to taste with salt and pepper.

RAVIOLI WITH ZUCCHINI AND LEMON THYME

YIELD: 10 APPETIZER OR 6 MAIN COURSE PORTIONS

This is one of the loveliest, most delicate pasta dishes I have ever tasted. Its lightness and gentle, fragrant lemon scent make it a perfect first or second course in a meal where the main course is a white fish, such as bass or snapper. The dish comes from the Caterina de' Medici restaurant at The Culinary Institute of America, and should be attributed to chefs Dwayne LiPuma and Gianni Scappin. By the bye, the 00 flour specified below refers to the Italian practice of labeling flour according to how finely milled it is. "00" or *doppio zero* is the finest and is usually the choice for both pastas and pizza dough. It is readily available in specialty stores and from baker's supply houses.

RAVIOLI STUFFING

Olive oil	1 Tbsp	15 mL
Finely chopped shallot	2 Tbsp	30 mL
Zucchini, seeded and cut into brunoise (skin on)	2 cups	480 mL
Leeks, white and pale green parts only, washed and cut into brunoise	3/4 cup	180 mL
Parsley chiffonade	1 Tbsp	15 mL
Chopped mint	2 Tbsp	30 mL
Chopped lemon thyme (may substitute lemon verbena)	1 1/2 tsp	7.5 mL
Fresh goat cheese log	8 oz	227 g
Ricotta impastata	8 oz	227 g
Grated Parmigiano-Reggiano or Grana Padano	1 cup	240 mL
Eggs, beaten	2	2
Kosher salt	as needed	as needed
Freshly ground black pepper	as needed	as needed

FRESH PASTA DOUGH

00 flour	13 oz	369 g
Semolina durum flour	3 oz	85 g
Large eggs	4	4
Olive oil	2 Tbsp	30 mL
Salt	1/2 oz	14 g
Warm water	as needed	as needed

(Continues)

ASSEMBLY

Vegetable or chicken stock, homemade or low-sodium	2 cups	480 mL
Ravioli	60	60
Butter	4 oz	113 g
Small zucchini, split lengthwise, seeded, and cut into 1/4 in/6 mm crescents	1 lb	454 g
Grated Parmigiano-Reggiano or Grana Padano	1 cup	240 mL
Roughly chopped parsley	1/2 cup	120 mL
Salt	as needed	as needed
Ground black pepper	as needed	as needed

METHOD

1. For the stuffing: In a large sauté pan over low heat, add the oil and sweat the shallots until translucent, about 3 minutes. Add the zucchini and leeks and cook until just tender, about 3 more minutes. Remove from heat and stir in the herbs. Allow to cool to room temperature.

2. Combine the cheeses and the eggs in a large bowl. Gently mix the zucchini mixture into the 3 cheeses. Season the mixture with salt and pepper.

3. For the pasta dough: Add the flour to the bowl of an electric mixer fitted with a dough hook or a food processor with a dough blade. Mix the eggs, olive oil, salt, and water together and pour the mixture into the bowl. Start mixing on first speed or pulse in the food processor until combined. Mix the dough until it pulls away from the sides of the bowl and is smooth and elastic, about 5 minutes for the mixer or 2 to 3 minutes for the food processor. Remove the dough from the bowl and let it rest, covered in plastic wrap, for at least a half hour.

4. Roll the pasta dough into very thin (about #7 on a pasta machine) strips 5 in/13 cm wide. Cover the strips with a damp towel or plastic wrap until ready to stuff them. Do not lay the strips on top of each other unless they are well dusted with semolina flour.

5. Make the ravioli with one teaspoon of filling each. To make round ravioli, place the filling close enough to the bottom of the pasta strip that you can fold the top half over and cut with a 2-in/5-cm round cutter. Pick up each piece and gently squeeze the edges to seal them. For half-moon ravioli, the pasta strips can be narrower, still folded over and cut with a round cutter. Make sure to squeeze out any air bubbles while sealing them, otherwise the ravioli may burst while being boiled.

6. Bring 2 qt/1.92 L of water to a boil in a 3-qt/2.88-L saucepan. Add 1/4 cup salt and blanch the zucchini crescents, drain, and then shock in ice water. Drain and hold aside until needed.

7. Bring a large pot of water to a boil. Salt the water liberally and add the ravioli. Meanwhile, in a sauté pan, heat the vegetable stock over medium heat until steaming. Mount the butter into the stock and reduce to a sauce consistency, about 5 minutes. When the ravioli float to the top of the cooking water, after 4 to 5 minutes, drain with a colander or large strainer, reserving about 1 cup of the cooking water to thin the sauce with, if necessary. Add the blanched zucchini and ravioli to the sauté pan that the sauce is in. Stir the grated cheese and parsley into the sauce and adjust seasoning with salt and pepper if necessary.

8. Place ravioli into the serving bowl, and spoon the sauce over the ravioli.

MIDNIGHT MOON CHEESE SOUFFLÉ

YIELD: 4 APPETIZER OR 2 MAIN COURSE PORTIONS

When I was a kid and we had leftover ham after whatever holiday dinner, my mom would occasionally whip up a cheese soufflé to accompany it. Even though it wasn't the hardest thing to prepare, the light, fluffy side dish made the last slices of ham seem as special as the first had been. If my mom had been able to get Cypress Grove's Midnight Moon aged goat cheese back in those days, I'm pretty sure she would have used it.

Butter, plus soft butter as needed to coat soufflé dish	1/4 cup	60 mL
Grated Grana Padano	1/2 cup	120 mL
All-purpose flour	1/4 cup	60 mL
Whole milk	1 3/4 cups	420 mL
Salt	1/2 tsp	2.5 mL
Black pepper	1/4 tsp	1.25 mL
Grated Midnight Moon (about 8 oz/227 g)	2 cups	480 mL
Eggs, separated	4	4

METHOD

1. Preheat oven to 375°F/191°C. Lightly coat the bottom and sides of a 2-qt/1.92-L soufflé dish with butter. Dust the inside with the Grana Padano.
2. Melt the 1/4 cup/60 mL butter in a saucepan over medium heat. Add the flour and cook, stirring, until it doesn't smell raw, about 2 minutes. Whisk in the milk, stirring constantly to blend. Add the salt and pepper. Bring the mixture to a boil. Reduce the heat and simmer, stirring, until thickened, about 5 minutes. Add the grated cheese and stir until melted. Remove from heat. Beat the egg yolks lightly. Add some of the cheese sauce to the yolks to temper them, then whisk the yolks into the rest of the cheese sauce. Allow to cool a bit.
3. Beat the egg whites until stiff and smooth, about 4 minutes. Stir a spoonful of the whites into the cheese mixture to lighten it. With a rubber spatula, gently fold cheese mixture into remaining egg whites.
4. Spoon into the prepared soufflé dish and bake until browned on top and an inserted skewer comes out dry, 35 to 40 minutes. Serve immediately.

TARTIFLETTE AMERICAINE

YIELD: 6 SIDE DISH OR LUNCH PORTIONS

Dishes like this have a long history in European alpine regions, but the original *Tartiflette* comes from Savoy, and is only a few decades old. Rumor has it that the Reblochon A.O.C. trade group created the dish to increase sales of that cheese. In order to make it more American, this recipe uses ingredients from closer to home, especially the cheese and potatoes. As for the bacon, get the best apple wood smoked version available from your nearest smokehouse. The cheese that this recipe calls for is Eden from Sprout Creek Farms in Poughkeepsie, NY. It's a washed rind cheese that is a little stinky—around the same level as Reblochon. Feel free to use the rind in the recipe, or you can remove some of it to tone down the funk. If you can't find Eden near you, use any local washed rind cheese that tends toward the mild side and has a semi-soft texture. As a lunch, serve with an endive or watercress salad.

Rose Finn or any other Fingerling Potatoes	6 cups	1.44 L
Butter	2 Tbsp	30 mL
All-purpose flour	1/3 cup	80 mL
Whole milk	2 cups	480 mL
Salt	as needed	as needed
Freshly ground black pepper	as needed	as needed
Apple wood smoked bacon, cut into lardons (see page 145)	12 oz	340 g
Grated Sprout Creek Farms Eden	1 1/2 cups	360 mL
Parsley chiffonade	1 Tbsp	15 mL

METHOD

1. Wash the potatoes and cook them in boiling, well-salted water until just tender, about 10 minutes. Drain and let them cool until they can be handled, and cut them on a bias into slices 1/4 in/6 mm thick. Set aside.
2. Melt the butter in a medium saucepan and add the flour. Stir and cook the roux until it loses its raw smell, about 2 minutes. Whisk in the milk to distribute the roux and cook over medium heat until it thickens to a sauce consistency, 7 to 8 minutes. Season with salt and pepper and set aside.
3. Heat the oven to 450°F/232°C.

(Continues)

4. Cook the bacon lardons over medium-low heat in a medium sauté pan to allow them to render much of their fat and brown, about 8 minutes. Remove with a slotted spoon to a few layers of paper towels to drain.

5. In a large bowl, toss together the potatoes, bacon, half of the grated cheese, and enough of the béchamel to bind them. Add a few grinds of black pepper and check for salt, adding if necessary. Place the mixture in a buttered 2-qt/1.92-L gratin dish and top with the remaining béchamel and then cheese.

6. Bake until well browned on top and bubbling, about 20 minutes. Sprinkle with parsley and serve.

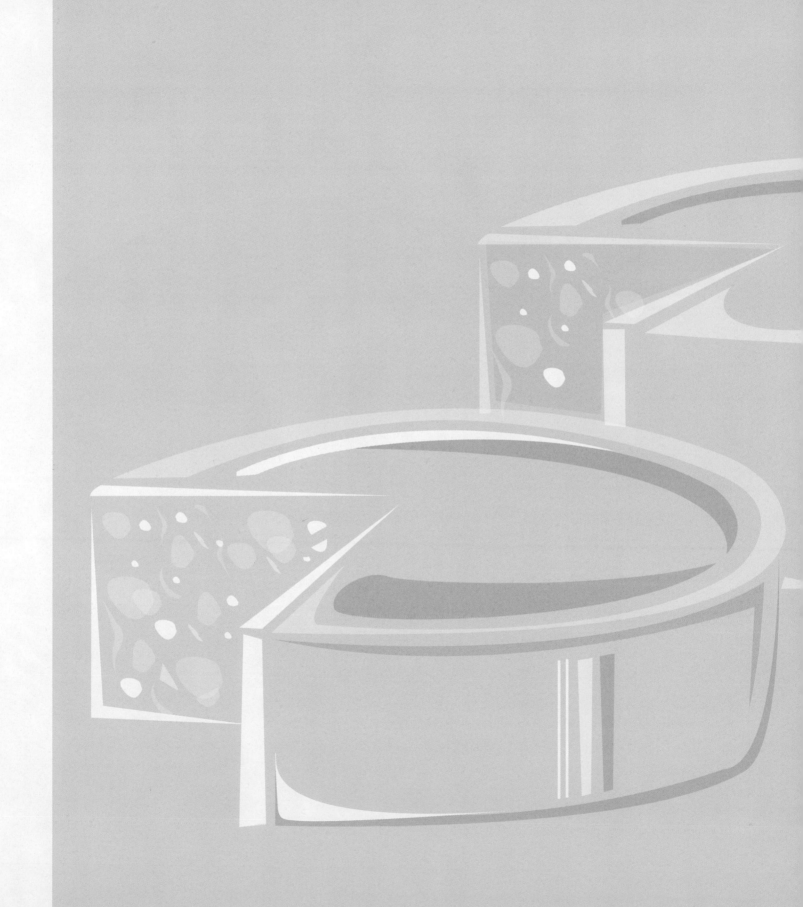

FONDUE

YIELD: 4 PORTIONS

Depending on when you were born, the fondue pot in your house either got a lot of use or sat in the closet. This dish is to blame for the bottle of Kirschwasser that lurks at the back of many liquor closets, and for the pangs of guilt whenever you see those long, color-coded forks. Well, it's time to pull out the Kirsch and grate some cheese, because tonight is fondue night!

Garlic clove	1	1
Dry white wine	1 2/3 cups	400 mL
Grated Gruyère	1 lb	454 g
Cornstarch	2 tsp	10 mL
Kirsch	1/4 cup	60 mL
Ground white pepper	as needed	as needed
Freshly grated nutmeg	as needed	as needed
Baguette, cut into 1-in/3-cm cubes	1	1
Apples, cored and cut into 1-in/3-mm cubes	2	2

METHOD

1. Cut the garlic clove in half and rub the inside of the fondue pot with the cut sides of the garlic. Turn the heat to medium under the pot.
2. Toss the grated cheese with the cornstarch and set aside for the moment.
3. Add the wine to the fondue pot, turn heat to medium-high, and bring to a simmer. Add the cheese, a handful at a time, waiting for the previous bit to have melted. Stir in a figure-eight pattern rather than in a circle to avoid roping.
4. When all the cheese has been incorporated, add the Kirsch, white pepper, and a few gratings of nutmeg.
5. Serve with the bread and apple cubes, keeping the fondue steaming, but not boiling.

Chef's Note: In case you didn't read the beginning of this chapter, two factors keep the cheese from seizing up in the pot. One is the saltiness of the Gruyère and the other is the acidity of the wine. So, if you sense that the cheese is getting too "ropy," you can save the day either with a splash of wine or a squeeze of lemon juice — don't add more salt because the cheese is salty enough.

GNOCCHI ALLA ROMANA

YIELD: 4 PORTIONS

During my discovery of true regional Italian food at Mark Strausman's Campagna Restaurant in New York City, these gnocchi were served as an appetizer with Fonduta, the Italian version of fondue. You can serve them as a starch with main courses, but then you should leave off the creamy cheese sauce and just bake them with a little grated Parmigiano on top.

This is as comforting as comfort food gets, and makes the perfect *secondo* (second course, usually starch or pasta) for a cold, blustery night. If you live in L.A., turn up the air conditioning.

Whole milk	3 cups	720 mL
Semolina flour (about 3/4 cup)	7 oz	198 g
Salt	1 tsp	5 mL
Butter, plus some melted as needed for brushing	2 Tbsp	30 mL
Grated Grana Padano or Parmigiano-Reggiano	1 cup	240 mL
Egg, beaten	1	1
Fonduta	2 cups	480 mL
Fresh white truffles *(optional)*	1/2 oz	14 g

METHOD

1. Heat the milk in a saucepan over medium heat until steaming. Whisk in the semolina and add the salt. Simmer over medium heat, stirring with a whisk or wooden spoon, until the mixture is thickened and pulling away from the sides of the pan, about 8 minutes.
2. Stir in half of the grated cheese and the beaten egg. Pour the mixture onto a buttered half sheet pan and spread out to about 1/2 in/1 cm thickness. Allow to cool.
3. Using a 3-in/8-cm round cutter or drinking glass, cut into 1/2-in/1-cm thick crescent moons.
4. Place the gnocchi in a buttered baking dish, either shingled (no fonduta) or with a little space around them. Brush with butter, top with the remaining cheese and bake in a 400°F/204°C oven until lightly browned, about 10 to 12 minutes.
5. Place the cooked gnocchi on individual serving plates and coat with the Fonduta, if using. If desired (and possible), shave fresh white truffle over the top just before serving.

FONDUTA

YIELD: 4 PORTIONS

This is the Italian version of fondue. It is used as a sauce or coating as well as the more traditional dipping medium in its home region of the Val d'Aosta, whence come the best versions of Fontina cheese.

Whole milk	1/2 cup	120 mL
Fontina, grated	8 oz	227 g
Heavy cream	1/2 cup	120 mL
Unsalted butter	1/4 cup	60 mL
Egg yolks, lightly beaten	4	4
Salt	as needed	as needed
Ground white pepper	as needed	as needed

METHOD

1. Place the milk, cheese, and cream in a bowl and allow to sit for at least 1 hour, refrigerated.
2. Heat the butter in a saucepan until melted. Whisk in the cheese/milk/cream mixture a bit at a time until it is completely incorporated and melted. Remove from heat, temper the egg yolks with a bit of the cheese, then add the egg yolks to the rest of the cheese. Adjust seasoning as needed.

GOUGÈRES

YIELD: 2 DOZEN PIECES

This is one of those little dishes you might not think is within your grasp. "Cheesy poofs? I'm not a baker!" Well, making these is almost more like cooking than baking. They are a perfect complement to cocktails and aperitifs, and are perfect finger food (no sticky sauce).

Water	1 cup	240 mL
Salt	1 tsp	5 mL
Unsalted butter	1/4 cup	60 mL
All-purpose flour	1 1/2 cups	360 mL
Eggs	3	3
Grated Grana Padano or other parmesan-style cheese	1 1/2 cups	360 mL
Grated Mimolette (aged at least 18 months) or another sharp cheese	1 cup	240 mL
Cayenne pepper	1/4 tsp	1.25 mL

METHOD

1. Preheat the oven to 450°F/232°C. Prepare a half sheet pan, either by greasing it, or using pan-release spray or a silicone mat.
2. Heat the water, salt, and butter in a 2- to 3-qt/1.92- to 2.88-L saucepan until it is just boiling and the butter is melted.
3. Add the flour all at once and stir over medium heat until the dough forms a ball, about 6 to 8 minutes.
4. With the heat still on, add the eggs one at a time, stirring forcefully to incorporate them before the next addition. It is done when the dough pulls away from the sides of the pan and its exterior is glossy.
5. Mix in 1 cup/240 mL of the Grana Padano, all of the Mimolette, and the cayenne.
6. Scoop the dough into a pastry bag with a 1/2-in/1-cm straight tip. Or, using a 1-oz/30-mL disher (ice cream scoop) sprayed with cooking spray, either pipe or scoop the dough onto the prepared sheet pan. There should be about 30 one-inch diameter gougères.
7. Sprinkle with the remaining grated cheese, and bake in the oven until golden brown, 12 to 15 minutes.

OPTIONS:

- You can use any number of cheeses for this, but they should be rather sharp for the flavor to be strong enough in the final product.
- Double their size (and cook at 400°F/204°C), and stuff with smoked chicken and apple salad, or whatever you want.
- Deep-fry them for only a minute or two at 350°F/177°C for a crisper, richer puff.

RACLETTE

YIELD: 6 PORTIONS

This is not so much a recipe as it is a method with some ingredients. Raclette is very popular in the northeastern part of France and French-speaking areas of Switzerland. The dish was created by cowherds who would take half a wheel of cheese and face the cut side toward their campfire. They would then scrape the melted cheese onto pieces of bread, hence the name Raclette—the French verb *racler* means "to scrape."

There are two ways to make this dish. The traditional method is to place half a wheel of Raclette (also the name of the cheese) in a rack under a heat lamp, then scrape the melted cheese onto the diners' plates. The more modern method uses a Raclette grill that provides each diner with a small pan that slips under the grill's heating unit.

Traditional accompaniments for both methods include boiled potatoes, gherkins, and pickled onions. More modern Raclette parties will also include various raw vegetables as well as cured and air-dried meats. The traditional beverage accompaniment is hot tea, as it is supposed to aid digestion. However, most modern Raclette lovers will serve a dry white wine from either Savoie or Valais. It's probably easier to find either a Pinot Blanc or Pinot Gris from Alsace, either of which will be fine.

Be forewarned that this is not an odor-free meal. In fact, some Raclette fans will leave a clove-studded orange on the dining table for a day after the meal to eliminate any unpleasant scent memories of the dish.

Small waxy potatoes such as Yukon Golds or Red Bliss	2 1/2 lbs	1.134 kg
Raclette	2 1/2 lbs	1.134 kg
Gherkins	1/2 cup	120 mL
Pickled onions	1/4 cup	60 mL

Assorted fresh, cut vegetables such as sweet peppers, tomatoes, mushrooms, and sweet onions or scallions

Assorted slices of cured or dried meats such as prosciutto, bresaola, and salami

METHOD

1. For either method, boil the potatoes (washed, but not peeled) in salted water until just tender. When done, drain and keep warm (wrapped in a tea towel, for instance).

2. When using a heat lamp: Place the cut side of the cheese facing the heat lamp and wait for the cheese to melt. Slice the boiled potatoes and place on individual plates. Scrape the cheese onto the potatoes and accompany with gherkins and pickled onions.

3. When using a Raclette grill: Because the top of the grill is usually a griddle, diners can cook vegetables to their liking, then put the vegetables in their individual pans, place a slice of cheese over and slide the pan under the heating element of the grill. When the cheese has melted, pour the contents of the pan over sliced boiled potatoes. Accompany with various pickles and sliced meats.

WARM MOZZARELLA APPETIZER

YIELD: 4 APPETIZER PORTIONS

I first saw this dish made by Paola Marracino of Paola's Restaurant on 84th Street (now 92nd & Madison Ave.) on Manhattan's Upper East Side. This appetizer's simplicity is outdone only by the pure luxury of the warm, soft cheese. You can garnish it with whatever is appropriate to the season, but a drizzle of pesto is perfect, maybe with a few olives scattered around. Even a few drops of extra-virgin olive oil and good balsamic vinegar with some basil chiffonade are enough to properly adorn this dish.

Whole milk	2 cups	480 mL
Salt	8 oz	227 g
Water, heated to 180°F/82°C	1 gal	3.84 L
Fresh cheese curd (whole milk preferred, but part-skim is okay), cut into 4 oz/113 g portions	1 lb	454 g

METHOD

1. Pour the milk into a shallow pan or dish large enough for the four pieces of cheese, and let it come to room temperature.
2. Add salt to the water and heat to 180°F/82°C.
3. Put the pieces of cheese curd in a shallow, flat heat-proof dish or pan. Pour half of the water over the curd and allow to sit for a minute or two. Pour off the water.
4. Add the remaining water to the pan and watch for signs of melting in the curd — the edges will look soft, and when pulled, the cheese will form a spiderweb shape easily.
5. Pour off the water again, and form each piece of curd into an egg shape by turning the cheese under itself. Pretend you're trying to make it into a sea urchin shape, rounded on top with its mouth underneath. As the "eggs" are formed, place them in lukewarm water for 2 minutes.
6. Place each piece of mozzarella on paper towels to dry off the bottom, then place on plates. Garnish with whatever you've chosen and serve while still warm.

Chef's Note: For bocconcini, follow the steps outlined in the photos on the following two pages.

(Continues)

FIGURE **6.1** Break the curds into small pieces and place in a large, shallow dish or pan

FIGURE **6.2** Carefully pour the hot water over the curds

FIGURE **6.3** Gently stir the water to facilitate the curds' melting

FIGURE **6.4** The curds should meld together into an elastic mass

FIGURE **6.5** When the mass is homogenous and stretchy, the cheese is ready to be shaped

FIGURE **6.6** Pull a piece off of the mass, and use your hands to stretch and mold the cheese into a ball. Drop the formed balls into ice water to firm

RISOTTO WITH TALEGGIO AND ARUGULA

YIELD: 6 APPETIZER OR 4 MAIN COURSE PORTIONS

Risotto scares a lot of people. Having worked in a number of Italian restaurants, I have seen (and eaten) a fair amount, and know that it is hard to mess up if you bear a few things in mind.

1. You *must* use short-grain rice, but it needn't be Arborio. It can be Carnaroli rice, which is actually preferred by many because of its larger kernel size and ability to hold shape a bit better than Arborio. In a pinch, any short-grain rice will do, because this type tends to have a higher starch content that will add to the creaminess of the risotto. The more compact shape also aids in the retention of the kernels' integrity.

2. Don't skimp on the amount of cooking liquid. Tastes vary regarding the consistency of the final product, but nearly all risotto cognoscenti agree that the dish should be able to flow — some refer to "all'onda," or on a wave, as the perfect consistency. That is, when you shake the pan, waves should form. This texture might be too loose for some, but the rice should never be allowed to seize up into a clump of goo.

3. The stirring needs to be often, but not necessarily continual. Adding a ladleful of liquid at a time while stirring constantly is unnecessary, although it will result in a slightly creamier consistency. At the very least, the stock should be added four times during the cooking, allowing it to be absorbed each time. The fourth time is the most critical with regard to doneness and final consistency. The rice should be *just slightly* underdone when the pan is being removed from the flame for the last time.

This specific risotto is luxurious, with the creamy richness of cheese and butter, but lightened somewhat by the peppery arugula. Americans don't *cook* with arugula often enough, usually just throwing it into salads. In this case, it awakens the risotto from its dairy-induced torpor. Use this dish as a *secondo* in a traditional Italian three-course meal. It would best precede a somewhat light main course, such as a roast chicken with lemon and fresh herbs. If using store-bought stock, cut its strength by half with water.

Chicken or vegetable stock	1 1/2 qt	1.44 L
Butter	2 Tbsp	30 mL
Olive oil	1 Tbsp	15 mL
Large shallots, minced	2	2
Short-grain rice (preferably Carnaroli or Arborio)	1 1/2 cups	360 mL
Dry white wine (no residual sugar)	1/2 cup	120 mL
Salt	as needed	as needed
Freshly ground black pepper	as needed	as needed
Taleggio, cut in 1/2 in/1 cm cubes (rind on, unless you want less funk)	5 oz	142 g
Grated Parmigiano-Reggiano	1/2 cup	120 mL
Arugula, washed and chopped into 1 in/3 cm pieces	1 1/2 cups	360 mL

METHOD

1. Heat the stock in a saucepan until boiling, then turn the heat down to keep it warm. Place on a burner near where you will be making the risotto.

2. Heat a 3 1/2-qt/3.36-L saucepan over medium heat. Add the butter and olive oil and wait for the butter to foam and subside. Add the chopped shallots and cook, stirring, until translucent, about 2 minutes. Add the rice and stir over medium heat until the kernels look a little translucent, about 2 more minutes. Turn down the heat if the shallots are browning.

3. Add the wine, and allow it to evaporate. Add a healthy pinch of salt and a couple of grinds of black pepper.

4. Using a 6-oz/180-mL ladle, add the stock one ladle at a time. Stir often, and wait for the stock to be absorbed each time. Essentially, the rice should neither be floating in stock, nor be a near-solid mass.

5. As you approach the 20-minute mark, taste a few kernels to check for doneness. When they are still slightly *al dente*, lower the heat and stir in the Taleggio, Parmigiano, and chopped arugula. Allow to come back up to temperature, check for consistency, and add a bit more stock if necessary. Remove from the heat.

6. Serve immediately on heated plates or pasta bowls. If you like, garnish with small slices of Taleggio and arugula chiffonade.

FRESH HERBED CHEESE SPREAD

YIELD: ABOUT 1 LB/454 G OF SOFT CHEESE SPREAD

Real fromage fort is not for the weak. Traditionally made in France, it means "strong cheese," and is ... as is this recipe ... a use for leftover hunks of cheese. The real deal is made by taking some chunks of leftover cheese and putting them into a vegetable broth or milk, then allowing it to ferment in the basement for a week or two; the longer the stronger.

The spread from this recipe will not scare small children, and can be used on crackers or slices of bread, and even browned under the broiler. Put it on a burger, use it in a chicken sandwich ... eat it with a spoon, whatever makes you happy.

The cheeses and fresh herbs used are completely up to you, although you will want to match the power of the herbs with that of the cheese. Parsley and chives will be fine for all, whereas fresh rosemary and oregano should be reserved for stronger partners. Pepper will almost always be welcome, but be careful with salt depending on the saltiness of the cheeses used.

Garlic clove	1	1
Leftover cheeses (cheddar, Swiss-types, Brie, anything)	1 lb (total)	454 g (total)
Dry white wine	1/2 cup	120 mL
Fresh herbs	1/4 cup	60 mL
Salt	as needed	as needed
Freshly ground black pepper	as needed	as needed

METHOD

1. Turn on the food processor and drop in the garlic clove, covering the opening with your hand to keep it from escaping. The clove will bounce around, gradually becoming finely minced.
2. Add the cheeses, cubed if soft or semi-hard, grated if hard. If used, the flavor of blue cheese will dominate, so be aware.
3. Add the wine and herbs and pulse the mixture until smooth. Adjust the seasoning, if necessary, and use immediately or store in small containers for up to a week.

LEEK TART WITH OSSAU IRATY

YIELD: 6 TO 8 APPETIZER OR 4 TO 6 MAIN COURSE PORTIONS

If you like Quiche Lorraine, but are looking for something with a bit more subtlety, this sublime egg-custard tart might be the one. Although bacon is magical, it is also a strong flavor, perhaps too much to precede a delicate main course. A little switcheroo happens here, though. Most Flamiche recipes that include cheese call for Gruyère, which can be a bit strong for the gentle eggs and sweet leeks. Instead, this recipe calls for Ossau Iraty, a delicious Brebis (mountain sheep's milk cheese) from the French Pyrénées. Serve the tart with a lightly dressed salad of Mâche or other tender greens, either as an appetizer or simple main course.

Savory tart dough, such as Pâte Brisée (page 170)	12 oz	340 g
Leeks	1 lb 8 oz	680 g
Unsalted butter	2 Tbsp	30 mL
Whole milk	1 cup	240 mL
Heavy cream	1 cup	240 mL
Large eggs	5	5
Salt	1/2 tsp	2.5 mL
Freshly ground black pepper	1/4 tsp	1.25 mL
Grated Ossau Iraty	1 cup	240 mL

METHOD

1. Preheat the oven to 325°F/163°C. Roll out the pastry to 1/8-in/3-mm thick and line a 12-in/ 30-cm tart pan with it. Line the pan with parchment and fill with beans or pie weights. Blind bake until pale blonde in color and its surface looks dry.

2. Trim and wash the leeks, discarding the dark green leaves. Cut the white and pale green areas into a 1/4 to 1/2 in/6 mm to 1 cm dice (about 2 cups/480 mL raw).

3. Sauté the leeks in the butter in a sauté pan over medium heat until softened, about 5 minutes. Allow to cool to room temperature.

3. Heat the milk and cream in a small saucepan over medium-low heat until steaming. Remove from the heat.

4. Whisk the eggs until well blended but not too frothy. Whisk in the milk/cream mixture, slowly at first to avoid curdling the eggs. Season the mixture with salt and pepper.

5. Place the leeks and grated cheese in the bottom of the tart shell. Pour in the warm custard mixture, and place the tart on a sheet pan or cookie sheet.

6. Carefully place the tart in the oven. Starting after 30 minutes, watch the flamiche carefully. When you jiggle the tart, its center should still move a little. In fact, when a 2-in/5-cm circle in the middle is still wiggly, pull the tart out of the oven and allow carryover cooking to finish the job. Allow it to cool 5 to 10 minutes before serving.

PÂTE BRISÉE

YIELD: 12 OZ

Cold unsalted butter, cubed	4 oz	113 g
All-purpose flour	1 1/3 cups	320 mL
Egg yolk	1	1
Ice-cold water	3 Tbsp	45 mL

METHOD

1. Rub the butter into the flour until a light, sandy texture is achieved; there should be small pieces of butter within the mixture. These will give the pastry a flaky texture when it's cooked.
2. Mix the egg yolk with the water and pour it over the flour mixture. With an open hand, work the moisture into the mixture until all of it becomes a little sticky, and then simply push it together to form a fairly firm, but not dry ball.
3. Rest the dough in the refrigerator for at least 1 hour before using.

SPIEDINI ALLA ROMANA

YIELD: 6 APPETIZER PORTIONS

This caloric splurge of an appetizer seems to be the offspring of a fried mozzarella stick and a grilled cheese sandwich. The sauce provides a sharpness that brightens the bland richness of fried bread and cheese, if not lowering the fat quotient. The dish is a favorite at many Italian-American restaurants in the New York City area and is worthy of export to your region.

Italian bread, medium-sized loaf	1	1
Fresh mozzarella	1 lb	454 g
Canola or vegetable oil, for frying	as needed	as needed
Eggs	3	3
Salt	as needed	as needed
All-purpose flour	1 cup	240 mL

SAUCE

Extra-virgin olive oil	1/4 cup	60 mL
Garlic cloves, smashed	3	3
Anchovy filets, roughly chopped	6	6
Capers, rinsed	2 Tbsp	30 mL
Lemon juice	2 Tbsp	30 mL
Dry white wine	1/4 cup	60 mL
Chopped flat-leaf parsley	3 Tbsp	45 mL
Freshly ground black pepper	as needed	as needed

METHOD

1. Cut the crust off the loaf of bread to form a large crustless rectangle. Slice into 18 half-inch/1-cm thick slices, about 2 by 3 in/5 by 8 cm each.
2. Slice the mozzarella 1/4 in/6 mm thick, or thin enough to get 12 slices that are just smaller than the bread slices.

(Continues)

3. Warm the oven to 200°F/93°C, and put a sheet pan with paper towels or a rack inside.

4. Layer three slices of bread with two slices of cheese to make six double-decker cheese sandwiches and push two 5-in/13-cm skewers through each one.

5. Add the oil to a pan large enough to fry three sandwiches at a time, to a depth of about 1 1/2 in/4 cm. Heat the oil to 350°F/177°C.

6. Whisk the eggs, adding a little water to thin them a bit. Add a pinch of salt.

7. Right before frying, coat each sandwich lightly with flour, then roll through the egg mixture, to coat but not to soak.

8. Fry the sandwiches, maintaining a 350°F/177°C oil temperature, until golden brown on all sides, about 5 minutes per side. Drain on paper towels or rack in the warm oven.

9. For the sauce: In another pan, heat the olive oil over medium-high heat and add the garlic. When the garlic is lightly browned, about 3 minutes, add the anchovies. As the anchovies break up a bit, add the capers and let them sizzle and dry out a bit.

10. Add the lemon juice and wine, and allow to reduce until slightly thickened. Add the parsley and a few grinds of black pepper, and remove from the heat.

11. Serve the Spiedini either on a platter or plated individually, with the sauce spooned over at the last minute.

ROQUEFORT AND WALNUT PITHIVIER

YIELD: 6 TO 8 APPETIZER PORTIONS

The classic Pithivier is a puff pastry-enclosed tart with a sweet almond filling. This cheese-based version is a simple and extendable appetizer, especially when served with a small green salad. To dress it up even a bit more, add some sliced fresh pears to top the salad to complement the blue cheese and nuts inside the Pithivier.

Roquefort, broken into 1-in/3-cm chunks	3/4 cup	180 mL
Roughly chopped, toasted walnuts	1/2 cup	120 mL
Fresh bread crumbs	1 cup	240 mL
Salt	as needed	as needed
Freshly ground black pepper	as needed	as needed
Eggs	3	3
12-in/30-cm puff pastry rounds, 1/4 in/0.5 cm thick	2	2
Egg wash	1/4 cup	60 mL

METHOD

1. Preheat oven to 350°F/177°C.
2. In a stand mixer, cream together the Roquefort, walnuts, and bread crumbs with a mixing paddle and adjust seasoning, as needed. There should be enough salt because of the cheese, but you may want to add some black pepper. Stir in the eggs.
3. Place a puff pastry round on parchment paper on a half-sheet pan or baking sheet. Mound the filling in the center, leaving a 1 1/2- to 2-in/4- to 5-cm border. Brush the border with water, milk, or egg wash and place the other round on top. To seal, either crimp the edges with the back of a fork or create a decorative scalloped edge. You may also want to cut a simple floral spiral design on top which is traditional.
4. Place the Pithivier in the oven, and leave door closed for at least the first 15 to 20 minutes so the pastry will puff. Cook until Pithivier is golden brown all over, turning it during cooking to achieve even browning, about 30 minutes. Allow to cool for 5 to 8 minutes before cutting with a sharp serrated knife.

Chef's Note: As with a classic Pithivier, the texture of the interior is a bit dry by design. Consider serving it with a green salad as an appetizer, or with a creamy cheese sauce such as the Fonduta on page 157.

GOAT CHEESE AND PECAN NAPOLEON

YIELD: 4 APPETIZER PORTIONS

This is a light, elegant appetizer that can be easily increased to serve more people. It is best to assemble the layers as close to service time as possible to keep them from getting soggy, but they can still hold well for at least an hour or so. The napoleon is inspired by a recipe from Mark Erickson, CMC and Vice President and Dean of Culinary Education at the CIA, and offers a range of soft, crunchy, and crisp textures along with elegant flavor profiles.

Puff pastry sheet (12 by 18 in/30 by 46 cm)	1	1
Hazelnut oil, or as needed	2 Tbsp	30 mL
Hazelnut oil	4 oz	113 g
Whole hazelnuts, toasted	1 cup	240 mL
Sliced chives	1/2 cup	120 mL
Cayenne pepper	pinch	pinch
Salt	as needed	as needed
Finely ground black pepper	as needed	as needed
Heavy cream	1 cup	240 mL
Powdered gelatin	1 Tbsp	15 mL
Fresh goat cheese	12 oz	340 g
Eggs, separated	6	6
Dry white wine	1/2 cup	120 mL

METHOD

1. Preheat the oven to 350°F/177°C.
2. Place the sheet of puff pastry on a half sheet pan lined with parchment paper. Brush the pastry with hazelnut oil, top with another sheet of parchment and then another half sheet pan. This will keep the pastry flat while still allowing flakiness to form. Bake until golden brown, turning the pan around as necessary to cook evenly, about 20 minutes. Remove from the oven and set aside in a warm place.
3. Cut the pastry into twelve 3- by 6-in/8- by 15-cm rectangles, with three pieces for each Napoleon.
4. Chop the toasted hazelnuts somewhat coarsely, and toss with 1 oz/30 mL of hazelnut oil, chives, and cayenne. Season the mixture with salt and pepper.

(Continues)

5. Heat the heavy cream in a small saucepan over medium-low heat until warm, and sprinkle the gelatin evenly over the surface. When the gelatin is thoroughly moistened, whisk it in and heat until it melts. Allow it to cool to room temperature.

6. In a large stainless steel bowl, mix the cream mixture into the goat cheese until smooth.

7. Make a sabayon with the 6 yolks and white wine by whisking them together vigorously over a hot water bath (or in a double boiler) until they are pale lemon yellow and hold a soft peak. Set aside. Whip the 6 whites into meringue with stiff peaks, fold into the sabayon, and then fold both into the cheese and cream mixture. Adjust seasoning as needed.

8. Allow the mixture to cool slightly, at which point it will begin to set up. Transfer the mousse to a pastry bag fitted with a 1/2 in/1 cm straight tip.

9. Pipe a half-inch layer of mousse onto 8 of the rectangles and stack 2 rectangles to form the beginnings of 4 napoleons. Place a third piece on top of each napoleon and garnish each napoleon with 2 tablespoons of the hazelnut mixture.

HOMEMADE RICOTTA

YIELD: 1 LB/454 G

This, for many, is the first step into the world of cheesemaking. It really could not be easier and yields a wonderfully fresh cheese with no additives or preservatives. It also allows you to control how rich the final product will be, because you can use skim or low-fat milk instead of whole milk. If you want it to be richer, you can even add a cup of heavy cream. This is something you might want to do if you'll be using the cheese for desserts such as cannoli. Most people are happy with leaner versions though, and the original versions of this cheese are made from whey. In fact, ricotta (which means "re-cooked" in Italian) is a natural companion to mozzarella and provolone production, utilizing the whey from the making of either to yield some lovely fresh curds. Omit the salt if using the ricotta for desserts.

Whole milk	1 gal	3.84 L
Lemon juice or white vinegar	1/3 cup	80 mL
Salt	1 tsp	5 mL

METHOD

1. Heat the milk, lemon juice/vinegar, and salt to 185°F/85°C, stirring often to prevent scorching. Skim away the foamy film as it rises to the surface.
2. When the milk reaches 185°F/85°C, turn off the heat and allow the milk to set for 10 minutes.
3. Pour the curd into a colander lined with damp cheesecloth or a cheesecloth bag set over a bowl.
   Refrigerate for at least 1 hour and up to 3 hours to drain. The longer it drains, the drier and more crumbly the final product.
4. Serve immediately or transfer to a storage container, cover, and refrigerate for up to 1 week.

(Continues)

FIGURE **6.7** As you heat and stir the milk mixture, curds will form

FIGURE **6.8** Pour the mixture through a sieve lined with cheese cloth

FIGURE **6.9** Hang the cheesecloth to allow the whey to drain

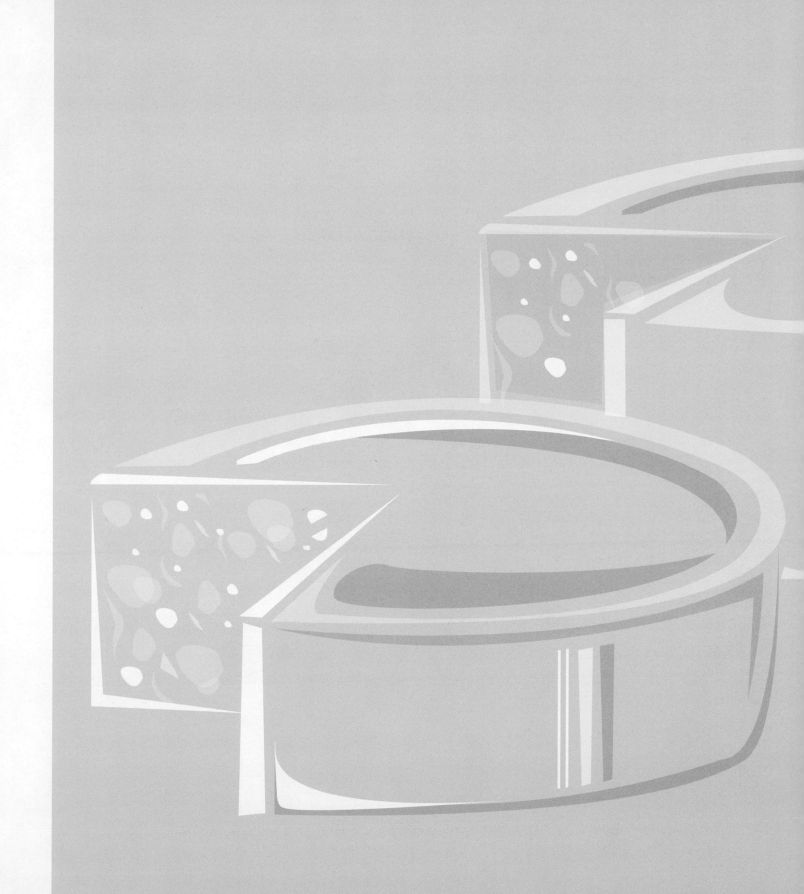

HERB-MARINATED YOGURT CHEESE

YIELD: 8 APPETIZER PORTIONS

This is a versatile preparation that can be used as a spread for crackers or bruschetta. It can also be molded in a ramekin and turned out onto a composed plate that includes a combination of raw or grilled vegetables such as fennel, radicchio, artichokes, and olives; all dressed with olive oil and sprinkled with fennel pollen.

Plain yogurt (whole, low fat, or fat free)	2 lb	907 g
Salt	1 tsp	5 mL
Ground black pepper	1 tsp	5 mL
Chopped oregano	2 tsp	10 mL
Chopped thyme	1 tsp	5 mL
Red chile flakes	1/2 tsp	2.5 mL
Bay leaf	1	1
Extra-virgin olive oil	1 cup	240 mL

METHOD

1. Mix the yogurt, salt, and pepper and let drain, refrigerated, for 3 days in a cheesecloth-lined colander or a cheesecloth or muslin bag set over a bowl. There must be space underneath the sack to allow the whey to drain.
2. Divide the cheese into 2 oz/57 g portions and place on parchment-lined trays. Allow to drain and dry on a rack uncovered overnight, refrigerated.
3. Combine the remaining ingredients to make marinade. Add the cheese, and marinate 12 to 24 hours before serving.

(Continues)

FIGURE **6.10** Pour the yogurt into a sieve lined with cheesecloth

FIGURE **6.11** Hang the cheesecloth and allow the yogurt to drain

FIGURE **6.12** After draining, divide into individual portions to marinate

BELGIAN ENDIVE AU GRATIN

YIELD: 4 APPETIZER OR 8 SIDE DISH PORTIONS

It is a shame that, as with arugula, Belgian Endive is rarely cooked in the United States. Although its slight bitterness when raw can be off-putting to some, that same taste becomes part of a more complex set of flavors when the pale, beautiful vegetable is cooked — especially browned. While the preparation here is vegetarian, a popular variation is to wrap or cover the cooked endive with a piece of cured ham before coating with the cheese sauce and baking. Both are delicious, but the version without the ham allows the cheese and vegetable to dance as partners without anyone cutting in.

Butter	1 1/2 Tbsp	22.5 mL
All-purpose flour	1 1/2 Tbsp	22.5 mL
Whole milk	1 cup	240 mL
Grated Beauvoorde (Parano may be substituted)	1 cup	240 mL
Belgian endive heads	4	4
Water	as needed	as needed
Olive oil	1 Tbsp	15 mL
Salt, plus as needed	1/2 tsp	2.5 mL
Black pepper	as needed	as needed
Grated Parmigiano-Reggiano (or other Parmesan-style cheese)	1/4 cup	60 mL

METHOD

1. Heat oven to 400°F/204°C.
2. Melt the butter in a small saucepan, and add the flour. Cook until it loses its raw smell, about 2 minutes. Add the milk, whisking to prevent lumps. Simmer over low heat until thickened, about 8 to 10 minutes, and stir in 3/4 cup/180 mL of the Beauvoorde cheese. When melted thoroughly, adjust seasoning with salt and pepper.

(Continues)

3. Trim the bottoms off the endive if browned or dry, then cut in half lengthwise.

4. In a sauté pan large enough to accommodate all 8 pieces, add enough water to come to a depth of 1/2 in/1 cm, and the olive oil. Add salt and pepper. Bring to a simmer and add the endive pieces, cut-side down.

5. Cook, covered, until endive is almost tender or has slight resistance to a paring knife, about 8 minutes. Remove the cover, and raise the heat to boil off the water. Over medium-high heat, allow the cut sides to brown, then turn over and brown slightly. Arrange the endive cut-side up in a roasting dish just big enough to hold them all.

6. Pour the sauce over the endive pieces and sprinkle the remaining cheeses over the top. Bake in the oven, uncovered, until browned on top and the sauce is bubbling lightly, about 20 to 30 minutes.

7. Serve 2 pieces as an appetizer, or in a dish on the table as a side.

GRILLED TREVIGIANO WITH SMOKED SCAMORZA

YIELD: 4 TO 8 APPETIZER PORTIONS

I was first introduced to this dish while working for Mark Strausman at Campagna Restaurant in Manhattan. It was largely from Mark that I learned how incredibly thrifty Italians can be regarding the number of ingredients in a dish, while still creating astonishing results. This dish does exactly that, yielding a range of flavors, textures, and colors, using only two main ingredients.

Trevigiano or Treviso (substitute Radicchio if not available)	2 large or 4 small heads	2 large or 4 small heads
Smoked Scamorza (substitute smoked mozzarella if not available)	8 oz	227 g
Extra-virgin olive oil	as needed	as needed
Salt	as needed	as needed
Freshly ground black pepper	as needed	as needed

METHOD

1. Preheat the grill and the broiler.
2. Remove the outer leaves of Trevigiano if wilted. Cut small heads in half and larger heads in quarters. Leave the stem intact to hold pieces together while grilling. Drizzle all sides sparsely with oil and season with salt and pepper.
3. Slice Scamorza lengthwise into 1/4-in/6-mm thick slices.
4. Grill Trevigiano pieces until the edges are slightly burnt, and the inner leaves begin to look tender, 8 to 10 minutes. Remove from grill and put on a sizzle platter or broiler pan, cut side facing up.
5. Arrange the cheese slices over the Trevigiano pieces. The cheese does not need to completely cover the Trevigiano. Place under the broiler until cheese is melted and lightly browned on top, 4 to 5 minutes.
6. Serve as is, or put a few drops of balsamic vinegar and good olive oil on the plate as a functional garnish.

PANEER PARATHA

YIELD: 20 PIECES

DOUGH

Whole wheat flour	12 oz	340 g
Bread flour	4 oz	113 g
Water	10 1/2 oz	298 g
Clarified butter	1 1/2 oz plus as needed	43 g plus as needed
Salt	1/2 oz	14 g

STUFFING

Paneer cheese, crumbled	1 lb 14 oz	850 g
Ground turmeric	1/4 tsp	1.25 mL
Minced Thai Bird red chilies	1 tsp	5 mL
Finely chopped cilantro	4 tsp	20 mL
Salt	4 tsp	20 mL
Minced red onion	6 Tbsp	

METHOD

1. For the dough: Combine all of the ingredients and mix together on low speed until the dough comes together in a homogenous mass, about 6 minutes.
2. Cover the dough and rest it for 30 minutes.
3. Scale the dough into 1 1/3-oz/38-g pieces. Shape the dough pieces into balls and keep them covered with a moist towel and plastic wrap. Allow the shaped dough to rest for 15 minutes. While the dough is resting, combine all of the ingredients for the cheese stuffing and mix thoroughly.
4. One at a time, roll the dough into a 5-in/12.7-cm circle. Place 1 1/2-oz/43-g of the cheese mixture into the center of the dough, and gather the edges around the cheese. Pinch the dough together, and turn it over. Roll the dough into a 6-in/15.25-cm circle. Repeat with the remaining balls of dough.
5. Heat a small sauté pan or skillet over medium-high heat. Cook the flatbread over dry heat until browned on one side and puffed slightly, about 2 minutes. Flip the bread over and cook until it is golden brown on the second side, about 1 1/2 minutes. Remove the bread from the skillet, and brush with clarified butter. Serve immediately.

WHAT'S WITH THIS CHEESE?

It is rare that you will eat cheese without accompaniments. You might at the cheese store, when the cheesemonger reaches across the counter to offer you a morsel, but usually cheese will be served with something else, either on the plate with it or in a glass alongside. First let's cover cheese-friendly beverages, and then move on to potential plate mates.

WASHING IT DOWN

Most Americans believe that wine and cheese are perfect for each other. There could be nothing better . . . it's a match made in heaven. I hate to put a crimp in your plans for a wine and cheese extravaganza, but wine doesn't always play well with cheese. In fact, red wine (the assumed best pal of cheese) tends to be less accommodating with cheese than many whites and rosés. This is not to say that your party will be a bust . . . no, indeed there are ways to ensure that the combinations you choose will work well. But, you can't just pull out a bottle (or jug) of something red to go with all of the fine cheeses that you brought home from the store.

Now, there are some very knowledgeable and talented wine and food professionals who recommend specific wines for specific cheeses. I can only imagine that they spent hundreds of hours trying different combinations to see which ones work well. This is impressive work, but it won't help you when you're at the wine or cheese shop, trying to figure out what to serve at your party that night. So, below you will find some guiding principles rather than specifics.

First of all, what *is* a good combination? The best pairing of any two ingredients is when their flavors enhance each other to the point that it almost seems like a third

WEIGHT CONCERNS

What is body? It's the weight or richness of food or beverage in your mouth. In other words, water is light-bodied and cream is full-bodied. Although not talked about by many wine professionals, the body of a wine is as important to the matching process as are the flavors and acidity. Ideally, the body of the beverage and food should be similar — that is, a big fat Chardonnay from Napa will blow away a fresh little goat cheese, and the opposite will occur when you put a light, refreshing Sancerre in the ring with some Roquefort. Switch the pairings, though, and you have a match. The body of food is usually related to its fat content or richness. With wine and other alcoholic beverages there are two determining factors, sugar and alcohol. Sugar adds viscosity to beverages just as it does to syrup, so sweet wines will tend to feel heavier on the palate. In dry wines, though, there tends to be more body as the alcohol percentage increases. So a dry wine with 10 to 11 percent alcohol content will be relatively light whereas a 14.7 percent Syrah from California or Australia (Shiraz down under) will have a fuller body, feeling thicker on the palate. Luckily, it's pretty easy to figure out what the body of the wine will be largely because of its provenance. Wines from colder regions tend to be lower in alcohol because the grapes don't get as ripe. Less sugar, lower alcohol, lighter body. Conversely, wines from warmer regions will tend to be fuller bodied. If you have no idea where the wine is from, look at the alcohol percentage on its label — it's required by law in the United States. Oh, and how will you know if it's a sweet wine? If there's no clue in its name or on the label, ask!

Not-so-hot pairings can still be okay in that the wine or beer will wash down the food in an innocuous way. Bad combinations, though, make you want to wipe your tongue off. They can happen, and they're not fun. Rather than get caught up in why bad pairings can happen (and frankly, sometimes they just do, despite thoughtful choices), there are a few general rules that apply specifically to cheese/beverage pairing, but are largely based on principles for all foods.

set of flavors emerges. My wife calls this "a direct hit," and it is an always-welcomed happenstance — and happenstance it is, because although good pairing is not that difficult, *perfect* pairings require some luck because of the many tiny variables that are hard to predict or keep track of. So, a good pairing is when the flavors complement each other, the acidity or bitterness in the wine or beer can help to balance, or mitigate the richness of the food, and the body is similar in each.

GROWS TOGETHER, GOES TOGETHER

There is a scientific side to this axiom, but the most useful part of it lies in the long experience (sometimes centuries) that people have had eating and drinking traditional foods and local beverages. It's the reason that rosé from Provence is so darned good with Bouillabaisse, that Brunello di Montalcino rocks with wild boar sauce on pappardelle — and why beer is just about the only choice for Cheddar. Traditional combinations work because the combinations that didn't work did not become traditions! That said, those of us in the New World do not have legacy to rely upon. We do not have the same conditions or traditions that exist in older cultures . . . but we can draw upon them. In that there are very few "new" things in the food world, almost every New World cheese has an Old World counterpart somewhere, and that is where you should look for the grows together, goes together pairing. Extra-sharp New York State Cheddar would be pretty tasty with a Hurricane Kitty IPA from Keegan Ales in Kingston, NY, and this pairing mirrors that of a farmhouse cheddar from England with a *true* IPA. So, when trying to find something to drink with a New World cheese, find a similar type of cheese from the Old World, and find out what is its usual counterpart.

SWEETER IS SAFER

If you remember from the cheesemaking chapter, virtually every cheese has salt added to it. The amount of, and when the salt is added are variables that largely control how salty the final product is. But certainly, virtually every cheese has salt in it. That said, one of the most dependable pairing strategies is to match sweet with salty. Peanut butter and jelly, chocolate-covered pretzels, brown sugar-glazed ham — there are many more examples.

This is why I often recommend a dessert wine be served with cheese. Because the cheese course is traditionally served after the main course and before (or sometimes in place of) dessert, it's the perfect time for a little sweet wine. In fact, most of the famous blue cheeses have classic dessert wine counterparts. Roquefort is often paired with Sauternes (from nearby Bordeaux), and Stilton has a willing and able partner in a glass of vintage Port. Having tried these combinations more than once, I know that there are few better in the world of wine and cheese. If you like, mix in "grows together, goes together" and find a sweet beverage, alcoholic or not, from the region whence the cheese came. One favorite for an aged Mimolette from Normandy is a hard cider. Salty, sweet, and from the same region. It had better work!

WHITER MEANS LIGHTER

I learned this phrase from Laura Werlin, author of several excellent cheese books. The fact behind the driving concept here is that whiter cheeses tend to be younger. Younger cheeses are less intense and lighter in body than their aged counterparts, and so a lighter-bodied wine will complement their youth. As cheeses age and develop a fuller body, partly because of water evaporation, the body of the accompanying wine should increase alongside. Thus, a brand-new bright white Crottin de Chavignol would be great with a crisp Sancerre. Once that little cheese has gotten waxy and has taken on an ivory color, perhaps a bigger Pouilly-Fumé or even a Savennières would have more heft, and would be better with the more intense cheese.

THE FUNK FACTOR

Stinky is as stinky does. The washed-rind cheeses are particularly hard to match because of their inherent power. They can lay to waste many wines that are fine for other cheeses, and need a firm hand to keep 'em in line. So, you might now know what funky cheeses are like, but how does funk translate to beverages? Well, earthiness, like that in red Burgundy, has been known to pair well with Epoisses. The wild aromas of a Vendange Tardive (i.e., late-harvest) Gewürztraminer from Alsace can be just the thing for a *real* Munster, and a *Gueuze* beer from Belgium could tame the wild Limburger. But just as the stinky cheeses have individual (and strong) personalities, so do the funkier beverages. Tasting, looking, asking, and listening is how you will find them, either at the beer store, wine shop, or cheese shop. For instance, when buying a stinky cheese that you've never had before, ask the counter person if there is a good beverage match for it. And don't forget grows together, goes together . . . it can often lead you in the right direction.

DON'T FORGET THE BEER!

Beer has already been mentioned as a fitting partner for cheese. There are two factors that support this; one being that many cheesemaking regions are also far enough north that beer is more common than wine anyway and, grows together . . . you got it. The other is that beer is a very good partner for a wide range of food — and sometimes the best choice. Although wine has better potential for perfect pairings, the chances are still rather slim that it will happen. Beer is more gregarious, and will make a broad range of cheeses taste good, if not great. This is because beer has two major flavor components; sweetness in varying degrees comes from the malt, while bitterness is from hops. Now consider the amount of alcohol and you have an idea whether the beer has light or full body. There are obviously complex aromas at work here, but the basics of sweet, bitter, and body are the framework. Sweetness is great with the saltiness of the cheese, bitterness helps balance the richness, and the body should keep up with that of the cheese as well. That said, a lighter lager would be better with younger, less intense cheese, whereas an aged hard cheese could do well with a higher-alcohol blonde beer from Belgium. For strong stinkers, a big malty doppelbock from Germany has the funk and the power to partner.

Looking at the history of beer with cheese in Europe it's no surprise that the monks of Chimay in Belgium have been making both cheese *and* truly great beer since 1862. And for many years, the German traditional dinner was light (lunch having been the main meal of the day) and would often consist of local cheese, cured meats, pickles, and beer, with some rye or black bread and mustard on the side.

ON THE PLATE

BREAD

Bread and cheese. The most basic of (almost) complete meals. For many cultures, it has been the most meager (but satisfying) of sustaining rations for millennia. However, there is a subtle, simple perfection here. A piece of cheese can be delicious and satisfying on its own, but somehow a hunk of bread with it seems to complete the composition. Certainly, other accompaniments are welcome and nutritionally necessary, but the protein, fat, and carbohydrates have been taken care of.

It's pretty easy to get carried away while selecting breads to go with your cheese, but it's usually best to stay rather neutral. The more complex the flavors in a specific cheese, the simpler the bread should be—you're looking for support, not competition. White and whole-wheat breads are fine, semolina and the like are nice as well, but avoid strongly flavored seeds (sesame, caraway) or herbs (rosemary) and other "inclusions" unless you've tried them with the cheeses you'll be offering. Nuts, black olives, raisins and other dried fruit can be lovely with some, but could overpower the more delicate cheeses on the board. Some stronger and saltier cheeses can be nicely complemented by sweetness, so raisin breads and sweeter crackers provide a very tasty contrast. Blues especially seem to have an affinity for crumbly, slightly sweet graham crackers.

Once you've chosen them, the crackers are ready to use, but the bread should be sliced to make it easier to transport the cheese to your gaping maw. The rusticity of torn hunks of bread is fine for a picnic, or for yourself at home, but in a restaurant or when entertaining, slicing the bread (*just* before service) makes it easier to serve, and neater for the guests to consume.

DANCING PARTNERS

There are some accompaniments for cheese that have complementary flavors and can be used to create a more complete — even controlled presentation of flavors. These foods usually have one or several qualities that work well as contrasts for their lactic partners.

SWEETNESS

One of the most famous pairings in the cheese world is Manchego with Membrillo, a Spanish quince paste. Manchego is rather salty, and can have a slightly dry texture; the sweet, soft quince paste completes the picture. An unflattering, if largely accurate comparison would be to the combination of peanut butter with jelly.

BALSAMIC

Balsamic vinegar is sweeter than people think. In fact, the real stuff is not technically a vinegar at all; it's a reduced grape must that is *protected* (usually by reheating) from the acetic bacteria that create real vinegar. The progressive aging process of true balsamic yields a concentrated acidity *and* sweetness, as well as depth and complexity of flavor. The sweet, sour power of its flavor goes well with hard aged cheeses, especially Parmigiano-Reggiano, but you should try it with other cheeses that share qualities with that Italian masterpiece.

FRUIT

Fresh fruit is a natural partner for cheese, though some are better than others. Ripe pears marry very well with a broad range of cheeses, from Ricotta Salata all the way up to strong blues such as Roquefort and Gorgonzola. In fact, there is a saying in Italy that translates to "don't tell the peasants how good pears are with cheese." Mean-spirited, but accurate. Apples do well, particularly with cheddars. In fact, even cooked apples can work well, hence the adage "apple pie without the cheese is like a hug without the squeeze." Perhaps the most convenient fruit for your platter is fresh grapes. Their light sweetness, bright acidity, and juiciness make them both fitting partner and welcome refreshment.

Goat cheese has a few popular partners, and one is a vegetable. Beets and goat cheese are in combination on so many menus these days that it might be considered annoying — if it wasn't so darned good. Earthy, moist sweetness from the beets and the slightly dry, tangy character of the fresh cheese work perfectly together, and the combination anchors many great salads. A more recent trend has developed (although with some history) of goat cheese with watermelon. Here again we have the complementary nature of lightly sweet and refreshing with slightly tart and dry. To round out the list of fruits worth trying, consider figs, persimmons, plums, and fresh apricots, but most citrus and tropical fruits don't have a place here. It is also worth noting that dried fruits can nicely complement some slightly stronger cheeses. Raisins, dried apricots, dried figs, even dates can be lovely with aged or strong cheeses. But keep in mind that older cheeses and dried fruit are both dry. Be sure that you provide moisture in some form, whether in another accompaniment on the plate, or in a glass alongside. Whatever you do, try new combinations, including non-traditional fruits, especially with cheeses that have no traditional partner — maybe you'll find that partner.

HONEY

Fruit and fruit products can be lovely with many cheeses, but for a hand-in-glove pairing, try some good honey drizzled over a piece of aged cheese. Honey was the first sweetener, long before cane sugar, and it has a wonderful affinity for dairy products. You might think first of "milk and honey," but cream, butter, and, of course, cheese are lovely with the stuff. The cheeses to consider for this pairing are those that will benefit from a sweet counterpart, therefore sharp, strong, and salty attributes can all be mollified with a drizzle of honey. That is not to say that some calmer cheeses won't play along, in fact, a piece of bread with fresh farmer's cheese and some local honey make for a lovely breakfast.

As for the choice of honey, the commercial brands are fine, but are usually a blend from many hives, covering a very broad area. To get honey with some interesting flavors, visit your local farmer's market and ask where the honey is from. The added benefit of eating local honey (within 40 to 50 miles) is that it can calm pollen-related allergies. Another aspect of honey to attend to is its pollen source. Because bees tend to all feed from one type of blossom at a time until that source is exhausted, varietal honeys are available. I first learned of this at a honey shop in Italy, where they had everything from a yellow-gold and perfumed Acacia honey, to the dark, brooding, and pleasantly bitter Chestnut version. Try using the latter with a powerful stinky cheese.

The best way to incorporate the honey on your cheese plate is to just drizzle it over individual servings of cheese right before it's being served. On a larger platter, you could put the honey in a pot and allow the server or guests to do their own drizzling, or even put a piece of honeycomb on the platter for a very dramatic presentation. And frankly, the best part of this pairing is that there is no cooking or complicated preparation involved, but the results are seductive.

SALTY

OLIVES

I honestly don't know why olives work so well with cheese. Salty, strong, and rich olives with salty (perhaps strong) and creamy cheese sounds like too much. Somehow, though, olives and cheese do provide a good contrast for each other. Perhaps it is more that they are well matched regarding saltiness and power, and the relative bitterness of the olives cuts through the richness of various cheeses. Whatever the mechanics are, it is a tried-and-true combination that is worth considering when putting a cheese platter together. One caveat is that olives before dessert can overpower the subsequent sweets, so only use olives when the cheese is an appetizer or the final course, not to be followed by dessert.

NUTS

There are some nuts that seem to keep showing up with cheese. Walnuts have a noticeable level of tannin in their skin, and the concomitant bitterness can work nicely. Hazelnuts are nice, and those lovely Marcona almonds from Spain provide a nice crunch along with a roasted (if you roast them, and you should) sweetness. If you want to get fancy, nuts can be candied while roasting, but taste them with the target cheese to make sure that it's still a good pairing.

This group of cheese-producing nations can hardly be referred to as secondary. In fact, some of them produce and export almost as much cheese as do the French. But there is a unifying feature here; while most of these countries might have very high dairy production levels, their residents are not engaged with cheese the way that the French, Italians, and many Americans are now. Sure, they produce and eat billions of pounds a year, but a lot of it is good, well-made, basic types (such as Swiss and Emmenthaler) from pasteurized milk. There is nothing wrong with that, of course, but there don't seem to be many cheeses that would make someone say, "Now *that's* a great cheese . . . I've never had anything like it before!" In that a tremendous amount of cheese is imported from these countries to the United States,

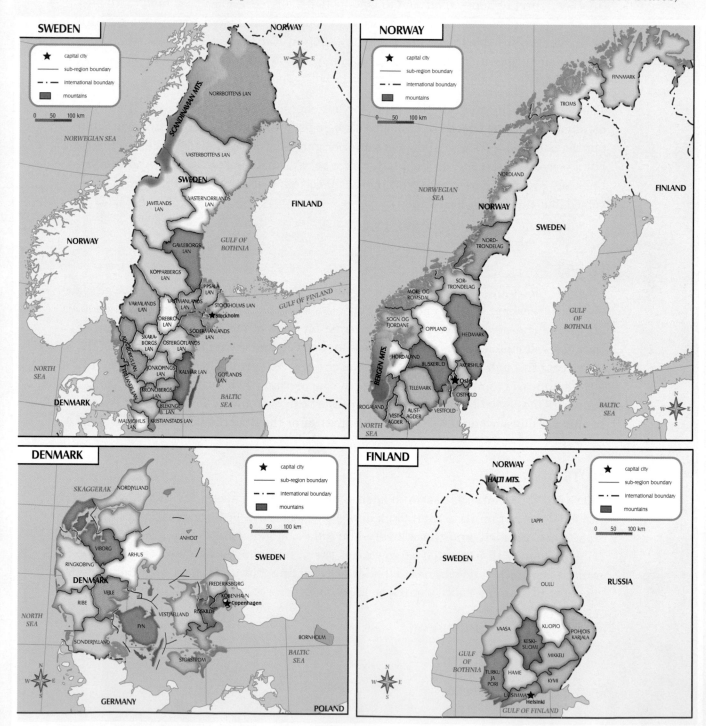

they need to be mentioned. As with many other high-volume food producers, big cheese companies are to be commended for the ability to turn out such consistent products. Their cheeses can be relied on to be well-made, clean, and dependable. They are cheeses that will be appreciated by most Americans.

Nordic Countries

The countries in question are Denmark, Sweden, Finland, Norway, and Iceland. Many of their residents come from one of two cultures, the Sami (sometimes called Laplanders) in the northern part of the region, and the Norse in the south. Because of these simple beginnings, many of the residents of different countries can understand each other's languages — and cultures. Similar climates lead to like cuisines, based largely on fish, meat, root vegetables, and grains. Other than northern Finland (which borders western Russia), most of the countries have a surprisingly mild climate for the latitude. This is due largely to a branch of the Gulf Stream current (called the North Atlantic Drift) that brings warm water to northern Europe. Although a lot of the region is warmer than one might expect, it isn't exactly a tropical climate either, so the cuisines tend to focus on meat, potatoes, bread, and cow's milk cheeses. Whereas these countries do not have a surfeit of famous, uniquely named cheeses, there is quite a bit made . . . and exported.

A lot of cheese is imported into the United States from Denmark and Finland; in fact, Denmark was the fourth largest exporting nation to the United States in 2003. Finland sends a lot of cheese here, especially the Finlandia Brand, which claims to be the top-selling imported cheese at American deli counters. Much of this cheese would fit in the category of factory-made volume cheeses, and the quality is quite high. Many of the varieties mimic popular styles from other countries, such as Gorgonzola (Danish Blue) and Gruyère (Swedish Graddost). These, along with Swiss, havarti, the aforementioned blue, cheddar, and gouda account for almost all of the cheese made in, and exported from, there.

There are a few more unique regional cheeses made there, of course. Denmark is the source of Tilsit, a slightly funky semi-firm cheese, as well as Danish Blue, which is available from a number of producers, all of whom make a consistent and versatile cheese. Norway sends Jarlsberg, which is one of the most popular imported cheeses in the United States. Gjetost comes from Norway as well, although the same cheese is produced under different names in the other countries, too. Most of Sweden's production stays in Sweden, and they also import quite a bit of cheese from France, Italy, and the United States.

The Netherlands

It's not just Holland — that name only refers to part of the country; Dutch is the proper word to use when referring to the people, products, and language of The Netherlands. It borders Belgium, Germany, and the North Sea, and has a rather moderate climate due to the prevailing southwesterly winds that bring relatively warm, moist air in off the ocean. Although the Dutch are known for their high level of industry and technology, their agricultural sector produces a surplus, and in 2005, according to the United States Department of Agriculture (USDA), they were the second-largest exporter (in value) of farm products in the world, tucked between the United States and France. Many of their exports are from the world of ornamental flowers, plants, and bulbs but tomatoes, peppers, and cucumbers are grown in very high volume as well.

The conditions are also perfect for raising dairy cattle, and the cows produce about 11 billion kilos of milk a year; in 2007, over 730 million kilos of cheese were produced. Butter, milk powder, and whey powder are among the other important dairy goods produced, and 60 percent of Dutch production is exported. Their most important cheese is Gouda. With a rich history that goes back hundreds of years, there are both industrial and artisanal versions available, with only the Noord-Hollandse Gouda being name-protected in the European Union. Because of this, Gouda is produced all over the world with varying levels of quality. Aged genuine Gouda is perhaps the most compelling of any gouda and is widely available in the United States.

The second-most-important cheese from The Netherlands is Edam, an almost spherical cow's milk cheese whose export version sports the familiar red wax coating (black if aged) that can be found on Gouda.

Its popularity during the age of sailing ships was due to its supreme ability to age. And it was even copied by the French when Louis XIV discouraged the purchase of foreign products — because Edam was perfect for long ocean voyages, a French version of Edam (Mimolette, page 86) was created in the city of Lille.

Industrial milk products (along with all those tulips) are more important contributors to the agricultural profits in The Netherlands, but there are still some unique cheeses to look for . . . and frankly, the industrial cheeses are made at a very high level of quality, and might be what you're looking for.

Belgium

The kingdom of Belgium is an intriguing place. At first glance, an American foodie notices the "important" stuff — the chocolate (Callebaut and Godiva), some of the finest beers in the world, the eponymous waffles, and of course the fries. Belgium is nestled among some of the greatest food and beverage-producing (and -consuming) nations in Europe, namely France, Germany, and The Netherlands, and England is just across the Channel. The climate is mild for the latitude because of maritime influence and is made up mostly of plains, plateaus, and rolling hills. Many of the most famous food specialties from Belgium come from around the capital region of Brussels, an officially bilingual, but functionally quadrilingual (French, Dutch, German, and

English, the first two being official) region that is home to NATO as well as effectively being the capital of the European Union.

It's ironic, then, that Belgium is a starkly divided country. In the north, the Flemish Belgians speak their dialect of Dutch and eat Waterzooi, a (usually) chicken stew that is richened with a liaison of eggs and cream at the end of cooking. In the south, the French-speaking population, many of whom are descended from the Walloons, eat French-influenced cuisine, perhaps with less wine, more beer, and higher calories than in France. They like their mayonnaise here. And if you are driving across the border of these two regions, be prepared for the road signs to change. In addition to the cultural differences, economic imbalance fuels the debate on separatism. The Flemish are especially interested in breaking the country in two, mostly because the north's prosperity subsidizes the somewhat financially unproductive south.

This political strife doesn't seem to have changed much in the world of food and drink, though, as the chocolate, cheese, and beer seem to be flowing into the United States unabated. Speaking of beer, it must be mentioned again that some of the best beers in the world come from Belgium. Some are made by monks, and there are still six working Trappist breweries there. But abbey-style beers and others such as the controversially named Delirium Tremens from the Huyghe Brewery in Ghent are standards by which many other beers should be measured.

Bringing it back to cheese, the cheeses of Belgium are generally made from cow's milk and are semi-soft, with varying degrees of stinkiness. The monks of Chimay, the most famous of the Trappist beer in the United States, make some very good cheese. Based on local cow's milk, Chimay cheeses are semi-firm with increasing aroma as they age. The other, most popular style of cheese in Belgium is Herve, named for its town of origin in the province of Liège. It is similar to Pont l'Évêque and is a square little stinker made with cow's milk. Ironically, it seems that there are more Belgian-*style* cheeses in America than the real thing. Limburger from Landhaus in Wisconsin, Hooligan from Cato Corners in Connecticut, and

Grayson from Meadow Creek Farms in Virginia are all directly or at least indirectly based on Belgian styles of cheese. At least you'll know what to drink with them . . . Belgian beer!

Germany and Austria

My wife was born in Germany, and when I asked her if she remembered any specific cheeses from her childhood, she said "No, but I remember that my mom often had some cheese that was so stinky that she kept it in its own container in the refrigerator so as not to stink up the whole house." Reinforcement

of this comes from Steven Jenkins, author of the *Cheese Primer,* who says,

> ". . . to my mind German cheeses, while standing tall in aroma and flavor intensity, fall short when it comes to depth and nuance of flavor and are only somewhat less disappointing in terms of texture and visual effect. Strong German and Austrian cheeses are often only that — *strong.*"

Germany has the largest population of any country in the European Union and is one of the most influential and richest countries therein. It is a big country, with highly varied geography, from the Alps to the two sea coasts (North and Baltic). Winters tend toward the mild because of maritime influence, but it's still not a hot country — in summer, temperatures rarely top 86°F (30°C) anywhere in the country.

The Germans are often the world's largest exporter of goods and have the largest economy in Europe. They can pretty much afford any cheeses they might want. Despite what may have sounded like disparaging remarks before, many of the cheeses produced are meant for indigenous consumption, and are pleasing to a vast majority of Germans. Very often, the cheeses are served with dark bread, onions, beer, and mustard as a simple meal. The stinky simplicity that many of them exhibit is exactly what many Germans are looking for.

German wine is a subject worthy of its own book, and can hardly be given its due here. But, the Germans produce some of the finest white wines in the world, and their Rieslings range from shatteringly dry to syrupy sweet, with all variants between. Historically, many of the wines have had residual sugar, and therefore some sweetness. Of late, their wines have been getting a bit drier, but both sweet and dry are appropriate for a range of foods. The wines with sweetness can pair marvelously with cheese, and stronger cheeses will be able to handle even sweeter wines. Lighter cheeses tend to go with lighter wines.

There are some cheeses that are unique in style from both Germany and Austria. Rauchkäse (smoked cheese) is a semi-soft smoky cheese also known as Brüder Basil. Halfway between smoked mozzarella and smoked gouda, it is great with beer and rustic accompaniments for lunch or a snack. Perhaps more famous is Tilsit or Tilsiter, made from partially skimmed cow's milk and washed enough with brine and whey to give it a bit of stink, but still preserves the cheese's gentle texture. It is produced in both Germany and Austria, with some of the more artisanally produced versions made in the latter. Lastly, although some turophiles will roll their eyes when the industrially produced Cambozola is mentioned, there is truly a luxurious experience awaiting the less jaded. If you enjoy the richness of Camembert and the blue mold of Gorgonzola, this cheese is a perfect combination (in name, as well). Made by Käserei Champignon, a century-old company based in Allgäu, Germany but also with an office in Englewood Cliffs, New Jersey, it is very rich with a touch of blues power. Clean and industrially produced, yes, but a simple hedonistic pleasure as well.

Austria sits below the southern border of Germany and is a much smaller country. In fact, its population is one tenth that of Germany. It is a largely alpine region, with borders on the Czech Republic, Slovakia, Slovenia, Hungary, and Italy. This assortment of bordering countries leads to a somewhat more varied cuisine than in Germany. Even its wines are their own in that the premier grape in Austria is Grüner Veltliner, which produces a world-class white wine deserving of a lot more notice than it currently receives. Riesling is another important grape here, and the wines in general are finely crafted and precise in flavor. Unfortunately, most Austrian cheeses have not followed suit yet, although there are a few exceptions. Bachensteiner, from the Bregenz Forest in the Voralberg region is a well-made stinky cheese. As you may have gleaned by now, Germans and Austrians like stinky cheese. There are some very good not-so-smelly styles, though, like Munsters, and Bergkäse Alt, also from Voralberg, is a very good aged mountain cheese.

It's still a mystery to me that the countries that brought us Beethoven, Mozart, Brahms, Mahler, Porsche, BMW, Brecht, and the Bauhaus do not have a higher profile in the world of cheese. The climatic and geographical conditions exist to produce fine and complex cheeses in both of these countries, and yet most of the huge volume of cheese produced and consumed in Germany and Austria are either imitations of unique styles from other countries, such as gruyère, or rather simple and forward versions of smoked or stinky cheeses. Perhaps it is the slightly colder climates that won't support the type of affinage that is possible in France or Italy; or maybe they're just happy with what they have. As the wines of Germany and Austria and global changes in cuisine take place, perhaps this will change.

COMPOSED CHEESE PLATES

One of the most efficient and helpful things you can do for your guests is to put together a combination of one cheese with accompaniments as a plated course. A few possibilities are:

- Ricotta Salata with ripe Comice Pears and a grinding of black pepper
- A few rough chunks of Parmigiano-Reggiano with a drizzle of 20-year-old balsamic vinegar and a piece of crisp flatbread
- Well-aged (2 or 3 years) cheddar with sliced Macoun apples and golden raisins
- Maytag Blue with some fresh figs

These work well on dessert menus because the combinations have already been put together for the guests, and the plates are executed in the kitchen. This can be much more efficient than having the waitstaff serve cheese from a cart.

FIGURE **7.1** An individual, composed cheese plate

CHEESE CARTS

So you didn't like the idea of individually plated cheeses. Putting a cheese cart together is the culmination of creating a cheese program. If the pressure of putting together a well thought out and composed cheese platter is too much for you at first, perhaps a few composed plated cheeses (as described above) would be a good first step into a cheese program.

Cheese carts are like wine lists. They can be big or small, with each having particular needs. The larger the cheese board, the more confusing it can get. So there has to be some sort of organizing structure that will help the guest to make decisions. That structure can exist on the board itself (organized by rinds, or countries, or milks), or

FIGURE **7.2** A cheese cart presentation

in the head of the person selling the cheese. Either way, the guest needs structure, either explicit or implicit, when more than ten cheeses are available. For example, in an American restaurant, you could have a board with a fresh Crottin from Vermont Butter & Cheese, Hudson Valley Camembert from Old Chatham, Eden from Sprout Creek, Midnight Moon from Cypress Grove, Bobolink Cave-Ripened Cheddar, and Point Reyes Blue. With these six cheeses, there is a gradually increasing intensity of flavor from start to finish, and a variety of milks, rinds, and textures. There are two goat's milk, one sheep/cow's milk blend, and three cow's milk, roughly representing national averages of cheese production. There's one fresh cheese, one smear-ripened, and two bloomy rinds. Also there is a mix of states represented. Most importantly, they all taste great and have individual personalities.

A smaller selection is simpler to choose from, but now the challenge is to provide enough of a variety for the guest to have a chance to try a range of flavors and textures. Here again, there are various ways to look at the selection process—if they all have to be French, you should have a few different milks, rinds, and ages of cheese available. You should have at least five cheeses on the board, and they must be chosen carefully. Think of it as having a "best of breed" for each cheese . . . the best bloomy rind you know, your favorite hard cheese, and a blue that leaves diners speechless along with a few other fine examples. Honestly, a small selection is more difficult to do well because there is less room for error. Larger selections offer more freedom to include a range, giving the guest an opportunity perhaps to try three very different stinkers. Still, the previously mentioned structure is necessary to keep the guests from getting lost in a miasma of information.

HOW MUCH CHEESE?

One way to figure out how much cheese to serve someone is to consider the cheese for what it is—a rich source of protein. If the cheese course is part of a larger meal, five 1-ounce pieces of cheese is about all the guests can handle, especially when dessert sits on the horizon. As the number of cheeses to sample increases, the portion should decrease, down to 3/4 to 1/2 ounce of each. Keep in mind, though, that too many cheeses can befuddle a guest, leaving them with no clear memory of what they had. Remember also that 1-ounce portions of sixteen cheeses will add up to a pound for each person. That's way too much, even for the most dedicated.

CUTTING DIRECTION

Whether creating a composed plate or a board, pay attention to how both the individual portions and larger pieces look. The simplest view to take is that the pieces should refer back to the shape of the cheese when it's whole. Wheels should be cut into pie-shaped wedges, logs into disks, and pyramids into triangles. Extremely large round cheeses will invariably be shaped like various Platonic Solids even directly from the cheesemonger, but then you just want to present the final portions neatly.

Some of the hardest cheeses, especially those of the *grana* style from Italy, are supposed to be served in irregular chunks that have been pried off the bigger chunk.

Various spades and chisels are available to do just this, and it is the most authentic presentation of these great cheeses, especially Parmigiano-Reggiano. The so-called "shards" that are made with vegetable peelers are okay on salads and the like, but remember that they dry out very quickly, and should only be prepared right before use.

The softest cheeses don't respond well to cutting with a knife, and sometimes a spoon or spreader will work better. The most famous spoonable cheese is Époisses, and to serve it you can use two small spoons to break open the top, then spoon out the unctuous interior.

CHEESE DESERVES SOME WARMTH

Even though different families of cheese require different storage conditions (see following), all cheeses should be served at room temperature, or somewhere between 65° and 72°F/18° and 22°C. Since you probably don't have a cheese cave (yet), your refrigeration is more likely to be somewhere

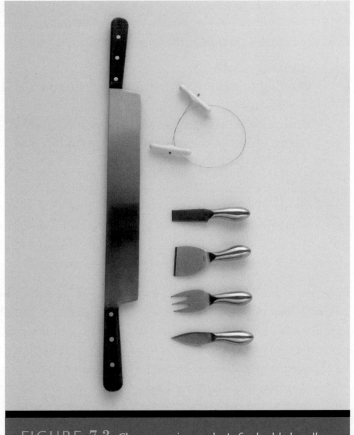

FIGURE **7.3** Cheese-cutting tools. Left: double handle cheese knife; Right, from top to bottom: cutting wire, cheese knife, cheese plane, cheese fork, cheese knife

around 36°F/2°C. This is far too cold for the cheese to show its best characteristics. At that temperature the texture will most likely to be too firm and the aromatic molecules won't be as available as they would in a warmer cheese. They shouldn't get too warm either, because they might start to sweat or ooze some butterfat that should still be in the cheese when it's eaten. A good rule of thumb is to take the cheeses to be served out of the refrigerator about an hour before service.

STORAGE

The storage of cheese is not difficult if you look back to why cheese came to be in the first place. As a preservation method for milk, different types of cheese evolved in different places, and the best storage conditions for each type are available in the homelands of those cheeses. Look at the map and you will realize that most of the French bloomed-rind cheeses are from around Paris. Many washed-rind cheeses come from places near water, especially oceans (as in Normandy). Whatever the type of cheese, if it was created before the advent of refrigeration, it was stored under available natural conditions.

If only one storage area is available for all of your cheeses, it is best to stay at or near 50°F/10°C and 80 percent humidity. But following are some more specific conditions that are best for certain categories of cheese.

Natural rinds: 49° to 51°F/9° to 10°C, 88% to 90% humidity
Washed (smear-ripened) cheese: 52° to 54°F/11° to 12°C, 94% to 96% humidity
Bloomy and Goat cheeses: 48° to 50°F/9° to 10°C, 88% to 90% humidity
Large cheeses (Gruyère, Emmenthaler, Parmigiano-Reggiano): 48° to 52°F/9° to 11°C, 88% humidity.

In general, blue cheeses should be kept separate from other cheeses, especially bloomy rinds (to avoid turning *everything* blue), and at a colder temperature to keep the interior mold from spreading too much. A good base temperature would be 38° to 40°F/ 3° to 4°C with 64 to 66 percent humidity. These are also good conditions for other cheeses that you don't want to ripen any further.

Cheeses should be left whole for as long as possible, because once they're cut, they begin to lose moisture. With large whole cheeses, you should only cut out (or off) the amount that is going to be used for service, and the rest should be wrapped lightly to preserve moisture. You should never wrap cheese tightly in plastic wrap, as it should be allowed limited access to air. This is because many cheeses, especially those made with raw milk, are "living," developing things, and need to breathe. So, parchment paper, waxed paper and semi-permeable cheese paper are all viable wrapping stock.

Younger cheeses, presumably with higher moisture content, should be turned over every other day or so to maintain the consistency of its paste, because fat is lighter than water.

WHEN GOOD CHEESE GOES BAD

There are a few signs that a cheese has reached its peak and is now going down the other side of the hill. Some are more obvious than others, and some may surprise you.

- Too runny — Strangely, it seems that many Americans will think that the Brie is perfect when it is cut open and runs out all over the board. This is actually a sign that the cheese has gone too far and the protein molecules have lost their structural integrity. Most bloomy cheeses and many other soft ones should bulge slightly when cut open, not leak out onto the plate.
- Too stinky — Even the stinkiest and funkiest washed-rind cheeses will slip past their *à point* or "perfect stage" and become repulsive. One clue here is the amount of ammonia odor. Because ammonia is a natural product of bacterial activity, the smell of ammonia in a cheese cave is to be expected. But when the cheese has been allowed to air out and warm up a bit, the smell should be gone. So believe it or not, there is good stink and bad stink. Bloomy cheeses are definitely past their prime if there is a whiff of ammonia.
- Shape shifting — If a whole cheese starts to collapse, it is likely that the paste is breaking down and no longer in viable condition. Even scarier, a cheese that starts growing is usually doing so because of excessive gas production in the paste.

- Blue mold in a non-blue cheese — It's usually not a good idea to make your own blue cheese just by being patient. Some Brits will do so with their cheddars, but they are mold experts. You should be wary of any non-blue cheese that starts to form blue veins. A bit of mold on the surface is, however, not a problem. Just cut off the offending section. Keep in mind, though, that the rest of the piece now has mold spores on it that are ready to erupt . . . use it before they do.
- Dried-out pieces — If you have a dried-out piece of cheese, you either cut too big a piece for service and tried to save the leftovers for service the next day, or you didn't preserve the "mother" piece well enough. The dry small piece should be chucked out, or you can make *fromage fort* with it. The bigger piece should be trimmed back to expose the edible surface, and then you should take better care of it.

BUYING CHEESE

Now that you are suitably wary of storing cheese, here's some advice. When you buy cheese, buy the smallest amount practical and buy it from someone who knows cheese. There are now great cheesemongers in just about every major city, and if you're not near a city, many of them will ship cheeses properly so that they arrive in excellent shape (see Appendix B on page 230 for a list of some reputable firms).

The great benefit to buying from a good cheesemonger is that he or she knows when the cheeses are at their best and can give you solid advice regarding seasonality . . . and can even advise you on which cheeses make sense for your needs. When you're dealing with such a complex product, expert advice is valuable, but doesn't cost much more than buying cheese from your regular wholesaler. The best part of buying from someone who knows cheese is that you will learn something along the way. As you become more knowledgeable and a better judge of both quality and style, you will become a better customer, as well as more capable when selling cheese to *your* customers.

If there is no way for you to buy from a specialty cheese seller, it will be up to you to judge the quality of the cheeses coming in to your home or business. Because each cheese has its own qualities, even personality, this is not going to be easy. The final decision is yours, and should depend on two things: Does the cheese taste good to you?, and Do you think others will like it? Fittingly, the end of this book leaves it up to you and your subjective taste. Everything up to this point should help to inform your decisions regarding the remarkable and venerable product that is cheese — but the information herein can only help you to answer the ultimate question: Do you like it?

GLOSSARY

À Point—The stage at which a cheese has been aged to its perfect state.

Acid—A substance having a sour or sharp flavor. A substance's degree of acidity is measured on the pH scale; acids have a pH of less than 7. Most foods are somewhat acidic. Foods generally referred to as acids include citrus juice, vinegar, and wine.

Affinage—Period of aging or maturing during which cheese is ripened. Cheese becomes what it was meant to be by reaching optimal moisture content, texture, and flavor.

Al Dente—Literally, "to the tooth"; refers to an item, such as pasta or vegetables, cooked until it is tender but still firm, not soft.

Appellation Contrôlée Laws—French. Set of laws that govern the production of France's finest agricultural products including wines, spirits, oils, and cheeses. They are premised on the notion that particular products are inherently connected to a region of origin or appellation, and they use guidelines of production to encourage quality rather than quantity.

Appellation d'Origine Contrôlée (AOC)—French. Formal and legally binding phrase indicating "controlled naming of origin," and implying a full set of appellation contrôlée laws that control the production of high-quality agricultural goods in France.

Artificial Rind—A coating that did not originate on the cheese. These rinds can be completely natural, and serve to protect the cheese but can also add flavor.

Bacteria—Microscopic organisms. Some have beneficial properties; others can cause food-borne illnesses when contaminated foods are ingested. Broad subcategories of bacteria have different effects on cheese.

Béchamel Sauce—A white sauce made of milk thickened with a light roux and flavored with white mirepoix. One of the Mother sauces.

Bloomy Rind—A cheese rind or coating that is actually a type of mold which causes ripening to occur from the outside in; the middle of the cheese is the last to ripen and become soft. The rind that forms appears white, soft, and often a little fuzzy. These molds originally occurred naturally, but now the cheeses are often inoculated with a specific strain of mold, usually from the *Penicillium* or *Glaucum* genus.

Blue Cheese—also "bleu" cheese; a classification of cow's, goat's, or sheep's milk cheeses which have come in contact, or have been inoculated with penicillium cultures so that the final product is spotted or veined throughout with blue, blue-gray, or blue-green mold, and carries a distinct smell.

Body—Tactile sensation of weight or fullness on the palate, usually from a combination of alcohol, extracts, glycerin, tannin, or other physical components in wine. Body in foodstuffs largely depends on richness (fat content).

Brie—Soft cow's milk cheese named after the province in which it originated with a soft and creamy texture, pale ivory in color under a white mold; savory with a hint of mushroom aroma.

Brine—A solution of salt, water, and sometimes seasonings used to flavor and preserve food.

Broil—To cook by means of a radiant heat source placed above the food.

Brunoise—Diced cubes 1/8 in/3 mm. For a brunoise cut, items are first cut in julienne, then cut crosswise. For a fine brunoise, cubes are 1/16 in/1.5 mm, cut items first into fine julienne.

Buffalo's Milk—Milk from the popular water buffalo of tropical Asia. This domesticated animal has been brought to parts of Italy and the United States, and is used for dairy production. Higher in butterfat than cow's milk, it has a rich texture and taste.

Caramelization—The process of browning sugar in the presence of heat. The temperature range in which sugar begins to caramelize is approximately 320° to 360°F/160° to 182°C.

Caseificio—An Italian cheese production facility.

Casein—One category of milk proteins.

Cheddaring—A cheesemaking activity during which whey is removed through cooking, grinding, and pressing. The product has high acidity due to the lactic acid bacteria and the proteins form longer strands which result in a flaky texture.

Chèvre—Cheese made from goat's milk.

Chiffonade—Leafy vegetables or herbs cut into fine shreds; often used as a garnish.

Composed Cheese Plate—A cheese plate where the items are carefully arranged and chosen to complement each other. Each cheese has specific accompaniments and is served as a plated course.

Cottage Cheese—A kind of fresh cheese curd product that is not pressed so some whey remains, giving it a high moisture content. Very mild flavor is typical.

Cow's Milk—A milk from cows which is often used to make cheeses in temperate climates. It usually has around 3.7 percent fat and 87 percent water. Bacteria can be found in cow's milk cheeses as well, many of which can be beneficial to the cheesemaking process.

Curd—The varying size masses of milk proteins produced by curdling.

Curdling—Effect of bacterial activity, acid, and/or rennet on milk to coagulate it and provide solid masses of milk proteins, called curds. The type of curd achieved is basic to the final product; softer cheeses start out as larger curds, harder cheeses are originally cut into smaller curds which results in lower water content.

Deep-Fry—To cook food by immersion in hot fat; deep-fried foods are often coated with breadcrumbs or batter before being cooked.

Denominazione di Origine Controllata (DOC)—Italian. A phrase indicating legally protected naming of an origin for cheese production. This system also controls other agricultural products including grapes, oils, cured meats, and spirits.

Denominazione di Origine Protetta (DOP)—Italian. Protected designation of origin which protects the names of foods which can only be labeled by their famed name if they have come from its specific region. These appellation laws eliminate the unfair competition and misleading of consumers by non-genuine products, which may be of lesser quality or have a different flavor.

Farmer's Cheese—Pressed cottage cheese, maintaining mild flavor but with a slightly firmer texture and less moisture.

Fermier—French. "Farm-made."

Fondue—Directly translating to "melted." A Swiss communal dish where diners use forks to dip bits of food (most often bread) into a warm semi-liquid, commonly cheese, sauce.

Fresh Cheese—Young cheeses that do not need to age at all, often high in moisture content and highly perishable. The main flavor profile is that of the milk they were made from and thus are sometimes considered bland.

Fromage Fort—Literally, "strong cheese"; refers to a recipe utilizing scraps of cheese which are placed in a vegetable stock or milk and allowed to ferment, eventually becoming a cheese spread.

Fromage Blanc—A young cheese with crumbly texture and very mild, slightly salty flavor. These cheeses do not melt when heated. In Mexican cuisine often referred to as queso blanco.

Gjetost—A brown Norwegian whey cheese in which the whey of cow's or goat's milk is cooked until the lactose is caramelized.

Glutamate—A non-essential amino acid that provides a unique umami flavor to foods through carboxylate anions and salt.

Goat Milk—Chalky white milk from goats that has lower lactose levels than cow's milk making it desirable for children and lactose-intolerant adults. Cheese from this milk was originally available to areas with limited food supply due to the animal's versatile living conditions and ability to survive in arid regions.

Grand Cru—French for "great growth"; used to designate a high-quality product or one with a favorable reputation.

Gratin—Cheese or bread crumb topping browned in an oven or under a salamander/broiler (au gratin, gratin de).

Grill—A cooking technique in which foods are cooked by a radiant heat source placed below the food. Also, the piece of equipment on which grilling is done. Grills may be fueled by gas, electricity, charcoal, or wood.

Julienne—Vegetables, potatoes, or other items cut into thin strips; 1/8 in by 1/8 in by 1 to 2 in/3 mm by 3 mm by 3 cm to 5 cm is standard. Fine julienne is 1/16 in by 1/16 in by 1 to 2 in/1.5 mm by 1.5 mm by 3 cm to 5 cm.

Latticeria—An Italian dairy or cheese shop.

Loire Valley—Also known as the Garden of France, this valley that runs through much of France is known for producing excellent goat's milk cheese.

Microbes—Specifically bacteria and fungus, which are responsible for decomposition and much of cheeses' flavors and textures, are used in many areas of cheese production.

Mild Aged Cheeses—Young cheeses that have only been aged slightly, thus retaining water content and mild flavor. These cheeses can vary but have not had the time to break fat and protein down into the more intensely aromatic molecules.

Mold—A type of fungus. Although some molds cause disease or food spoilage, others can be helpful in the production of various foods, like some cheese. Different molds affect cheese differently; blue molds lead to veined cheeses whereas white molds need more oxygen and grow on the surface of bloomy-rind cheeses, like brie.

Monosodium Glutamate (MSG)—A flavor enhancer derived from glutamic acid, without a distinct flavor of its own; used primarily in Chinese and processed foods. Controversy swirls around this product, which is assumed to be the cause of allergic reactions in some. Technically, one could be sensitive, not allergic to it, and there has been no conclusive scientific proof either way.

Monté au Beurre—Literally, "lifted with butter." Refers to a technique used to finish sauces, thicken them slightly, and give them a glossy appearance by whisking or swirling whole butter into the sauce until just melted.

Mozzarella—A type of Italian cheese made by heating curds, then spinning, cutting (hence the name; the Italian verb *mozzare* means "to cut"), and dropping it into cool water. There are three main types of mozzarella; unsalted, salted, and smoked.

Mozzarella di Bufala—High in protein and fat, this rich cheese is made from the milk of water buffalo occupying the province of Campania, Italy. It is made using the pasta filata, or spun paste, method.

Mozzarella Fior di Latte—Cheese made from Italian cow's milk through the pasta filata or "spun paste" method.

Natural Rind—A cheese rind that forms naturally when the outside of the cheese hardens from contact with air. These rinds are sometimes maintained by brushing or rubbing with a cloth.

Pasta Filata—An Italian term meaning "spun paste." This process of cheesemaking involves heating up the curds in liquid, removing them, and then stirring or kneading them until the desired stringy texture is reached. Mozzarella and provolone are produced in this manner.

Pasteurization—A process in which food products are heated to kill microorganisms that could spoil the milk.

Pâté—Interior of the cheese; also called paste.

Pithivier—A round, enclosed pastry, usually made with puff pastry.

Raclette—A semi-firm salted cow's milk cheese and also a traditional Swiss or French dish in which the cheese is melted and then scraped over vegetables or potatoes.

Reduction—The product that results when a liquid is simmered or boiled to decrease its volume. The result has a thicker consistency and/or concentrated flavors.

Rennet—A natural complex of enzymes produced in the fourth stomach of young ruminant mammals that helps to digest milk. Rennet also occurs in some plants and microbes, and can now be produced through genetic engineering. All of these types are used in cheesemaking. Cheeses made with rennet yield a more durable, strong, and elastic curd.

Ricotta—A kind of whey cheese translating to "re-cooked," it is made by reheating the whey.

Rind—Outside covering of some but not all cheeses. Rinds provide protection, texture, flavor, and can even help with the identification of a cheese.

Ruminants—A mammal that digests plant-based food by initially softening it within the animal's first stomach, then regurgitating the semi-digested mass, now known as cud, and chewing it again. The process of rechewing the cud to further break down plant matter and stimulate digestion is called "ruminating." Ruminant animals include cows, goats, sheep, buffalo, water buffalo, and others.

Sheep's Milk—Milk from sheep often raised on foothills. This milk has more fat and protein than cow's or goat's milk, and more minerals as well. Diverse flavors of sheep's milk cheeses exist from Roquefort to Pecorino.

Smoking—Any of several methods for preserving and flavoring foods by exposing them to smoke. Methods include cold smoking (in which smoked item are not fully cooked), hot smoking (in which the items are cooked), and smoke-roasting.

Soufflé—Literally, "puffed." A preparation made with a sauce base (usually béchamel for savory soufflés, pastry cream for sweet ones), whipped egg whites, and flavorings. The egg whites cause the soufflé to puff during cooking.

Swiss Cheese—A generic name for several related varieties of cheese, all of which resemble Emmental. Some types of Swiss cheese have a distinctive appearance, with holes known as "eyes."

Triple-Crème Cheeses—Cheeses required (in France, at least) to have a minimum butterfat content of 75 percent solids, achieved by adding cream or milk to curds during production. Soft, smooth cheeses often with salty, earthy flavor profiles.

Turophile—A connoisseur of cheese.

Umami—Describes a savory, meaty taste; often associated with monosodium glutamate (MSG), mushrooms, Thai fish sauce, and many cheeses.

Washed Rind—A coating created by bacteria belonging to the "smear" family. The cheeses are washed with a solution of brine, wine, beer, or spirits during ripening. This liquid promotes the growth of certain bacterias, which cause the cheese to grow an exterior that in turn creates a brightly colored orange-red coating, robust flavor, and renowned stink.

Water Content—The amount of moisture in a product; harder cheeses have lower water content and softer cheeses higher. The lower the moisture content the lower the melting point of a cheese.

Whey—The liquid remaining after milk has been curdled and strained in the process of cheesemaking. Also called "milk plasma," it is a complex liquid containing, among other things, proteins. It can be difficult to dispose of ecologically, but can be used to feed livestock or even make a second type of cheese.

Whey Cheese—Cheeses made from utilizing the remaining liquid after milk has been curdled in a non-acidic process. This type of whey is referred to as "sweet."

Wine—Alcoholic beverage produced by fermenting fruit juice (generally grapes).

READINGS AND RESOURCES

Home Cheese Making: Recipes for 75 Delicious Cheeses
Ricki Carroll, Storey Publishing, LLC, 2002

Cheese Primer
Steven Jenkins, Workman Publishing Company, 1996

French Cheeses (Eyewitness Companions)
Kazuko Masui, Tomoko Yamada. Gillian Emerson-Roberts ed., Dorling Kindersley Publishers, 2005

Cheese: A Connoisseur's Guide to the World's Best
Max McCalman and David Gibbons, Clarkson Potter, 2005

The Cheese Plate
Max McCalman and David Gibbons, Clarkson Potter, 2002

On Food and Cooking: The Science and Lore of the Kitchen
Harold McGee, Scribner, 2004

Atlas of American Artisan Cheese
Jeffrey Roberts, Chelsea Green Publishing, 2007

*The Cheese Chronicles: A Journey Through the Making and Selling of Cheese in America,
From Field to Farm to Table*
Liz Thorpe, Ecco, 2009

The New American Cheese
Laura Werlin, Stewart, Tabori and Chang, 2000

*American Cheeses: The Best Regional, Artisan, and Farmhouse Cheeses, Who Makes Them, and Where to Find
Them*
Clark Wolf, Simon & Schuster, 2008

Web Sites

American Cheese Society
http://www.cheesesociety.org/

Wisconsin Cheese Board
http://www.eatwisconsincheese.com/

California Cheese Board
http://www.realcaliforniamilk.com/

Vermont Cheese Council
http://www.vtcheese.com/

Food and Agriculture Organization of the United Nations – global food information
http://www.fao.org/

Alsace Tourism – local food and drink
http://www.tourisme-alsace.com/en/gastronomy/

Caseophile – cheese professional's blog from France
http://fromagium.typepad.com/caseophile/

Paper by Bart Gietema on Modern Dairy Farming in Warm Climates
http://www.fastonline.org/CD3WD_40/LSTOCK/001/agrodoks/EM-23-e-2005-digitaal.pdf

La Cucina Italiana Magazine – includes a cheese guide
http://lacucinaitalianamagazine.com/

Pecorino Romano Consortium – requires registration to view
http://www.pecorinoromano.com/en/

Italian Trade Consortium – Food and Wine information
http://www.italianmade.com/home.cfm

USDA Economics, Statistics and Market Information System (ESMIS)
http://usda.mannlib.cornell.edu

Dutch Dairy Board
http://www.prodzuivel.nl/

Canadian Dairy Council
http://www.cdc-ccl.gc.ca/cdc/index.asp

milkproduction.com – Technical U.S. Dairy Farming Information
http://www.milkproduction.com

CÁIS – The Association of Irish Farmhouse Cheesemakers
http://www.irishcheese.ie/

Appendix A: Tables
Quick Reference Tables by Chapter

CHAPTER 2						
CHEESE	**MILK TYPE**	**ORIGIN**	**RIND**	**PASTE**	**AGE**	**CULINARY USES**
Cottage Cheese	Cow's, sheep's, or goat's milk	Cottages of colonial Europeans	N/A	Curds and whey, drained	Fresh	Eaten with fruit, in salads, or used in many dessert recipes
Farmer's Cheese	Cow's, sheep's, or goat's milk	Individual farms	N/A	Curds and whey, drained and pressed	Fresh	Often in blintzes, sprinkled on soups or salads, or even used for cheesecake
Brousse de Rove	Goat's milk	Provence, France	N/A	Soft, liquidy, creamy	Fresh	Sprinkled with sugar and eaten, used in an omelet
Cervelle de Canut	Goat's milk	Lyon, France	N/A	Soft, spreadable	Fresh	Used as a spread mixed with shallots, garlic, and fines herbes
Chèvre Frais	Goat's milk	Loire, especially Berry, France	N/A	Soft, creamy, will not go stringy when melted	Fresh	Often rolled in herbs or spices, pairs well with white wine
Fontaine-bleau	Cow's milk	Fontainebleau, France, outside Paris	N/A	Soft, cream cheese-like	Fresh	Mixed with cream and eaten as a sweet dessert with fruit
Fromage Frais de Nîmes	Cow's milk	Languedoc, France	N/A	Soft, creamy	Fresh	Used as a dessert or mixed or flavored with fruit

(Continues)

	CHAPTER 2 (CONTINUED)					
CHEESE	**MILK TYPE**	**ORIGIN**	**RIND**	**PASTE**	**AGE**	**CULINARY USES**
Gastanberra	Sheep's milk	Aquitaine, France	N/A	Milky flavor with a more solid texture	Fresh	Pairs well with fruity red wines
Petit-Suisse	Cow's milk	Normandy, France	N/A	Creamy, rich, and sweet	Fresh	Served with bread, jams, and coffee
Queso Blanco	Cow's, or cow and goat's milk	Spain, and eventually Mexico	N/A	Crumbly texture, slightly salty	Fresh	Served as topping for Mexican dishes or atop soups and salads
Mozzarella di Bufala	Buffalo's milk	Campania region of Italy	N/A	Spun and cut, tender, elastic, rich and creamy	Fresh	Served alone, in caprese salads, atop pizza, or on sandwiches
Mozzarella Fior di Latte	Cow's milk	Italy	N/A	Spun and cut, tender, creamy, with grassy aromatics	Fresh	Served alone, with prosciutto or tomatoes in salads, sandwiches, and pizzas
Ricotta	Cow's or sheep's milk	Italy	N/A	Grainy, creamy white, slightly sweet in taste	Fresh	Used in cheesecakes and cannoli, can also be used for pasta filling
Gjetost	Cow's or goat's milk	Norway	N/A	Spreadable or hard, with sweet taste and caramel color	Fresh	Served with dark bread or flatbread as a dessert cheese

CHEESE	MILK TYPE	ORIGIN	RIND	PASTE	AGE	CULINARY USES
La Tur	Cow's, sheep's, and goat's milk	Italy, Piedmont, Alta Lange, Caseificio Dell'Alta Langa	Natural, beginning to form bloom	Velvety, creamy mousse-like center, with hint of runny creaminess near the surface	15 days at the caseificio. Should be eaten fresh	Nice addition to cheese plate with buttery texture, goes well on warm baguette
Coulommiers	Cow's milk, pasteurized	Île-de-France, France	Bloomy	Light to bright yellow, creamy, sometimes with a chalky center	1–4 weeks	Brie-like cheese good melted on sandwiches or served on a cheese plate
Fougerus	Cow's milk, pasteurized	Île-de-France, France	Bloomy, with a fern on top	Yellow-light gold, creamy, sweet	4 weeks	Brie-like cheese good for many applications
Chaource	Cow's milk, pasteurized	Champagne, France	Bloomy	Chalky/velvety to creamy, depending on age	2–4 weeks	Pairs well with Champagne
Chabichou de Poitou	Goat's milk	Poitou-Charentes, France	Natural, off-white to beige (can have blue-gray mold as it gets older)	Chalky, pure white when young; acquires waxiness as it ages	≥10 days	A dessert cheese, best served at the end of a meal
Cabécou de Rocamadour	Goat's milk	Midi-Pyrénées (Quercy, historically)	Natural, mold with age	Chalky, creamy, tender	1–2 weeks, up to 4 weeks	Good on bread, in salads, or at the end of a meal by itself
Ricotta Salata	Sheep's milk	Southern Italy, originally Sicily and Lazio (Rome)	N/A	Chalky, smooth, crumbly, and firm with some moisture	3 months	Served in antipasto, grated over pasta or grilled vegetables, or with pear for dessert

(Continues)

CHEESE	MILK TYPE	ORIGIN	RIND	PASTE	AGE	CULINARY USES
Humboldt Fog	Goat's milk	Arcata, Humboldt County, California; Cypress Grove Chevre	Bloomy over ash	Chalky, moist, and pure white when young, a ribbon of ash through its center and under the bloom, creaminess increases as it ages	4 weeks for 1 lb size, 8 weeks for 5 lb before cutting	Served with fresh fruit as part of light dessert or on a cheese board
Wabash Cannonball	Goat's milk	U.S.A., Indiana; Capriole, Inc.	Bloomy over ash	Chalky but creamy and light, more crumbly as it ages	3 weeks	Great on a cheese board. Pairs well with Sauvignon Blanc and honey
Crottin de Chavignol	Goat's milk	France, Loire Valley, Central	Natural, can form spots of (edible) mold if aged	Chalky and smooth when young, turning waxy as it ages, eventually to a grating-only texture	10 days to 4 months	Fresh, it is good with fruit or atop a salad; aged, can be good grated over salads
Brillat-Savarin	Cow's milk, (pasteurized in U.S.)	Seine-et-Marne, Ile-de-France	Bloomy	Rich, smooth, creamy, salty, earthy but no overt ammonia smell. Should bulge slightly when cut, but not be runny	3–7 weeks	Pairs well with dates and champagne, good on a cheese plate
Explorateur	Cow's milk, (pasteurized in U.S.)	Île-de-France, Fromagerie Petit Morin	Bloomy	Rich, smooth, buttery, creamy, earthy	3 weeks	Delicious when served as dessert with fresh fruit, good on a cheese plate
Pierre Robert	Cow's milk, (pasteurized in U.S.)	Île-de-France, Fromagerie Rouzaire	Bloomy	Light, creamy, mouth-coating, yet delicate; with an earthy/salty character	3 weeks	Champagne Doux or Demi-Sec, strawberries

(Continues)

CHEESE	MILK TYPE	ORIGIN	RIND	PASTE	AGE	CULINARY USES
Hudson Valley Camembert	Sheep's and cow's milk, (BGH-free)	Old Chatham Sheepherding Company, Old Chatham, NY	Bloomy	Soft, creamy, buttery	18–20 days	Ripe pears and a glass of Moscato d'Asti make excellent dessert pairing
Camembert de Normandie	Cow's milk, unpasteurized	France, Normandy	Bloomy, *Penicillium camemberti*	Creamy throughout, bulging. Once it's runny, it has passed its peak	3–4 weeks	Good with other Normandy produce such as ripe pears and strawberries
Saint–Marcellin	Cow's milk, but historically goat's milk	France, Dauphiné Province (southeast, but north of Provence)	Natural but sometimes comes in a ceramic crock; develops a light white mold with age	Soft, creamy, becomes spoonable with age	2–6 weeks	Good on a cheese board or paired with red wine from Côtes du Rhône
Selles-sur-Cher	Goat's milk	France, Central Loire	Ash that encourages bloom	Chalky (but smooth) and dense when young, gaining creaminess with age	≥8 days	Pairs well with fresh fruit or wine from its region like Sancerre or Vouvray
Valençay	Goat's milk	France, Loire, Valençay (near the Touraine)	Bloomy, with a light layer of ash underneath	Pure white and chalky in the center, with a creaminess near the surface	8 days to 1 month	Goes well with crackers as an hors d'oeuvre
Morbier	Cow's milk	France, Franche-Comté (just south of Alsace on the Swiss border)	Natural, rubbed and washed with water	Semi-soft, creamy ivory, with a thin layer of ash separating the top from the bottom	2–4 months	Great on sandwiches, can be used for upscale grilled cheese

(Continues)

CHEESE	MILK TYPE	ORIGIN	RIND	PASTE	AGE	CULINARY USES
Wensleydale	Cow's milk	England, Yorkshire	Natural, clothbound	Slightly crumbly, fine and a little dry	3–6 months	Apples, pears, or some dried fruits. Also good with crusty bread, mustard, and ale
Caerphilly	Cow's milk	Wales and nearby England	Natural, medium brown brushed with some white mold	Somewhat dry and crumbly at 3 weeks. Creamy halfway in at 3 months	3 weeks to 3 months	Serve alone on dark bread with sliced tart apples. Also grated into scones or melted into fondues
Lancashire	Cow's milk, raw	England, Lancashire	Natural, clothbound	Crumbly but creamy	6 weeks to 8 months	Pairs well with lager or ale, melts well on bread
Tomme de Savoie	Cow's milk	France, Savoie	Natural, brushed with various white, red, or yellow mold spots. Slightly cratered	Semi-firm. Light yellow with small, randomly sized and placed holes	2–6 months	Works well paired with dried sausages, fruits, or bread
Fourme d'Ambert	Cow's milk	France, Auvergne	Natural, light brown	Creamy with abundant blue mold	≥28 days	Pairs well with ripe pears and Coteaux du Layon dessert wine
Bleu d'Auvergne	Cow's milk	France, Auvergne	None, foil-wrapped	Creamy with abundant dark blue marbling	4 weeks	Good in salad dressings, or with nuts and mushrooms. Pairs nicely with sweet wines like Port

			CHAPTER 4			
CHEESE	**MILK TYPE**	**ORIGIN**	**RIND**	**PASTE**	**AGE**	**CULINARY USES**
Mimolette & Boule de Lille	Cow's milk	Normandy & Lille, France	Natural, beige with pockmarks, looking somewhat like a cantaloupe	From semi-firm to hard, depending on age	3 months to 2 years	Excellent on the cheese board or in canapés and for grating (older cheeses)
Ossau-Iraty Brebis	Sheep's milk, raw, from Basco-Bearnaise or Manech ewes	Pyrénées Mountains of southwest France, from a number of small producers	Natural, light brown	Semi-hard with a slightly granular texture; but with a soft, creamy mouthfeel	Minimum of 60 days for the smallest cheeses, 80 days for larger, best after 5 months	Pairs well with fruits, like apples or pears, dry sausages and prosciutto, or with fresh vegetables and olives
Midnight Moon	Goat's milk	Cypress Grove, California, U.S.A.	Natural/black wax	Firm, with some granular texture	≥6 months	Works well with fig preserves, fresh fruit, or in grilled cheese
Cantal/ Fourme de Cantal (A.O.C.), Salers	Cow's milk, pasteurized or raw	Cantal and surrounding towns, Auvergne, France	Natural	Semi-hard, smooth ivory-colored, getting darker with age	30 days to 6 months	Can be used in soups, salads, fondue, and gratins
Emmental Grand Cru	Cow's milk, raw	Franche-Comté, Burgundy, Champagne, Lorraine, Rhône-Alpes, France	Lightly washed	Firm but supple with large circular holes	10 weeks	Good for fondue, before-dinner snacks, or cheese plates

CHEESE	MILK TYPE	ORIGIN	RIND	PASTE	AGE	CULINARY USES
Provolone Val Padana	Cow's milk	Northern Italy	Natural, smooth	Pale yellow, darkening with age	3–18 months	Used on sandwiches or pizzas
Brin d'Amour	Sheep's milk	Corsica, France	Natural, but coated with dried herbs	Pale ivory, softish, with a creamy chalkiness	1–3 months	Pair well with olives, fresh tomatoes, hot peppers, and other Mediterranean foods
Manchego	Sheep's milk	La Mancha, Spain	Natural, oil-rubbed, with cross-hatch pattern from the grass aging basket	Off-white to ivory, firm, dense, and slightly flaky, with a few small holes	2 months to 2 years, shows best character after at least a year	Popular with Serrano ham, and quince paste on a sandwich. Also good melting cheese
Zamorano	Sheep's milk, Churra breed (raw)	Zamora, Spain	Natural, oil-rubbed, with a herringbone pattern from the woven grass forms. Acquires a white mold that turns brown with age	Pale gold, dense, with very small holes	≥100 days	Similar to Manchego; pairs with good ham, fresh fruit, and quince paste
Asiago d'Allevo	Cow's milk	Northern Italy, particularly Veneto	Natural	Hard and deep ivory with a granular flakiness. Young versions are off-white and supple	Vecchio (most character) ≥9 months; Mezzano, 3–5 months; Fresco, 2–3 months	When young can be good on sandwiches; with age it can also be good on pasta. It is also a good eating cheese

(Continues)

CHEESE	MILK TYPE	ORIGIN	RIND	PASTE	AGE	CULINARY USES
Parmigiano-Reggiano	Cow's milk, raw	Emilia-Romagna, Italy (primarily the cities of Parma, Modena, and Mantua)	Natural, oiled and brushed regularly. Has dimpled impressions that spell out the name of the cheese and date of production	When fresh, it is semi-hard, with toothsome quality. It also has small, crunchy crystals of calcium lactate or tyrosine. The older, the harder	1 year (giovane, young), 2 years (vecchio, old), 3 years (stravecchio, extra old), and 4 years (stravecchione, extra extra old)	Excellent grating cheese. Also good eating cheese with bread, balsamic vinegar or honey, and Tuscan red wine
Mahón	Cow's milk (sometimes raw)	Menorca, Balearic Islands, Spain (in the Mediterranean)	Natural, rubbed with paprika or oil (the color will let you know)	Yellowish, getting harder with age. Eventually it acquires a crumbly texture but should never be dried out	Best age is añejo at 9–12 months. There are also curado at 3–6 months; semi-curado at 2 months; and tierno at 15–30 days old	When young, a good cheese on sandwiches. As it ages, can be a good grating or even dessert cheese with fruits
Sbrinz	Cow's milk, raw	Lucerne, Switzerland	Washed, brushed, and oiled	Lightly golden yellow	Minimum 18 months, but will do well past 2 years, and even up to 4 years	Eaten in slivers, chunks, or grated on top of pastas and gratins
Pecorino Romano	Sheep's milk	Southern Italy, originally around Rome	Natural	Hard and off-white to ivory	≥8 months	Grating cheese for pasta, like Bucatini all' Amatriciana, or vegetable dishes especially including fava beans

(Continues)

CHEESE	MILK TYPE	ORIGIN	RIND	PASTE	AGE	CULINARY USES
Mont St. Francis	Goat's milk, raw	Capriole Goat Cheeses; Greenville, Indiana, U.S.A.	Washed, with brine	Semi-hard, softening with age, but never runny	4–8 months	Pairs well with fortified and dessert wines, even Bourbon whiskey
Harvest Moon	Cow's milk	Bingham Hills Cheese Company, Fort Collins, Colorado, U.S.A.	Washed with brine and starter culture	Semi-soft, off-white and slightly chalky when young, becoming creamier and eventually runny with age	2 months	Good as a table cheese with acidic wine or hoppy beer. Also good on toasted rye bread
Red Hawk	Cow's milk, (organic) with the addition of heavy cream	Pt. Reyes Station, California, U.S.A.	Washed with brine	Soft and deep ivory to pale yellow with occasional small holes	6 weeks	Good eating cheese with sweet condiments, like honey or fruit. Also pairs well with sweeter Rieslings
Reblochon	Cow's milk	Savoie/ Rhône Alps, France	Washed, brine	Ivory, semi-soft to soft, with a slight stickiness	2–6 weeks	Important in tartiflette dish with potatoes, bacon, and béchamel
Pont l'Évêque	Cow's milk	Pays d'Auge, Normandy, France	Washed, brine	Ivory/creamy-white with small holes of different size throughout, soft but not runny at room temperature	40–45 days	Good eating cheese at room temperature, pairs nicely with hard cider

(Continues)

CHEESE	MILK TYPE	ORIGIN	RIND	PASTE	AGE	CULINARY USES
Époisses de Bourgogne	Cow's milk	Burgundy, France	Washed, both brine and Marc (pomace brandy, like French grappa)	Soft to runny, ivory to pale yellow	5–6 weeks	Pairs well with a Burgundy or spicy, aromatic white wine
Taleggio	Cow's milk	Lombardia, Italy	Washed, brine	Semi-soft to soft with age	35–40 days	Good in risotto or pasta. Excellent eating cheese
Tête de Moines	Cow's milk	Jura, Switzerland	Washed and brushed	Firm and ivory	≥3 months, on pine boards	Serve with grapes or other fresh fruit as part of a platter or substitute for a stronger flavored gruyère
Livarot	Cow's milk	Calvados, Normandy, France	Washed, brine	Soft to runny with age, and at room temperature. Small holes visible throughout	3 weeks to 3 months	Serve as an appetizer with crusty French bread. Serve as a dessert cheese with fruits such as apples, grapes, or pears
Maroille	Cow's milk, (raw if *fermier*)	Maroilles, France, Nord Pas de Calais region near the Belgian border	Washed	Ivory to pale yellow with some small holes; soft, oily texture	2 weeks to 5 months	Good paired with other strong components.
Munster-Géromé	Cow's milk	Alsace (Munster)-Lorraine (Géromé)	Washed with brine	Semi-soft to runny when ripe, ivory to pale gold	≥3 weeks, but 2–3 months is more often the case	Pairs well with wines from the region like Pinot Gris, Gewürztraminers, and Rieslings

(Continues)

CHEESE	MILK TYPE	ORIGIN	RIND	PASTE	AGE	CULINARY USES
Fourme d'Ambert	Cow's milk	France, Auvergne	Natural, light brown	Creamy with abundant blue mold	≥28 days	Good table cheese, pairs with ripe pear and Coteaux du Layon sweet wine
Bleu d'Auvergne	Cow's milk	France, Auvergne	None, foil-wrapped	Creamy with abundant dark blue marbling	4 weeks	Good in salads, or with nuts and fruit
Roaring Forties Blue	Cow's milk	King's Island, Australia	Dark blue wax coating	Firm but smooth and creamy; can have a yellowish tinge because of beta-carotene from fresh grass	4–5 weeks for blue mold development, coated with wax, and then 2–3 more weeks at creamery	Good eating cheese
Shropshire Blue	Cow's milk, pasteurized	Created in Scotland, now made in Nottinghamshire, England	Natural, browning and turning rough with age	Bright orange, with green-blue veining	3 months	Goes well with rich beers like English Stout or fortified dessert wines
Bleu des Causses	Cow's milk	Aveyron, South-Central France	Natural, moist in summer, drier in winter	Firm but creamy, with moderate bluing. Winter cheeses tend to be drier	≥70 days. Usually 3–4 months	Good at the end of a meal, or alternatively, melted in an omelet or crêpe or served as an enhancement to grilled meat

(Continues)

CHEESE	MILK TYPE	ORIGIN	RIND	PASTE	AGE	CULINARY USES
Persillé	Goat's milk	Savoie, Rhône-Alpes, France	Natural	Soft and dry to hard and very dry, depending on age	1–3 months, with further affinage of 1–4 months (4–7 total)	Good table cheese complemented nicely by Chenin Blanc sweet wine from the Loire
Maytag Blue	Cow's milk	Newton, Iowa, U.S.A.	Natural, foil-wrapped	White to ivory paste with prominent blue veining	6 months	A good eating cheese also, excellent with Anchor Porter beer
Stilton	Cow's milk	Leicester, England	Natural, with a reddish mold forming	Ivory with substantial blue-green veining	9–14 weeks	Pairs classically with a vintage Port
Roquefort	Sheep's milk (raw), mostly Lacaune sheep	Roquefort sur Soulzon, France (south-central)	Natural, foil-wrapped	Ivory with deep blue mold, with some holes of varying size	3–9 months, with at least 3 months in limestone caverns	Good table cheese and pairs well with Sauternes from nearby Bordeaux
Gorgonzola	Cow's milk, pasteurized	Lombardia and Piemonte, Italy	Natural	Ivory with plentiful veining, turning more yellow with age	2–4 months	Serve with pears, apples, peaches, nuts, or raisins. Melts well or is good atop salads
Cabrales	Cow's milk, (raw), traditionally with the addition of sheep's and goat's milk as well	Asturias, Spain (northwest)	Natural, foil-wrapped	Creamy but granular, off-white with a lot of blue veining	3 months	Should be served with a sweet Spanish wine and dried fruit

PERCENTAGE OF FAT, PROTEIN, LACTOSE, MINERALS, AND WATER IN TYPES OF MILK					
MILK	FAT	PROTEIN	LACTOSE	MINERALS	WATER
Human	4.0	1.1	6.8	0.2	88
Cow	3.7	3.4	4.8	0.7	87
Holstein/Friesian	3.6	3.4	4.9	0.7	87
Brown Swiss	4.0	3.6	4.7	0.7	87
Jersey	5.2	3.9	4.9	0.7	85
Zebu	4.7	3.3	4.9	0.7	86
Buffalo	6.9	3.8	5.1	0.8	83
Yak	6.5	5.8	4.6	0.8	82
Goat	4.0	3.4	4.5	0.8	88
Sheep	7.5	6.0	4.8	1.0	80
Camel	2.9	3.9	5.4	0.8	87
Reindeer	17	11	2.8	1.5	68
Horse	1.2	2.0	6.3	0.3	90
Fin Whale	42	12	1.3	1.4	43

McGee, p. 13

Appendix B: Resources List

Artisanal Cheese Shop
2 Park Ave
New York, NY 10016
(212) 532-4033
www.artisanalcheese.com

Bobolink Dairy
42 Meadow Burn Rd
Vernon, NJ 07462
(973) 764-4888
www.cowsoutside.com

Coach Farm
105 Mill Hill Rd
Pine Plains, NY 12567
(518) 398-5325
www.coachfarm.com

Cowgirl Creamery at Tomales Bay Foods
80 Fourth Street
Point Reyes Station, CA 94956
Phone (415) 663-9335
www.cowgirlcreamery.com

Murray's Cheese
89 E 42nd St
New York, NY 10017
(212) 922-1540
www.murrayscheese.com

Point Reyes Farmstead
PO Box 9
Point Reyes Station, CA 94956
Phone: (800) 591-6878
www.pointreyescheese.com

Sprout Creek Farm
34 Lauer Road
Poughkeepsie, NY 12603
845.485.8438
www.sproutcreekfarm.org

INDEX

Vella Cheese Company, 42
vendors, 209
Veneto, 33
Venezia-Giulia, 33
Vermont, 42–43
Vermont Butter & Cheese Company
    Bijou, 60, 61
    Coupole, 60
Vermont Cheese Council, 43
vinaigrette, white wine, 142
Vin de Pays de la Jardin de France, 14

W

Wabash Cannonball, 41, 60
washed rinds, 24–25, 101
water buffalos
    milk, 8
    mozzarella di Bufala, 8, 34, 38
Welsh, Tim, 110
Wensleydale, 70, 73
Westfield Farm, 31
whey, 20
    cheeses from, 39, 44
White, Jonathan, 109

White, Nina, 109
white wine vinaigrette, 142
Windham Foundation, 110
wine, 194–197
    Austrian, 204
    body of, 194
    dessert, 195
    French, 11–16
    German, 204
    Italian, 33–36
    Spanish, 88–91
    U.S., 40–43
Winnemere, 83
Wisconsin, 41, 81

Y

yogurt cheese, herb-marinated, 182–184

Z

Zamorano, 89, 106
zebus, 5
Zuker, Charles, 102

PHOTO CREDITS

KEITH FERRIS

Pages 8, 9, 17, 18, 19, 20, 21, 22, 23, 24, 28, 29, 30, 31, 37, 38, 39, 44, 48, 49, 50, 51, 52, 53, 54, 55, 57, 58, 59, 60, 61, 63, 64, 65, 66, 67, 68, 69, 72, 73, 74, 75, 76, 77, 81, 82, 83, 84, 85, 86, 87, 92, 93, 94, 95, 96, 97, 103, 104, 105, 106, 107, 108, 109, 110, 111, 113, 114, 115, 116, 117, 118, 119, 120, 121, 122, 123, 124, 127, 128, 129, 130, 131, 132, 133

BEN FINK

Pages 138, 140, 144, 146, 150, 154, 162, 164, 165, 174, 176, 180, 182, 184, 188, 190, 205, 207

We would particularly like to thank and give credit to the cheesemakers and farmers who allowed us access to their farms and creameries, and especially to Sprout Creek Farm and Coach Farm, who generously allowed us to photograph their establishments and animals. To a large degree, this book only exists because of them.

CIA CONVERSION CHARTS

TEMPERATURE, WEIGHT, AND VOLUME CONVERSIONS

TEMPERATURE CONVERSIONS

32°F = 0°C	205°F = 96°C	380°F = 193°C
35°F = 2°C	210°F = 99°C	385°F = 196°C
40°F = 4°C	**212°F = 100°C**	390°F = 199°C
45°F = 7°C	215°F = 102°C	395°F = 202°C
50°F = 10°C	220°F = 104°C	**400°F = 204°C**
55°F = 13°C	**225°F = 107°C**	405°F = 207°C
60°F = 16°C	230°F = 110°C	410°F = 210°C
65°F = 18°C	235°F = 113°C	415°F = 213°C
70°F = 21°C	240°F = 116°C	420°F = 216°C
75°F = 24°C	245°F = 118°C	**425°F = 218°C**
[room temp]	**250°F = 121°C**	430°F = 221°C
80°F = 27°C	255°F = 124°C	435°F = 224°C
85°F = 29°C	260°F = 127°C	440°F = 227°C
90°F = 32°C	265°F = 129°C	445°F = 229°C
95°F = 35°C	270°F = 132°C	**450°F = 232°C**
100°F = 38°C	**275°F = 135°C**	455°F = 235°C
105°F = 41°C	280°F = 138°C	460°F = 238°C
110°F = 43°C	285°F = 141°C	465°F = 241°C
115°F = 46°C	290°F = 144°C	470°F = 243°C
120°F = 49°C	295°F = 146°C	**475°F = 246°C**
125°F = 52°C	**300°F = 149°C**	480°F = 249°C
130°F = 54°C	305°F = 152°C	485°F = 252°C
135°F = 57°C	310°F = 154°C	490°F = 254°C
140°F = 60°C	315°F = 157°C	495°F = 257°C
145°F = 63°C	320°F = 160°C	**500°F = 260°C**
150°F = 66°C	**325°F = 163°C**	505°F = 263°C
155°F = 68°C	330°F = 166°C	510°F = 266°C
160°F = 71°C	335°F = 168°C	515°F = 268°C
165°F = 74°C	340°F = 171°C	520°F = 271°C
170°F = 77°C	345°F = 174°C	**525°F = 274°C**
175°F = 79°C	**350°F = 177°C**	530°F = 277°C
180°F = 82°C	355°F = 179°C	535°F = 279°C
185°F = 85°C	360°F = 182°C	540°F = 282°C
190°F = 88°C	365°F = 185°C	545°F = 285°C
195°F = 91°C	370°F = 188°C	550°F = 288°C
200°F = 93°C	**375°F = 191°C**	

WEIGHT CONVERSIONS

For weights less than 1/4 oz: use tsp/tbsp for U.S. measure with gram or mL equivalent (see specific conversion tables).

Formula to convert ounces to grams: number of oz × 28.35 = number of grams (round up for .50 and above)

1/4 ounce = 7 grams
1/2 ounce = 14 grams
1 ounce = 28.35 grams
4 ounces = 113 grams
8 ounces (1/2 pound) = 227 grams
16 ounces (1 pound) = 454 grams
32 ounces (2 pounds) = 907 grams
40 ounces (2 1/2 pounds) = 1.134 kilograms

VOLUME CONVERSIONS

Formula to convert fluid ounces to milliliters: number of fluid ounces × 30 = number of milliliters

1/2 fl oz = 15 mL	20 fl oz = 600 mL
1 fl oz = 30 mL	24 fl oz = 720 mL
1 1/2 fl oz = 45 mL	30 fl oz = 900 mL
1 3/4 fl oz = 53 mL	**32 fl oz = 960 mL [1 qt]**
2 fl oz = 60 mL	40 fl oz = 1.20 L
2 1/2 fl oz = 75 mL	44 fl oz = 1.32 L
3 fl oz = 90 mL	**48 fl oz = 1.44 L [1 1/2 qt]**
3 1/2 fl oz = 105 mL	64 fl oz = 1.92 L [2 qt]
4 fl oz = 120 mL	**72 fl oz = 2.16 L [2 1/2 qt]**
5 fl oz = 150 mL	80 fl oz = 2.4 L
6 fl oz = 180 mL	96 fl oz = 2.88 L [3 qt]
7 fl oz = 210 mL	128 fl oz = 3.84 L [1 gal]
8 fl oz = 240 mL [1 cup]	1 1/8 gal = 4.32 L
9 fl oz = 270 mL	1 1/4 gal = 4.8 L
10 fl oz = 300 mL	1 1/2 gal = 5.76 L
11 fl oz = 330 mL	**2 gal = 7.68 L [256 fl oz]**
12 fl oz = 360 mL	3 gal = 11.52 L
13 fl oz = 390 mL	4 gal = 15.36 L
14 fl oz = 420 mL	5 gal = 19.20 L
15 fl oz = 450 mL	10 gal = 38.40 L
16 fl oz = 480 mL [1 pt]	20 gal = 76.80 L
17 fl oz = 510 mL	25 gal = 96 L
18 fl oz = 540 mL	50 gal = 192 L
19 fl oz = 570 mL